LUTYENS
AND THE
GREAT WAR

£20 -
6/12

LUTYENS
AND THE GREAT WAR

TIM SKELTON   GERALD GLIDDON
FOREWORD BY GAVIN STAMP

F

FRANCES LINCOLN LIMITED
PUBLISHERS

Frances Lincoln Ltd
4 Torriano Mews
Torriano Avenue
London NW5 2RZ
www.franceslincoln.com

First published in the UK: 2008
First published in the US: 2009

A catalogue record for this book is available from the British Library.

ISBN: 978-0-7112-2878-8

Printed and bound in China

9 8 7 6 5 4 3 2 1

HALF TITLE Oxfordshire and Buckinghamshire Light Infantry Regiment Memorial, Cowley, Oxford
TITLE PAGE Orange Trench Cemetery
RIGHT Croisilles British Cemetery

To the
One Million
who did not return

CONTENTS

Southend-on-Sea War Memorial

FOREWORD
BY GAVIN STAMP

THERE WAS A TIME WHEN the only architect the English had heard of was Sir Christopher Wren. That is no longer the case; the name of Wren's great admirer, Edwin Lutyens, is now also well known, and some maintain that he was a much greater architect than the designer of St Paul's. Lutyens first made his name in the last decade of Queen Victoria's reign as the designer of romantic country houses; his later creation of a miniature house for Queen Mary caught the imagination of the public and today two of his houses are in the care of the National Trust. But it was not for his domestic practice that Lutyens was knighted but for his work in New Delhi and for the Imperial War Graves Commission, and if he is remembered today it is mainly for his war memorials: for the Cenotaph in Whitehall and possibly for the Memorial to the Missing of the Somme at Thiepval. The former, from the moment it was unveiled in its initial temporary manifestation, seemed perfectly to express the grief of a mourning nation and was indeed judged perfect in form; the latter — vast, complex, awesome — is arguably the greatest work of British architecture of the last, murderous century, even though it stands across the English Channel, in France.

The architecture of death came to form a major part of Lutyens's work and comprised not only official war memorials and war cemeteries but village memorials, institutional memorials and individual tombs. Like the other Principal Architects of the War Graves Commission — Blomfield, Baker, Holden and Burnet — Lutyens exploited the continuing resonance of the Western Classical tradition: one reason why the Cenotaph spoke and still speaks to so many. But he invested that tradition with a unique, personal character by developing and abstracting it, making it modern. What Christopher Hussey called Lutyens's 'Elemental Mode' proved ideal for memorials. Fortunate, indeed, is the architect who has memorials to design, for they need not be practical: they do not require windows or doors, do not need to be heated and have no chimneys which might smoke. In Lutyens's hands, they became ideal monuments, pure architectural forms whose sole function was to convey meaning and emotion. In the presence of a sublime structure like the memorial at Thiepval, the need for both words and figurative sculpture is transcended — although the monument is covered with names: names of just some of the victims of the European civil war, the orgy of industrialised slaughter we call the Great War.

What this book reveals is the astonishing range and variety of the memorials and cemetery buildings designed by Lutyens, some of which are little known and — despite the large literature on the great architect's work — have not been illustrated before. His three-dimensional imagination was perennially fertile and, with the war cemeteries in particular, he was able to compose many happy variations on a theme. The results are never dull, always different, usually with some felicity of design that marks them as works of their creator, assured in the use of brick and stone, and invariably responsive to site and landscape. Very few of Lutyens's contemporaries had this ability to re-invent and develop inherited architectural forms both to reiterate their familiar meanings or to give them new meanings: only Jože Plečnik, with his similar ability to 'metamorphose' Classical forms and make them modern, and Le Corbusier perhaps, using very different languages of expression. It is possibly an irony that the terrible war which brought to an end the complacent civilisation which sustained Lutyens's practice should also have given him the opportunity to rise to the highest levels of creativity.

Béthune Town Cemetery

INTRODUCTION

MY INTEREST IN LUTYENS began on a wet Easter Sunday in the early 1980s. I was at the Torbay Easter Hockey Festival and, as I didn't have a game and my wife and I needed something to occupy our time, Alison suggested that we visit Castle Drogo. I seem to recall that I was not particularly enthusiastic about the idea but I couldn't think of a better alternative so we drove to see it. How things have changed! As soon as I stepped inside the front door and saw the wonderful fireplace in the study I was hooked. On how many occasions since, I wonder, has Alison regretted her suggestion?

As a result, whenever we were at a loose end, we would go out, *Pevsner* in hand, looking for Lutyens buildings. As I continued my travels I realised that there was no definitive list of his work and such lists that existed contained inaccuracies and duplications. A short spell of redundancy in 1995 gave me the time that I needed to pull together some form of rudimentary database and I set myself the task of visiting the entries and recording their locations.

Open any book on Lutyens and the same images come tumbling out — a series of large exquisite houses designed for a series of wealthy clients in the twenty-five years before the outbreak of the First World War. And yet, as I developed my database I realised that such properties are in the minority and number but 13 per cent of the 700 or so built objects around the world to which Lutyens's name can be ascribed as designer. More than twice this number are the various memorials and cemeteries that he designed to commemorate those who died during the War.

As I continued with my research, I became increasingly intrigued by his war memorials which, the Cenotaph and Thiepval apart, seemed to be poorly documented. I was particularly incensed that the beautiful Spalding memorial (which I had passed close-by on numerous occasions without ever having realised it was there) had never appeared in any Lutyens book.

Scroll forward to 1999 and a suggestion from my brother Nigel that we should pay a visit to the Somme. Obviously Thiepval would have to be on our itinerary but I also wanted to look at some of the cemeteries that Lutyens had designed. As we travelled around for three days I could not believe what was unfolding before my eyes as I saw work after work that I had never seen illustrated, not even in the battlefield guides that I had consulted before our trip, which tend to concentrate upon individual gravestones rather than the cemetery buildings.

Needless to say, it was inevitable that we should return to the Western Front and, with Nigel an ever-willing chauffeur, we duly visited Ypres the next year. Thus it was that my head was turned away from my general Lutyens catalogue into a more in depth study of the architect's work in connection with the War and we made a further series of trips with a view to looking at all of Lutyens's cemeteries.

I always had it in mind that, one day, my work might be a suitable subject for a book but, like a lot of people with a full time job, I saw it as a potential retirement project. Then Gerald Gliddon appeared within my orbit. As a member of the Lutyens Trust, I would, from time to time, field enquiries about the war memorials and one day I was forwarded an email from Gerald seeking

Monchy British Cemetery

information about Lutyens's work in this field. Gerald is a published author on the War, having written the acclaimed *When The Barrage Lifts* (now updated and reissued as *Somme 1916: A Battlefield Companion*) and was contemplating writing a book about Lutyens and his memorials. He gave me the impetus that I needed to get the fruits of my labour into print, and with Gerald in his self-confessed role as 'part researcher and part encourager', our co-operation, and this book, was born.

One of the matters with which I have wrestled as I have travelled around in my search is how the work on the pages that follow fits within Lutyens's oeuvre. How does one equate, for example, the Viceroy's House in New Delhi with the absolutely exquisite approach to the war cemetery at Monchy (at which even Nigel let out an involuntary gasp when he saw it)? The key fact that struck me, and has stayed with me, is that bar one or two exceptions, everything on the pages that follow is accessible to the general public for whom it was created. It is not hidden behind high walls and available to a select few: it is architecture for Everyman. On the one hand Lutyens could design the equivalent of a royal palace, on the other he could give the same care and attention to the humble resting place of a fallen soldier. This is the true mark of his genius as an architect.

Tim Skelton
Milton Keynes, Summer 2008

ONE
TYRINGHAM

STANDING OUTSIDE THE Church of St Peter at Tyringham one could not be further removed from the horrors of the Western Front – the pastoral meadows alongside the River Ouse in this part of North Buckinghamshire form a stark contrast to the muddy and shell-ravaged landscape of Northern France and Flanders during the First World War. There is no village here, not even a hamlet, just a few estate cottages and Tyringham House, a large house rebuilt in the 1790s for the banker and MP William Praed by the fashionable architect of the time, Sir John Soane. Less than two miles along the road towards the market town of Olney is the straggling village of Filgrave, the residents of which have worshipped at St Peter's since their own church was pulled down around 1760 by one of Praed's predecessors.

By the time that the shooting of the Archduke Franz Ferdinand led the world into war in August 1914 the total population of the parish that supported St Peter's was around two hundred. Yet the 'War To End All Wars' touched even this quiet corner of Middle England for, just inside the door on the western wall of the church, is a small tablet of Carrera marble with two verdite swags that records the names of three local men who 'obeying their country's call laid down their lives in the Great War and helped to win the victory for freedom and right'.

Alfred Clench was the first to die, aged just twenty. The son of a local farm worker, he had left Tyringham in June 1914 to take up farming in Western Australia. Following the outbreak of war he enlisted in the Australian Imperial Force and, in September 1915, was posted to Egypt where he suffered a series of illnesses including appendicitis. Having recovered, he had been in France for barely two months when, during an attack on the Somme on 6 August 1916 (most probably near Poziéres),

The Church of St Peter, Tyringham

he was hit on the head and chest by a high explosive shell and died within two minutes. A colleague, writing to Clench's parents, reported: 'We were digging a new firing line ready for a charge. We had been out about eight hours and had just finished the first part when we got orders to stand to ready in case Fritz attacked us. About twenty minutes after we got the order word passed along that Arthur [sic] was wounded. When he got it he only said "I am hit" before he went unconscious and never spoke again. I hope that you will not feel Arthur's death too much, because I am sure he would be more happy if you did not worry.'[1] If Clench's colleagues subsequently had the opportunity to bury him then his last resting place was either destroyed by subsequent fighting or went unrecorded, because he has no known grave. Like many others who died in similar circumstances the name of Alfred Clench is recorded on one of a number of Memorials to the Missing in France and Belgium, in his case the Australian National War Memorial at Villers-Bretonneux.

Albert Miller was next. Employed in the Olney Tannery he enlisted in the Bedfordshire Regiment at the War's outbreak. He had twice been wounded in action before being shot in the abdomen during heavy fighting in April 1917, following which he was moved to the 13th General Hospital in Boulogne. A visitor to the hospital wrote to Private Miller's mother on 14 April: 'Your son has had another operation today, so is not too well. He is not improving very much at present but there are still hopes that he may get better in a few days. He is very brave for he has a great deal of discomfort but he does not complain at all.'[2] His mother must have feared the worst, and on 2 May she received news from the War Office that Albert had died four days previously. In common with other parents in a similar situation she received a message of sympathy from the King and Queen and from the Army Council. Miller was also twenty but,

REMEMBER WITH THANKFULNESS
AND IN ALL HONOUR
ALFRED CLENCH · ALBERT MILLER
FREDERICK GUBBINS
WHO OBEYING THEIR COUNTRY'S
CALL LAID DOWN THEIR LIVES IN
THE GREAT WAR AND HELPED TO WIN
THE VICTORY FOR FREEDOM AND RIGHT

MCM XIV

MCM XIX

1939

ALSO
HERBERT ARTHUR LANE

1945

LEFT AND ABOVE Tyringham War Memorial

because he died in a hospital, he was able to be buried with due dignity in a grave that is properly recorded – in his case in Boulogne Eastern Cemetery.

The third name on the tablet is that of the man who had worked for seventeen years as electrician and chauffeur at Tyringham House, which had been bought in 1903 by the Silesian banker Frederick König. Frederick Gubbins had joined up on 31 July 1916 as a driver in the Army Service Corps and was posted to German East Africa. He died of pneumonia at Lindi on 13 May 1918 and was buried in Lindi Cemetery in what is now Tanzania.[3] In addition to his name being recorded on the Tyringham War Memorial the Königs erected a private memorial to him in the form of a plaque on the south wall of St Peter's, recalling his service as a 'faithful servant' of the family.

The fate of Clench, Miller and Gubbins formed a microcosm of what was happening throughout the country as families and friends came to terms with the loss of their loved ones, and it led to a determination that their losses should be properly recorded, to be witnessed by future generations.

It was on Saturday 23 June 1921, nearly three years after the end of the War, that the war memorial in St Peter's Church was unveiled by Her Highness Princess Marie Louise, one of the many grand-daughters of Queen Victoria. After the service, König and his wife Gerda (who was one of the Princess's Ladies-in-Waiting) hosted a reception at Tyringham House for the dignatories together with members of the local War Memorial Committee; the nearest relatives of Clench, Miller and Gubbins

and the twenty or so local men who had fought in the War and survived. The war memorial's architect was also present and, with his ready wit and endless stream of puns, would have been an engaging guest at dinner at Tyringham House that evening. To him, as well as to countless other architects and designers, had befallen the task of ensuring that those who had died in the recent conflict would be remembered with a dignity worthy of the supreme sacrifice that they had made. A friend of the Königs through their interest in a religion shared with his wife, he had risen supremely to the task before him and, if his name was not necessarily familiar to all of those who he had met during the day, they would have at least been familiar with the memorial that he had designed that had already become the focus for national mourning – the Cenotaph in Whitehall.

The memorial at Tyringham was one of the smallest of more than sixty war memorials at home and abroad, designed by the most famous architect of his generation and the man who was described as the country's greatest architect since Sir Christopher Wren: Sir Edwin Lutyens.

TWO
THE ARCHITECT ESTABLISHED

BY THE TIME THAT BRITAIN declared War on Germany on 4 August 1914, following the latter's invasion of neutral Belgium, Edwin Landseer Lutyens was at the height of his powers. Born on 9 March 1869 to a father who had left the Army after nine years to earn a living as an artist with a particular interest in horses, he had studied architecture at South Kensington School of Art for barely two years before joining the architectural practice of Ernest George and Peto. His stay with George lasted a year until, with the precociousness of youth backed with the comfort of a commission for a substantial house from a family friend, he left to establish his own architectural practice at the tender age of nineteen.

One of the key influences upon his early professional life was Gertrude Jekyll, whom he had first met at a tea party in 1889. Described by Jane Ridley as a 'one-woman Arts and Crafts movement'[1] Miss Jekyll had also attended the South Kensington School of Art and became exceptionally skilled at embroidery, metalwork, gilding and carving before turning her hand to photography. Fading eyesight caused her to take up gardening and landscape design and, since 1881, she had been writing articles for *The Garden*, a magazine founded by William Robinson. In Lutyens (who was twenty-six years her junior) she found an architect who shared her ideals, and not only did she introduce him to a series of her friends who would provide him with a rich crop of clients, but she also commissioned a number of houses from him herself, including her own celebrated home, Munstead Wood. The two formed an enduring professional partnership with Lutyens designing the house and the architectural components of the garden while Miss Jekyll designed the planting. In the region of 100 properties were designed in this manner, many of

Munstead Wood (1896), the house that Lutyens designed for his close friend and collaborator, Gertrude Jekyll

which were featured in *Country Life*, whose founder Edward Hudson assiduously promoted Lutyens's interests, having even become a client himself. The names of the houses from this period – Deanery Garden, Goddards, Orchards, Folly Farm, Greywalls, Tigbourne Court and Lindisfarne Castle, to name a few – have become justifiably well known as some of the very best individual houses built in Britain in the nineteenth and early twentieth centuries.

Stylistically, Lutyens's early work was in the Arts and Crafts style that he had picked up from his journeys around the Surrey lanes in his youth when he would sketch buildings with a piece of soap on a sheet of glass. He had briefly flirted with Art Nouveau before, in 1906, designing his first complete Classical house in the unlikely setting of a quiet back street in the Yorkshire town of Ilkley. Continuing to pursue the 'High Game' as he termed it, his architecture then settled into a blend of classicism that he called 'Wrennaissance', after his great hero, Sir Christopher Wren.

Despite his achievements and popularity, Lutyens had little success in gaining any major public commissions until, in 1912, he was appointed as architect for the New Delhi Planning Commission, which had been charged with overseeing the design and construction of the new Indian capital. Realising that the task was far too big for him alone, he approached Herbert Baker to work alongside him. Baker, a former colleague from his time with Ernest George, had moved to South Africa in 1892 and had become the country's leading architect with a number of significant public commissions, including the Union Buildings in Pretoria, to his name. The two architects had last met in 1910 when Lutyens had visited South Africa to prepare plans for the Johannesburg Art Gallery, a visit that also saw him awarded the commission to design his first war memorial – the Rand Regiments Memorial – which took the form of a 65ft-high classical triumphal arch surmounted by an Angel of Peace carved by Naoum Aronson.[2]

Lutyens's progression from Arts and Crafts to Classical architecture. Clockwise from top left: Goddards, Abinger Common (1899); Heathcote, Ilkley (1906); The Salutation, Sandwich (1911)

By coincidence, Lutyens's wife, Lady Emily Lytton, whom he had married in 1897, was the daughter of a former Viceroy of India. She had married Lutyens on the rebound from an infatuation with an older womaniser and she saw in him an artistic champion. He was ardently in love with her but ill comfortable amongst her circle for which humour and puns became his successful defence. Despite her admiration for his work, Emily was painfully shy and, in spite of her social status, not at all at ease with the self-made businessmen who were the mainstay of her husband's clients.

The Lutyens marriage deteriorated when, in 1910, Emily became involved in the Theosophical Movement. She found solace in the quasi-religion that preached about reincarnation and a Second Coming and increasingly spent time in the company of Annie Besant, the movement's president, together with a young Indian boy, Krishnamurti, whom, Besant believed, represented the Second Coming of the World Teacher. Somewhat ironically, Lutyens had been the unwitting cause of Emily's interest in theosophy when he introduced her to one of his clients, Guillaume Mallet, for whom he had designed Le Bois des Moutiers near Dieppe in 1898, and who was also caught up in the movement.

In spite of their strained relationship, Lutyens and Emily were prodigious letter writers and they constantly wrote to each other as he travelled to meet his clients and visit his various projects. By July 1914 he was as busy as ever but, within a few weeks, everything was to change.

On 5 August 1914 he wrote to her:

So war was declared last night. I heard it in the Athenaeum too late to telephone you and the morning's newspapers would tell you as soon as I could. From the top balcony of the

Deanery Gardens, Sonning (1901–2) with its garden by Gertrude Jekyll is
widely regarded as one of the pair's finest compositions

Athenaeum we watched the German Embassy, but there as no
demonstration – a few boys booed and perhaps 12 policemen
moved them on gently and without effort. There was no stone
throwing. Rule Britannia was very badly sung – the
Marsellaise and God Save the King. The crowd was an offshoot
of the Buckingham Palace crowd on its return. I walked home
and got into bed about 12.20.[3]

The effect of the outbreak of war upon Lutyens's workload
was immediate. Not only did clients swiftly cancel their projects
but twelve of his staff signed up for the armed services in the general patriotic fervour that was sweeping the country. Fortunately
he was able to take refuge in his work on New Delhi, to which he
would make annual visits by boat, using his cabin as a drawing
office *en route*. However, his visit in 1916 proved the breaking point
in his relationship with Baker.

The centrepiece for New Delhi was to be a grand ceremonial
avenue, King's Way, laid out along the gentle incline of Raisina
Hill, and terminating in the largest building that Lutyens ever
designed – the Viceroy's House. More of a royal palace than a
house, it showed Lutyens at his supreme best and was designed in
a style that blended Western classicism with Indian vernacular
detailing. Framing the approach were two Secretariat buildings
designed by Baker to house the Indian Civil Service: it was a conjunction that was to cost the friendship dear.

As the overall plan for New Delhi was being finalised in
1913, it was agreed that the secretariats would be moved further
up King's Way so that they and the Viceroy's House could sit
together and form an acropolis. Lutyens readily agreed to the
change but it was not until January 1916, when building work
was progressing, that he realised full implications of the
change. It had always been his intention that the Viceroy's

ABOVE 'Bakerloo': the level of Baker's two Secretariat Buildings either side of
the rise up Raisina Hill partially obscured the view of the Viceroy's House and
blighted the relationship between the two men until Lutyens's death
LEFT Rand Regiments Memorial, Johannesburg: Lutyens's first war memorial

House would be fully visible along the whole of the rise up the hill but the need to create a level platform to accommodate all three buildings together had meant that the gradient of the final part of the road had to be altered. As a consequence, depending where one was on King's Way, the Viceroy's House was either fully or partially visible. Lutyens was distraught and quite how he made such an elementary mistake in not being able to interpret Baker's plans correctly has never been explained. It is to easy to allow him the defence that he was misled by a contemporary artist's impression by William Walcot that was drawn from a viewpoint in mid-air, but the probable explanation is that he just made a simple mistake. Unfortunately he was unable to swallow his dignity and launched an increasingly futile campaign to have the gradient reconstructed to the original design, even though it would have caused an unacceptably deep chasm between the Secretariat buildings. He badgered anyone who might have influence and who would listen to his pleadings but it was only after six years that a decision by the King himself to leave things as they were put an end to the matter. 'Bakerloo' (as Lutyens as subsequently to refer to the incident) is the single episode in his professional life from which he emerges with little credit. It

blighted the relationship between the two architects, even to the extent as will be seen in the following chapter, that Baker's reputation was to suffer unnecessarily, and it was only resolved when Lutyens died. The dispute seems all the more pointless when one considers that architectural critics are themselves divided upon whether the view would be better as Lutyens had originally designed it or as it now exists. Lutyens himself, as much as any architect, appreciated the importance of concealing objects from the viewer until the last minute, to heighten the sense of drama, and it is to his detriment that he was not able to revise his thinking about Raisina Hill in such a fashion.

Although his visits to India had isolated Lutyens from the War it had touched his wider family. Charles Lutyens was the first of five of the architect's nephews to die, when he was killed at Gallipoli in 1915. Cyril and another Charles were both killed near Ypres in 1917, as was Lionel a year later. Derek, also died in 1918, but in England. Cyril and Charles died barely three months after Lutyens had been asked to visit the Western Front, an event that was to have a profound effect upon him and was to influence the way in which his nephews and countless others, including Alfred Clench, Albert Miller and Frederick Gubbins of Tyringham, were to be commemorated.

THREE
THE WAR STONE

GERMANY'S STRATEGY at the start of the War was based upon the Schlieffen Plan, which had been developed as early as 1905. The plan sought to avoid the need to fight a war on two fronts by making a swift strike through neutral Belgium to precipitate the surrender of France by capturing Paris within six weeks of the initial mobilisation. However, the German army was thwarted by dogged resistance from French, Belgian and British troops. Both sides then tried unsuccessfully to outflank the other in a 'Race to the Sea' with the result that the Western Front was born – a network of trenches and supporting infrastructure that stretched from Switzerland to the North Sea. The quality of the defences, coupled with the fact that both armies were evenly matched in terms of weaponry and manpower, meant that, despite a limited series of successes on each side from time to time, the War soon developed into a static war of attrition.

The scale of casualties that resulted from such a stalemate was unprecedented in any form of warfare and brought with it the attendant logistical problem of what to do with the bodies of the fallen. The response of the British and Empire Armies to such a challenge was shaped by Fabian Ware, a powerful and energetic man who had arrived in France in September 1914 shortly after the first troops. He had already achieved distinction in a number of positions, particularly as an administrator in South Africa under the High Commissioner Lord Milner,[1] and latterly as the editor of the *Morning Post*; however, aged forty-five, he was too old for active service. He had therefore joined the Red Cross to run the 'flying unit' responsible for searching out wounded soldiers and stragglers. It soon became apparent to him that there was no formal procedure for marking and recording the graves in the cemeteries that had already begun to appear throughout the battlefields and alongside the hospitals and Casualty Clearing

Stations behind the Front Line. His visit to the town cemetery in Béthune the following month was to give him the focus for the remainder of his working life as he was disturbed to find a number of British graves for which, not only was there no evidence that their location had been formally recorded, but also that there were no arrangements for ongoing maintenance. The Red Cross subsequently agreed to provide money for proper, durable inscriptions and gave Ware the support to develop this particular aspect of his work which, in March 1915, was formally recognised when his Unit was renamed the Graves Registration Commission (GRC).

The War Office in London became increasingly supportive of Ware's operations, recognising that the proper treatment of the bodies of the dead soldiers would also contribute to the morale of those men still serving. As a result, and with Ware's full support, they assumed full responsibility for the GRC from the Red Cross in October 1915 and Ware was given the rank of Major to give authority to his work. By the end of the year his discussions with the French authorities about the long term future of the cemeteries had led to the French Government passing a Bill to allow its Ministry of War to acquire land for cemeteries in '*sepulture perpetuelle*' that it could then pass to the British Government for future maintenance.[2]

The early cemeteries consisted of little more than rows of wooden crosses set in grass, although there was an early proposal that they should be planted in themes to accord with the nationalities of the people who were buried there, for example maple trees in the Canadian cemeteries and, in the Australian ones in Gallipoli, wattle. However, Ware's imagination was sparked by requests that had been received from relatives who wished to plant flowers by the graves of their loved ones, and as a result, in 1916, the Director of the Royal Botanic Gardens at Kew was asked to send a 'a practical man' to France to advise

Bucquoy Road Cemetery

upon the 'shrubs, grasses and so on which would give the best results having regard to the soil and aspect of each cemetery'.[3] The Assistant Director, Arthur Hill, was chosen and during his tour he visited thirty-seven cemeteries, before producing a report detailing the types of plants suitable for the conditions that he found. The initial planting schemes of annuals and grass were modest but, by 1917, shrubs and trees had begun to be added and, to emphasise the importance with which the GRC viewed the matter, four nurseries had been established. Particular attention was paid to the forward cemeteries close to the Front Line, causing Hill to write: 'The sowing of annuals is of considerable value; they help to brighten places often very barren and desolate; they cheer our men who are constant visitors to our cemeteries and who frequently pass these cemeteries when on the march.'[4]

Although the GRC had secured the future ownership of the cemeteries, there were no formal arrangements regarding their maintenance once the War was over. There was a view that responsibility should be given to the Government's Office of Works, but Ware envisaged a separate, permanent body that would operate on behalf of all of the imperial countries and not just the UK. This was not without controversy but, on 21 May 1917, the Imperial War Graves Commission (IWGC) was created to care for the graves of all of those from the Dominions who had died on active service. It had the power to acquire land and erect suitable memorials and, critically, to prevent others erecting permanent memorials in its cemeteries. The Prince of Wales was the Commission's first President, the Secretary of State for War (Lord Derby)[5] its Chairman and, appropriately, Fabian Ware its Vice-Chairman and, de facto, Chief Executive.

Within a week of his appointment Ware had received a letter from Lutyens. Clearly the two men were on familiar terms, with Lutyens addressing Ware as 'Mon General', but how they first met is not recorded. The matter of commemoration of the war dead had clearly been playing on the architect's mind and he excitedly poured out his thoughts

On platforms made of not less than 3 steps the upper and the lower steps of a width twice that of the centre step: to give due dignity: place one great stone of fine proportion 12 feet long set fair and finely wrot – without undue ornament and tricky and elaborate carvings and inscribe thereon one thought in clear letters so that all men for all time may read and know the reason why these stones are so placed throughout France – facing the West and facing the men who lie looking ever eastward towards the enemy.

After this you can plant to desire and erect cloisters – chapels – crosses buildings of as many varieties as to suit the always varying sites.

Every grave enclosure should be made for permanence and to have one covered permanent building wherein a roll of honour may be kept indelible'[6]

The letter also contained what Lutyens referred to as a 'stoneology' in which he ran through the potential alternatives names for his 'great stone' (see page 25):

'Altar' – The Stone – The War Stone – The Great Stone	
The Great War Stone	The Battle Stone
The Dedication Stone	The Stone of Peace
The Achievement Stone	The Stone of Pity
The Commemoration Stone	The Waiting Stone
The Foundation Stone	The Stone of Sleep
The White Stone	The Stone of Attendance
The Stone in France	The Stone of Righteousness
The Stone of France	The Stone of Right
The King's Stone	The Stone of Might
The King Emperor's Stone	The Watching Stone
Our Stone	The Stone of Victory
The Command Stone	The Stone of Fame
The Stone of Prayer	The Famous Stone
The Stone of Praise	The Stone Prostrate
The Stone of Appeal	The Stone of Thought
The Stone of Reverence	The Memorial Stone
England's Stone	The Memory Stone
The Stone of Britain	The Image Stone

Lutyens completed this section of the letter poignantly: 'For "God made man in his own likeness the image of his Eternity" for they are gods these men.'[7] He had written a similar letter to his close friend the author James (J.M.) Barrie, with whom he had been discussing the matter. It reached Ware at an appropriate time. He was conscious that he needed to make progress on the permanent design of the cemetery at Etaples, which was one of the main British bases and hospital areas, and had asked Charles Aitken, the Director of the Tate Gallery, to go to France accompanied by a small working party to advise him on how it and ten other typical cemeteries should be designed. Ware suggested that the party should comprise Lutyens and Herbert Baker, Lutyens's collaborator in New Delhi, together with one other. Owing to the bureaucracy involved in funding such a trip it would, wrote Ware, be 'greatly simplified' if the two architects went as volunteers and did not require fees for their time and advice. The question of a wider 'Advisory Committee' to deal with design of the cemeteries once the working party had reported their findings had also been discussed between the two men and Aitken (who was not Ware's initial choice – he had originally contacted Charles Holmes, Director of the National Gallery) had suggested the names of Sir

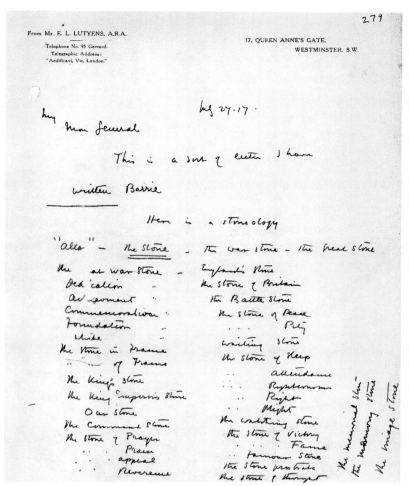

Lutyens's letter of 27 May 1917 outlining his initial thoughts on the
War Stone to Fabian Ware

Robert Lorimer, Mervyn Macartney, Inigo Thomas and Charles
Holden as being suitable, in addition to Lutyens and Baker.

Lutyens and the rest of the Working Party left for France on 9
July 1917. The effect of the trip upon him was considerable and he
wrote to Emily on 12 July from a chateau near the British Army
headquarters in Montreuil:

Each day we have long motor drives, being billeted in a chateau
some way back from the front.

The cemeteries, the dotted graves, are the most pathetic
things, specially when one thinks of how things are run and
problems treated at home.

What humanity can endure and suffer is beyond belief.

The battlefields – the obliteration of all human endeavour
and achievement and the human achievement of destruction is
bettered by the poppies and wild flowers that are as friendly to an
unexploded shell as they are to the leg of a garden seat in Surrey.

It is all a sense of wonderment, how such things can be.

Men and lorries – motors without thought of petrol – fat

horses and thin men all in the pink of condition. Great in size
beyond imaginations and all so inexplicable that it makes writing
difficult and one dare not mention names of places etc.

One is seeing very little of all there is to be seen but the little
is ominous of what lies beyond a battlefield, with the blessed
trenches, the position of a machine gun by its litter of spent cartridges. The ruined tanks, the rough broken shell-hole pitted
ground, you assume was once a village. A small bit of wall of
what was once a church may stand but nothing else.

The half ruined places are more impressive for there you can
picture what a place might have been.

The graveyards, haphazard from the needs of much to do
and little time for thought. And then a ribbon of isolated graves
like a milky way across miles of country where men were tucked
in where they fell. Ribbons of little crosses each touching each
across a cemetery, set in a wilderness of annuals and where one
sort of flower is grown the effect is charming, easy and oh so
pathetic. One thinks for the moment no other monument is
needed. Evanescent but for the moment is almost perfect and

how misleading to surmise in this emotion and how some love to sermonise. But the only monument can be one where the endeavour is sincere to make such monument permanent – a solid ball of bronze!

For miles these graves occur from single pairs to close packed areas of 1000s on every sort of site and in every sort of position, the bodies laid to face the enemy. In some places so close one wonders how to arrange their names in decent order.

We have a lot more to see.

The question is so big, so wide that the most one can do is to generalise. General Ware, the Director, is a most excellent fellow and very keen to do the right thing without fear or favour of the present sentiment – a preference for the most permanent and perfect.

I am terrified of the censor. The mess here is delightful – a terrible chateau does not spoil it. A good view and fine trees. France – as France – is altered, becoming gentler and more sympathetic simply that they have not the labour to cut the trees so hard.

Tomorrow we go again to the battlefields – to a scene of obliterated villages, scarred soil and destroyed tanks etc.[8]

In addition to Aitken, Lutyens and Baker, the Working Party consisted of Ware, his deputy Lieutenant-Colonel Arthur Messer (an architect and the member of the IWGC's staff responsible for cemetery implementation) and Arthur Hill (who had continued his involvement with the cemeteries following his initial visit to France the previous year). They met in a formal session on 14 July to discuss their findings and, in general terms, even at this early stage, their recommendations formed the basis for the subsequent design of the cemeteries. In particular it was agreed that, although there should be an overall broad design theme, there should not be a prescriptive formula. Four types of cemetery were identified – those for which a monumental effect was required (such as High Wood, the scene of fierce fighting on the Somme); the special base, garden or forest cemeteries such as Etaples; town cemeteries (where a cloister might be appropriate); and village cemeteries (which, depending upon size, could either have a cross or Calvary, a shelter building or a chapel and care-taker's cottage as appropriate).

The Working Party also agreed that each grave should be individually marked and that there should be no private crosses or memorials in the cemeteries although all existing crosses made out of shells and cartridges should be preserved if possible. There was agreement with Lutyens's proposal that the cemetery boundary should be marked with a wall at least 9in high with the top parallel to the horizon but that existing hedges should not be removed without prior discussion. The landscaping treatment was critical and it was held to be important that both the appointed architect and the landscape architect should jointly inspect all the cemetery sites.

There was not complete harmony, however. The visit to France took place eighteen months after Lutyens had first discovered the true position regarding the approach to the Viceroy's House in New Delhi and the antipathy between him and Baker surfaced again in Northern France, this time over Lutyens's proposal for the War Stone. Lutyens reiterated the idea that he had previously advanced to Ware for a 'monolithic Altar set in dignity on steps should be placed in every cemetery' where it would be 'a permanent and reverent monument which should appeal to every feeling and denomination'.[9] He proposed that its actual function could be fluid: it could either stand alone or cover some of the graves and, in the larger cemeteries, there might even be two such stones; the inscriptions on them could vary and could either be a general one or, alternatively, have the names of the fallen or regimental names (depending on the cemetery's size). Lutyens envisaged that national materials could be used for the stones and they could also be used as a resting place for wreaths. He emphasised that using the stones would not exclude the use of a cross in any particular cemetery but 'What he wished to urge was the one note which would be continuous throughout British cemeteries in France'.[10]

Baker did not agree, because 'the symbolism of the Altar did not express the symbolism of the war'.[11] His preferred alternative, shared by Aitken, was for a churchyard cross.

Consideration was also given to the monuments in the Somme and the Butte de Warlencourt, High Wood, Thiepval and Delville Wood were suggested as potential sites. In an interesting comparison with what was to emerge later it was felt that at Thiepval 'the site here above the valley of the Ancre suggests a long terrace overlooking the battlefields in that valley (cf the long terrace at Duncombe Park, Yorkshire overlooks Rievaulx)'.[12]

Having returned to England further fractures appeared in the relationship between Aitken, Lutyens and Baker, even to the extent that they began to argue over matters upon which they had previously agreed whilst they were in France. Not only were Aitken and Baker adamant about preferring a cross to Lutyens's proposed Stone, but Aitken had even begun to doubt the overall principle of major expenditure at all. Foreshadowing the kind of argument that was to occur in towns and cities throughout the United Kingdom once their citizens started to consider their own war memorials, he expressed a preference that the commemoration of the War dead should serve some additional utilitarian purpose, such as housing or a national university.

Baker reiterated his views that the architecture should have a strongly symbolic theme. He saw the War very much as a crusade, even to the extent that, at one stage, he suggested to Ware that grave markers should incorporate the ship of Henry the Navigator, which, he felt, had been instrumental in helping to win

Bagneux British Cemetery

the Crusades. It is often quoted, based on a letter that Lutyens wrote to Emily on 23 August 1917, that Baker wanted the cemeteries to have a cross with five points, one for each self-governing Dominion ('Baker must be dotty! A five pointed cross for each of the colonies. Too silly. And India left out which will cause bitter hurt and what about the Jews and agnostics who hate crosses?' was Emily's reply),[13] but this was a fallacy and Lutyens was mistaken in his assertion: Baker had actually suggested that the cross should have a pentagonal shaft (one side for each Dominion) rather than a five-pointed cross and he clearly recognised that India could not be included in any memorial that included a cross. He had therefore proposed that, instead of continuing the symbolic theme and making the shaft hexagonal, those cemeteries containing Indian burials should be marked by a column in addition to the cross. He suggested that a suitable model for such a column would be the Asoka Column and, in the Wheel of Law and Authority at the top, there could be a swastika as the symbol of India or, if Muslims objected, the Star of India on a lotus capital or foliage.[14]

Developing this train of thought further, Baker then suggested that, if the Jews and Unitarians objected to the cross then they should have a pillar of their own. He made his views on Lutyens's War Stone clear: 'I feel strongly that from a purely architectural point of view you want more than a horizon line of the altar. . . . We have yet to consider the unidentified and the names without remains, and for this purpose I think that it would be fine to have Lutyens's idea of a great long flat stone, only it would be a tomb and not an altar, and much might be made of it with a fine inscription.'[15]

However, Aitken did not support the War Stone: 'I feel that a large monolithic altar in all graveyards, irrespective of size and character would be a mistake, as it would be out of scale and character in many of the small rural graveyards. Even in the larger cemeteries altars would be somewhat useless. I am of the opinion that the adoption of some form of churchyard cross as the distinguishing feature of all the graveyards would express better the spirit of the war and its use would be more harmonious with the surroundings in France.'[16]

Needless to say Lutyens was not prepared to let his idea fall by the wayside: 'They write about sympathy with France! And artistically − well − in a country of poplars you want your building lines horizontal and not vertical' was his comment to Ware.[17]

Over the next few months Lutyens advanced his ideas for his altar-cum-War Stone to an ever-widening group of potential supporters. Barrie had been an early ally and barely a week had elapsed following the Working Party's return from France when he wrote to Ware: 'I think that there is something rather grand in its simplicity about this proposal. The one stone means little enough, but that one in each of these consecrated places becomes impressive. If a happy name were found for this object it would begin to stand out in our minds, some name that would at least henceforth apply to nothing else. It should be like a new word added to the language. The poetry of the future should make it an immortal word. Lutyens's is one of the most imaginative minds I have ever known, and I'd like to see some practical development of this idea from him'.[18] It was a symbol of the closeness between them that Ware showed Barrie's letter to Lutyens: 'He referred to me so nicely. . . . It is pleasant to be thought to have imagination' he subsequently wrote to Emily.[19]

Barrie also had an idea of his own and proposed that each cemetery should contain a belfry. He envisaged that the bells could be briefly rung each evening and, as they stopped in one cemetery, the ringing would commence in the next to give a continuous peal, as if each cemetery was waking up its neighbour. It was a somewhat eccentric albeit worthy idea that was to progress no further and can be placed into the same category as one that was proposed many years later by Lord Milner whereby the memorials could be floodlit using parts from old cars.[20]

The next person to write to Ware was Lutyens's father-in-law, Lord Lytton, whose letter of 6 August almost gave the impression of having been drafted by Lutyens himself:

Bellacourt Military Cemetery

I have been talking to Lutyens about his proposals regarding the burial grounds in France and I am greatly impressed with them.

The monuments must be solemn and grand with dignity and simplicity. They must be silent not garrulous or fussy – they should inspire awe and reverence in a form that is really appropriate to all sites and needs.

Lutyens's proposals for a chain of great stone blocks raised on 3 steps seems to me to meet all these requirements and I am very enthusiastic about them. I hope that you also approve. Please let me know if I can do anything to forward the idea.[21]

Lutyens continued to drum up support and enlisted support from a group of former clients – David McKenna, Gertrude Jekyll, Arthur Balfour and Arthur Chapman – as well as Winston Churchill. He persisted in his arguments to Ware's receptive ear

'Labour members, Jews, Roman Catholics, non-conformists, ladies of fashion especially those who suffer a loss, all seem to like it and agree in the banality of the cross.'[22]

However, there was one body with whom he had not discussed his proposal – the Anglican Church: 'I have not had the courage to tackle a Bishop, but do you think it wise if I asked Cantuar to see me, he would I think, but if I catch sight of the apron it is apt, at a critical moment, to give me the giggles, especially when they get pompous and hold their hands across their knees – why?'[23] In the same letter he also referred to the place that was destined to provide his supreme creation on the Western Front:

It looks as though you will only want one monument for the Somme and that is the Boot!

Klein Vierstraat British Cemetery

Southampton War Memorial

Say you have a structure full of bronze columns bearing the names of the dead.

The walls inside might be cut and modelled and carved to make a plan of those battlefields. It might be very beautiful.

Lutyens duly plucked up courage and spoke to 'Cantuar' (Randall Davidson, Archbishop of Canterbury) a few days later at their Club, The Athenaeum ('this Pot House' as Lutyens called it to Ware): 'He said he was impressed and liked the idea, but could not give an answer at once. . . . He said he could certainly (my word) perform the Sacrament on such a stone and should think his RC brother of Westminster – as well as our Brer Hindu. . . . I hope he turns up trumps for the stone unless he can evolve something better.'[24]

On 20 August he wrote again to tell Ware that he might be expecting to hear from the Prime Minister, David Lloyd George about the War Stone and that Arthur Chapman, who had recently been dining with Davidson, reported that the latter was 'impressed favourably'.[25] Then, in a Machiavellian twist, he floated the idea to Ware that he should dismiss the '. . . genius committee. Then you settle on the big stone – and get us all to work again on another footing with the big stone settled'. Then, perhaps with a little much too enthusiam for his beloved War Stone, made the suggestion 'for each and every stone to spend a night rolled into the nave

of Westminster Abbey where all might see them touch them from King to itinerant pedlar or in the forecourt of Buck Palace'.[26]

As well as receiving support from his clients, Lutyens also received backing from Emily and it is one of the few occasions within their published letters on which she expresses her views upon a developing design of her husband's: 'I am very keen on your stone. It appeals to my side of life – as houses don't and I see so much true symbolism in it. I do hope you get it through'[27] and, a week later, 'It seems as if your stones are going well and I do hope for your sake that something will soon be settled so that you can set to and do the work. It would be the finest thing of your life if it comes off . . .'[28]

Shortly afterwards Lutyens wrote a memorandum 'Graveyards of the Battle Fields' that he sent to for Ware to encapsulate his thoughts upon the design of the cemeteries, which mostly reiterated the points discussed and agreed by the Working Party in France. He continued to advance the cause of his 'one great fair stone of fine proportions' (referring to it as the 'Great War Stone'[29]) which he felt, would suggest 'the thought of memorial Chapels in one vast cathedral whose vault is the sky'.[30]

The image that one has of Ware throughout all of this is of someone with a strong personality and a resolute sense of purpose and yet it seems as though the issue of religious symbolism was beginning to wear even him down. He confided to Lutyens that a letter about the matter from the Archbishop of Canterbury left

Chocques Military Cemetery

him 'shocked' and grieved' as he had been expecting a neutal attitude and 'not a narrow antagonistic view.'[31] The experience seems
to have left Ware feeling despondent, even to the extent that he
apparently informed Lutyens that he was even contemplating
passing responsibility for the war graves to the Office of Works. It
was a rare moment of self-doubt that soon passed. He did, however, comfort his architect with his belief that 'the "stone" will win
yet'.[32] Davidson reiterated his views when he and Ware met on 17
October, with the Archbishop expressing his disapproval of the
stone, as Ware's file note of the meeting explains: 'But then he
came back to the question of the Lutyens War Stone about which
he seemed to be, for him, rather agitated and thought that while
the Roman Catholics would want a Crucifix they would be satisfied with a Celtic cross such as that which had been erected at
Ebbsfleet to commemorate the landing of St Augustine. He
thought that a stone would be shapeless and meaningless and an
altar was useless', but 'he strongly approved of Kenyon [see below]
to decide on the artistic and architectural question'.[33]

Whilst Lutyens had been pursuing his idea for the War Stone,
he, Baker, Aitken, Ware and other members of the IWGC had
been developing their thoughts upon the cemetery designs in
accordance with their discussions in France in July. They met on
21 September at Winchester House, the Commission's London
headquarters, and the minutes record that 'plans prepared by Mr

Baker and Mr Lutyens respectively should be discussed by them
with Lt Hill'.[34] There was no indication of the detail of the plans,
albeit that it was noted that three cemeteries (Chocques, Contay
and Warloy-Baillon) were discussed and that there were to be further discussions with Baker over the former. There are, however,
plans from Lutyens's office dated October 1917 in the Archives of
the Reef Point Library at the University of Southern California at
Berkeley, which show proposals for five cemeteries —
Auchonvillers, Corbie La Neuville, Daours, Hersin and
Warlincourt Halte — so it is logical to assume that they would have
been discussed at this meeting.

As well as being involved in the 'Cross versus Stone' debate
between Lutyens and Baker, Ware also had to address the more
fundamental issue of Aitken's role. The existence of well-designed
cemeteries was fundamental to Ware's vision for the Commission
and he clearly could not continue by leaving responsiblity for the
matter in the hands of someone who did not support his overall
vision. He therefore began to look for a suitable replacement and
chose Sir Frederic Kenyon, Director of the British Museum, who
had been originally suggested for the role by Charles Holmes,
when he had turned down Ware's intial approach. An established
classical and biblical scholar, as well as an excellent administrator,
Kenyon was an inspired choice and he and Ware soon became firm
friends. Ware's valedictory letter to Aitken (written on 11

Bruay Communal Cemetery Extension

November 1917) praised his contribution: 'I shall always look back on your visit to us in France with real gratitude. Up till that time it had been impossible for us to get any clear idea of the best course to pursue in connection with the very difficult questions with which we were confronted as to permanent memorials and the planning of cemeteries. Thanks to the valuable advice that you, Lutyens and Baker gave us we have been able to get everything on to a more practical basis.'[35]

Having been appointed, one of Kenyon's immediate priorities was to visit the battlefields himself and to pull together the work of the Working Party and its subsequent discussions into a comprehensive report, which he submitted to the Commission in January 1918. He reaffirmed the general principles that had been originally agreed and, critically for Lutyens, endorsed the idea of the War Stone: 'at the eastern end of the cemetery will be a great altar stone, raised upon broad step, and bearing some brief and appropriate phrase or text'.[36] Bowing to the inevitable, Aitken also proposed that, as well as the War Stone, each cemetery should contain a cross 'as a symbol of the Christian faith and of the self-sacrifice of the men who now lie beneath its shadow'.

Once this key decision had been made, Lutyens refined the design of the War Stone by adopting the principle of entasis: putting curves into horizontal lines so that, to the viewer, they

appear straight. Thus the horizontal surfaces of the War Stone are parts of parallel spheres with diameter of 1,801ft 8in and the vertical surfaces taper to meet at 1,801ft 8in above the centre of those spheres.

Although he had designed it for the war cemeteries, the first potential use of the War Stone was as the centrepiece of a replacement for a Temporary War Shrine that had been erected in London's Hyde Park. Lutyens's design showed the stone raised on a substantial plinth, flanked by open pylons supporting fir cones, the symbol of eternity. Text suggested by Emily was to be carved on each pylon – 'God created man in his own likeness to be immortal' and 'and made him to be the image of his own Eternity'. S.J. Waring (of the furniture makers, Waring and Gillow) offered to meet the cost but the memorial did not proceed because the King (whose approval was required as Ranger of the Royal Parks) did not like the design. Lutyens was instructed by Sir Alfred Mond, the First Commissioner of Works, to prepare an alternative design but it was not progressed before the ceasefire occurred in November 1918. However, his work on the Shrine helped him to develop his thoughts on the words to appear on the face of the War Stone.

Writing to Emily in a train on the way back from Muncaster on 30 August 1918, Lutyens ran through the alternatives:

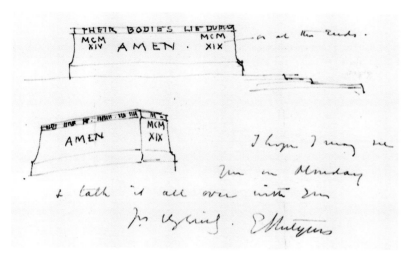

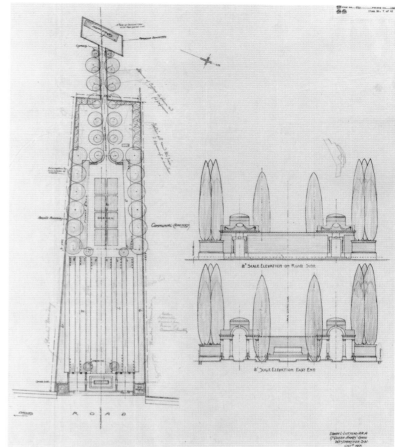

ABOVE Lutyens's letter of 19 October 1918 to Sir Frederic Kenyon made a suggestion for the War Stone's inscription

RIGHT Lutyens's initial plan for the Daours Communal Cemetery Extension was one of a number prepared upon his return from France in 1917. The eight formal planting beds in the middle of the cemetery were to contain herbaceous perennials such as bergenia, kniphofia, Michaelmas daisy and campanula

Kipling: Their bodies lie buried in peace(s!) but their names liveth for evermore.

Kenyon suggested the latter half would do, Their names liveth for evermore. But what are names? Even that is long to bear repetition thousands of times round the world's circumference.

You want a word like

Go losh

Though it suggest gums and slippers now it will mean *the* thing in the years to come.

Your other text, You live to die, die to live, does not appeal to me, it sounds helpless, hopeless and has the rhythmic action of a barrel organ.

(To those) (These are they) that came out of great tribulation

(For these) The trumpets sound from the other side

Barrie's 'All's Well'

Nicholson 'To the Brave'

I was glad when I found that both Waring the donor and Mond were anti Cross. I am coming to believe the Cross is the great anti-Christ of prophecy!

'Peace be with you'. Too churchy and Christian? There might be fine things in Bunyan.

The question is getting to a head, and if Kipling once says?? [*sic*] the Royal Commission will say 'Yes' and there will be no retraction.

And I want one phrase, one word and the same to ring the world.

OMNOPQRST

Is what I have put on the model, a block of alphabet, M to T with an O to begin with. It reads jolly well! You declaim it aloud. Nine letters. I can get them larger. Now a long inscription would not have the same effect at all.

One might get a phrase, cut it on the back of the stone, just like the initials GMMTBI on the face and in time they will be known like the splendid Roman SPQR.[37]

Emily responded: 'If you only want one word you should have Amen. It is the same really as the Indian OM and the Egyptian A-Men is the sacred word of the Aryan race.'[38]

Emily's letter clearly struck a chord and, writing to Kenyon about the matter two months later, Lutyens included two sketches showing 'AMEN', with the dates of the War either side of the inscription or at the ends of the stone. Somewhat clumsily, though, he suggested that the inscription could be carved in a continuous band on the small setback at the top of the stone.

In the end the Commission decided to adopt Kenyon's suggestion and truncate the phrase that had been chosen from the Book of Ecclesiasticus by Rudyard Kipling (who was one of the

IWGC's members and acted as their literary advisor). Discussing the matter nearly six years later, Kipling told Lutyens that the stone was 'an inspiration and it looked well no matter where it was put. The only mistake I made was to have an inscription on it. Even my proposed 'Amen'. It wanted no inscription. . . . It was nice of him'.[39]

The War Stone has tended to become somewhat overlooked in the consideration of Lutyens's total output, almost as if its ubiquity has rendered it invisible, and yet it was clearly something about which he cared with a very deep passion. One therefore senses that it was with a degree of some satisfaction that, in 1923, he wrote to the Archbishop of Canterbury 'I was glad to see in today's paper that the Great War Stone in a cemetery was used as an Altar for the administration of Holy Communion.'[40]

The development of the War Stone catches Lutyens at his best. Although not particularly religious, his experiences with Emily and theosophy had made him acutely aware of the 'tyranny of the enforced cross'[41] and that people should have a clear freedom of choice. The way in which he rallied supporters to his cause recalled the way in which he fought to secure the reconstruction of the King's Way in New Delhi, but there was a critical difference. His campaign on Raisina Hill was a fey rearguard action that stood little chance of success. With the War Stone, however, he had a well founded argument coupled with the ear of a sympathetic client. Not only did it become a key feature in many of the war cemeteries, as Lutyens had envisaged from the outset, but it was a component of many of the larger war memorials that he designed and, even if they were not included in the final schemes as built, they often appeared in the initial presentations that he made to his clients. Yet, it was very much the 'War' Stone, as he explained in a letter to Fabian Ware in 1920: 'As far as the War Stone is concerned, if it was used for any purpose but as a war memorial its whole intention would be destroyed – oddly enough I have been asked to put it up as a family monument in a cemetery – did you ever?'[42] As with the subject of the next chapter, Lutyens had brilliantly succeeded in designing an abstract memorial that had a wide and popular appeal.

Pernes British Cemetery

FOUR

SOUTHAMPTON AND LONDON: A TALE OF TWO CENOTAPHS

IN SUPPORTING LUTYENS upon the War Stone, J.M. Barrie had recognised the desirability that it should have a readily identifiable name, an 'immortal word'. No single word ever emerged and, even though Kenyon wrote a note to Colonel Durham, the IWGC's Commissioner of Works, stating that it should be called 'The War Stone',[1] it became known as the 'Stone of Remembrance' which, Kenyon considered, should be used as its description rather than its title. However, in deference to both Lutyens and Kenyon, it will be referred to by the name that Kenyon preferred for the remainder of this book.

By happenstance, the situation envisaged by Barrie occurred when, in mid-1919, the word 'cenotaph' appeared in the public lexicon to describe the next abstract memorial that Lutyens designed – the simple, temporary structure that was to become, by accident, Britain's national war memorial.

It is tempting to think that, of all people, it was Baker, with his suggestion that the War Stone could function as a tomb, who planted the seed of a cenotaph (which is derived from the Greek word kenotaphion meaning 'empty tomb') as an appropriate form for a war memorial in Lutyens's fertile mind. However, Lutyens had been familiar with it as a concept from Gertrude Jekyll's garden at Munstead Wood, where a large simple stone slab seat under a birch tree had been christened the Cenotaph of Sigismunda by her friend Charles Liddell, a librarian at the British Museum.

However, whatever its genesis, the idea of designing a cenotaph came into Lutyens's mind when, in early 1919, he was commissioned to design a war memorial in Southampton.

A public meeting had been held shortly after the Armistice and a resolution was passed that 'This meeting resolves to provide in Southampton a memorial to perpetuate the memory of those who have fallen in the Great War, and elects a Committee to give effect to this resolution and that its proposals be placed before another town's meeting.' A large committee was formed and the Lord Mayor, Sidney Kimber, was elected both Chairman and Honorary Treasurer. It, in turn, formed a smaller advisory sub-committee which, after considering the various proposals that had been made, decided that 'the people of Southampton would like to point to some really fine outstanding memorial in the best position of the town, always to remind them of the sacrifices made for them and others'.[2] One of the sub-committee members, the local architect Alfred Gutteridge, recommended Lutyens as a potential designer and, on 22 January 1919, the architect met Kimber, Gutteridge and others to discuss the matter and look at potential sites. As was to happen elsewhere, Lutyens rejected the initial site (on Asylum Green) that his clients had chosen and suggested Watts Park instead. However, his first design for a War Stone flanked by a pair of arches each topped by a recumbent figure resting on a bier was rejected by the committee because of its perceived cost (the architect had been given a budget of £10,000). In its place, Lutyens retained the upper part of the arch that contained the figure, but set it on a tall modelled pillar. He kept the War Stone and, in a nod to his proposals for the Temporary War Shrine (see pages 147–8), he included two smaller columns topped by pine cones.

The new design was approved with acclamation at a public meeting on 12 September 1919 and, with drawings that could now be shown to the public, fundraising began in earnest. Tenders were invited for the building work and, on 16 December, a bid of £8,500 was accepted from Messrs Holloway Bros of Westminster. Building work duly commenced and the memorial was completed in time to be unveiled on 6 November 1920 by General Seely, Lord Lieutenant of Hampshire. The unveiling itself, at which Lutyens was present, was a two-stage affair which Seely began by pulling a

The Cenotaph

Lutyens's initial proposal for the Southampton War Memorial was his first use of a cenotaph

cord that allowed a light canvas-covered structure that encased the memorial to fall away. He then addressed the crowd and released the Union Flag that covered the figure at the memorial's top. The ceremony concluded with the Last Post, two minutes' silence, the Lord's Prayer and the National Anthem, before Alderman Kimber, on behalf of the subscribers, formally handed over the memorial to the Council. A total of £9,485/17/3 had been raised which, after the deduction of costs, left a balance of £101/18/11 that was donated to the Hampshire County and Isle of Wight War Memorial Fund. It had taken less than two years from the initial public meeting to completion and was, especially in the light of delays that Lutyens was to experience elsewhere, an exemplary illustration of how to commission a public monument.

Kimber wrote fondly of Lutyens in his autobiography, referring to him as a 'most lovable man, a clever vivacious and most witty conversationalist'.[3] He had hoped to have a further Lutyens war memorial for the city in the churchyard at Highfield and Lutyens agreed to give him the design of his War Cross free of charge, but nothing came of it. They met again in 1929, when Lutyens was in Southampton to catch the *Aquitania* to sail to the USA and the architect professed himself happy at the colouring and weathering of the memorial and its maintenance.

Southampton is important because, as the first completed Lutyens war memorial after the Rand Regiments Memorial in Johannesburg, it helps to set the context for the designs that were to follow. It was Lutyens's first design for a cenotaph, although, architecturally, it can be considered a one-off as it is more ornate and lacks the subtlety of the cenotaphs that were to follow. The design is particularly notable for the amount of carving – not only is there the recumbent soldier himself but there are the city's coat of arms, wreaths containing the emblems of the Armed Services, two lions and, on one of the panelled sides of the main column, a sword on top of an inset cross.

The Southampton cenotaph was still under design when its more famous successor, in London's Whitehall, appeared in temporary form as part of the celebrations around the signing of the Peace Treaty that brought the Great War to its formal end. Although the fighting had ceased on 11 November 1918 (Lutyens was at home in London with Emily) it was still necessary to negotiate the full terms of the surrender and sign a formal Peace Treaty. In anticipation of this event a Peace Celebrations Committee (PCC) was formed under Lord Curzon and met for the first time on 9 May 1919. It planned four days of activities, initially for the period 2–5 August. The committee was keen to understand what the French were proposing and Lionel Earle, Permanent Secretary of the Office of Works, wrote to the Earl of Derby, the British Ambassador to France. Derby replied on 17 May with the information that the French were planning a procession from the Arc de Triomphe to the Panthéon with 'some form of monument or catafalque' as the centrepiece.[4] What happened next is, to a certain extent, conjecture but the Imperial War Museum has a drawing by Lutyens of the Cenotaph, largely as built, dated 4 June, i.e. barely a fortnight after Derby's reply would have been received. It is clear that Lutyens had received no formal commission at this stage but he had a close friendship with both Earle (who was the son of one of Emily's sisters as well as the godfather of their daughter Mary) and Sir Alfred Mond, the Minister for Works. It therefore seems that either or both of them might have discussed the principle of some form of monument with him.

However, there was no mention of this when the PCC met again on 18 June, although there was still concern about the French because the Minutes record that Lloyd George had spoken to his opposite number Georges Clemenceau and had been told that they were thinking of holding a formal military parade.

The signing of the Treaty of Versailles on 28 June gave a clear impetus for the celebrations and, when the PCC met for the third time on 1 July, it chose 19 July as the date for the formal ceremonies. The minutes note that Lloyd George had been told by Clemenceau that the French parade on 14 July would pass a 'great

Southampton War Memorial

Southampton War Memorial

catafalque, which they would salute in honour of the dead'.[5] There was a discussion about the principle of having something similar in the British parade and Mond and General Leach were deputed to consider the matter and consult a 'prominent artist' if they felt it appropriate. Lutyens was an obvious choice and was invited to 10 Downing Street where Lloyd George gave him the commission to design a suitable non-denominational catafalque; Lutyens famously replying that what was needed was not a catafalque, but a cenotaph. He then left Lloyd George to meet Sir Frank Baines, Chief Architect for the Office of Works, and sketched his proposal.

Lord Curzon approved the final design on 7 July, which left less than two weeks for the cenotaph to be constructed out of wood and plaster, work that was completed under the supervision of the Office of Works. There was no mention of a cenotaph in the minutes of the final meeting of the Peace Celebrations Committee on 9 July indicating, perhaps, that it was not seen as

having any particular significance.

Unfortunately the date of the meeting between Lutyens and Lloyd George, which is germane to the whole story of the Cenotaph, is not recorded. Christopher Hussey (Lutyens's biographer) puts it as 19 July (which is clearly wrong, given that it was the date of the parade for which it had been constructed). It is possible that it might have been 4 June but if this had been the case then Mond and Leach would not have been given their actions at the later meeting on 1 July. Alan Greenberg hypothesises[6] that Lutyens and Lloyd George met in early July, which would seem logical as it is supported by the available evidence. Unfortunately, the author of the sketch, Lutyens himself, is of not much help either. He wrote a 'Journal of Remembrance'[7] in 1931 to record his role in the Cenotaph and but did not provide a date for the meeting.

Southampton War Memorial

ABOVE The Peace Procession passes the temporary cenotaph, 19 July 1919
RIGHT Lutyens walks away from the temporary cenotaph, having not been invited to the official ceremonies

In the end, whether it was six weeks from drawing to completion or two is of little relevance. The subject of remembrance had been on Lutyens's mind for some time, stretching back to his first visit to France in 1917. He had been waging his personal battles over the War Stone and was beginning to receive commissions from towns and cities for their war memorials. The Rand Regiments Memorial apart, a war memorial was a new form of commission for him and he had to resolve, in his own mind, the most appropriate architectural style to adopt. If it was not to be in Whitehall then the Cenotaph as we know it would have appeared somewhere else in due course, albeit that it would it is unlikely that it would have received the same level of acclaim. The point to be made is that the concept appears to have been circulating in his mind for some time and, when the need arose to put pen to paper, the Cenotaph as we now know it appeared fully formed.

The memorial as built was largely similar to the '4 June' sketch albeit that there are various drawings in existence showing that Lutyens was experimenting with putting a smoking urn on the top (a matter to which he was to return on a number of subsequent occasions) or, on one drawing, a recumbent figure. Sketches also show either four soldiers or four lions at the base. The carving that was present on the Southampton memorial had gone and what remained was a 35ft-high memorial consisting of a chest tomb atop a rectangular pylon that featured a number of subtle setbacks throughout its height. Ornamentation was limited to three wreaths (one on each end and one on the top) and six flags on poles, three on each side.

The French Peace celebrations took place on 14 July as planned and the catafalque, which formed the centrepiece for the parade was referred to in *The Times*, whether by accident or design, as a 'cenotaph'. A report in the newspaper of 14 July had a sub-heading of 'The Glorious Dead', which, apart from the dates of the two World Wars, is the only wording that appears on the Cenotaph and was supposedly suggested by Lloyd George.

Even before it was unveiled 'R.I.P.' had written to *The Times*: 'The cenotaph in Whitehall is so simple and dignified that it would be a pity to consider it merely an ephemeral erection. It appears to be of more lasting material than the other decorative efforts, and I suggest that it be retained either in its present form or rendered in granite or stone with bronze wreaths to take the place of the evergreens. The absence of all ornament will dispose of any criticism on this score, and the simple inscription will be a constant reminder to us that will be far more poignant than any pile of sculpture or architecture.'[8]

The memorial was unveiled 'quietly and unofficially'[9] the day before the parade of 15,000 soldiers and 1,500 officers marched past it on their way to be reviewed by the King outside Buckingham Palace; famously Lutyens was not invited to the ceremony. Barely had the troops passed before queues began to form as people laid floral tributes around it and the surrounding area quickly became deep in flowers and wreaths.

The Cenotaph struck an immediate chord with the public. Its success owed much to its simplicity and its non-religious appearance. It was a blank canvas on to which people could project their own particular thoughts and, with its combination of simplicity, elegance and lack of triumphalism, the British took it immediately to their hearts. Four days after the Parade Captain Ormesby-Gore, the MP for Stafford, referred to it in the House of Commons and asked a question of Mond as to whether a permanent replica, to be made of Portland stone, should be commissioned. He was supported by other members of the House but Mond replied that the matter would have to be decided by the Cabinet and that he would inform Ministers of the wishes of the House.

However the acclaim for the Cenotaph was not universal. *The Builder* struck a discordant note: 'Notwithstanding the refinement and dignity in the Memorial to the Dead in Whitehall, one could hardly feel that it was a thing to stir one's pulse or adequately typify the reverential memory for millions of dead soldiers. We believe there may be a dramatic quality imparted into designs of this sort without which they signally fail their purpose.'[10]

However, such criticism was in the minority and support for Ormesby-Gore grew. *The Times* published a leader on 26 July calling for a permanent replacement, although it felt that the location in Whitehall was inappropriate due to the risks of accidents, considering that somewhere such as Horse Guards Parade would be more appropriate. Other letters of support appeared in the press and, bowing to the inevitable, the Cabinet meeting on 30 July announced that a permanent replacement would be built on the original site. Lutyens had written a moving letter that was read to the Ministers by Mond and referred to the fact that the Whitehall site had 'been qualified by the salutes of Foch and the allied armies and by our men and their great leaders. No other site would give this pertinence'.[11]

The decision gave Lutyens the opportunity to refine the design and, as with the War Stone, he used entasis, with the result that the horizontal surfaces are arcs of a circle with a centre 900ft below ground level. The vertical surfaces all taper so that they would meet 1,000ft above the ground if extended. The calculations were so complicated that they reputedly occupied thirty-three pages of a manuscript book.

The detailed design was submitted to Mond on 1 November 1919. Apart from subtle changes brought about by the entasis, there was one fundamental change proposed by Lutyens. He had been concerned that the silk flags used on the temporary structure would soon start to look unkempt and, in their place, proposed six furled stone flags. In submitting the design to Mond he wrote: 'As regards the flags, I propose that these should be of stone, and built in solid with the structure carrying them up as pinnacles. Sir Henry Jackson[12] is very kindly assisting me with the impregnation of the stone with colour, and by this means the flags will be constructed of stone in colours proper, and would have, I believe, a very fine effect. I have not been able to prove the possibility of this proposal.'[13]

Mond supported the idea of the stone flags and Lutyens engaged the noted sculptor, Derwent Wood, to carve both them and the wreaths, the latter to be in verdite.

Despite Cabinet approval for the Whitehall site there was still disquiet about the Cenotaph's location in the middle of a busy road. In early December the London Traffic Advisory Committee advocated that it should be moved to Parliament Square but, when the matter was raised again in the House of Commons in a motion to vote through £5,000 of the estimated cost of £10,200, Captain Ormesby-Gore again took a popular lead and, to loud cheers, said that it would be a profound mistake to move it and he was certain that the overwhelming sentiment was to keep it where it was. Stanley Baldwin, Financial Secretary to the Treasury, said that the overall cost included £200 for lighting and, also to further cheers, it was announced that Lutyens was giving his services for nothing. The motion to keep it in its original site was approved albeit that a leader in *The Times* on 18 December and Westminster City Council both called for the Parliament Square site.

The temporary Cenotaph was surrounded with black tarpaulins in January 1920 and the sarcophagus was removed to the Imperial War Museum, where it was used for that year's Armistice Day. The main structure was given to the St Dunstan's Blinded Soldiers' and Sailors' Hostel and used by them to raise funds – the wood being used for bases of bronze souvenir models of the memorial.

The question of road safety was still under discussion in February when Mond reported to Parliament that it was not proposed to construct subways under Whitehall to reach the

Cenotaph. Opposition to the site finally died away and the construction contract was awarded to Messrs Holland, Hannen and Cubitt Ltd and, by 8 May, *The Times* was able to report that the Cenotaph was under construction. It is noticeable that no completion date was given at the outset but it is reasonable to assume that 11 November was at the front of everyone's minds. *The Times* announced, to no surprise, that it would be unveiled by the King. Labour problems due to a shortage of manpower at the quarry in Portland were overcome.

There is, however, a curious interlude concerning the flags. It is received wisdom, based upon an entry in Lady Sackville's diary of 7 August, that Lutyens objected to the change of flags from stone to silk: 'McNed[14] says that his Cenotaph stone flags had been absolutely refused at the last Cabinet meeting, and he is wondering if Lord B [assumed to be Lord Balfour] could have any influence over Lloyd George in getting him to use stone flags instead of silk flags which are advocated by Lord Leigh [*sic*] and Eric Geddes, and which will get bedraggled and smear the Cenotaph. They will have to be changed constantly. Poor McNed says that they have no confidence in him. He took me to Hampton Court to see his beloved Wren's work, and told me how badly the great Wren had been treated.'[15]

However, examination of the files in the National Archives reveals that Lutyens had been aware of the decision for over six months. The prime mover for the change was the Minister of Agriculture and Fisheries, Viscount Lee of Fareham, who wrote a memo about it to his Cabinet colleagues in which he made it clear that Lutyens was aware of the possible change:

Now that the work of replacing the temporary cenotaph in Whitehall by a permanent replica is now actually in hand, I wish to call the attention of my colleagues to the rumour that an attempt is being made to reproduce the national flags which now decorate the structure in carved and dyed Portland stone.

Anything less calculated to inspire reverence or emotion than a petrified and raddled imitation of free and living bunting, which responds to every breeze and mood of nature, it is difficult to imagine, whilst one can easily foresee what its colours will be reduced to after one or two winters of London grime and fog.

It has been suggested, I believe, that in no other ways could the flags be made 'permanent' but is it necessary or desirable that they should be? The staffs could be a permanent as desired, but surely the bunting could be renewed, once a month if need be, at insignificant cost.

I am aware that Sir Edwin Lutyens originally favoured the idea of experimenting with dyed stone, but I discussed the matter with him before he left for India and he told me that he would be quite content to have real and renewable flags affixed to the permanent structure if they were considered preferable.

In 1938 Lutyens designed bronze barriers to be erected at either end of the
Cenotaph after Remembrance Day to protect the floral tributes from the traffic

The cult of 'Strawberry Hill gothic' demanded that every material should be outraged to represent something different; thus stucco was made to imitate wall paper, wall paper to imitate stucco, and metal coal-scuttles to resemble the stone capitals of cathedral columns. I venture to plead that our National flag may be spared from such misplaced ingenuity – which special circumstances would be almost an act of sacrilege.[16]

Lee's suggestion was supported and two days later Earle wrote to A.J. Thomas, Lutyens's assistant, to inform him of the decision. Why then did Lutyens complain about the decision to Lady Sackville when he seems to have been aware of it, if not complicit in it? The only logical explanation would seem to be that, somewhere along the line, he forgot to tell Wood of the alteration and, to save his embarrassment, sought to persuade the Cabinet to change its mind instead, to no avail.

Like the gradient on Raisina Hill, this was another matter in which Lutyens did not get his own way, however unlike the situation in New Delhi, he subsequently seems to have reached an accommodation in his mind about it, later noting that 'the flags themselves, always a flutter of colour in the breeze, seemed more fitting to those who mourned, and that was enough – more than enough'.[17]

Wood's work was not wasted, however, and the stone flags were to appear on many of the memorials that Lutyens subsequently designed – both painted as at Rochdale (page 64) and Northampton (page 72) and unpainted as at Etaples (page 111) and Villers-Bretonneux (page 145).

Whilst Lutyens, Wood and Mond were concerned about the flags there was a brief incident in which a monument appeared that could have supplanted the Cenotaph as the focus of the nation's remembrance of the War. Sir Frank Baines had been working on his own private proposal for a National War Memorial to be built at Hyde Park Corner and an MP, Major Henderson, had asked Mond if the drawings could be exhibited in a room in the House of Commons. *The Times* of 13 July reported that 'extraordinary interest' was being taken in the design however, when an artist's impression was published in the paper the next day showing a 160ft-high tower with flanking pavilions in an Egyptian style, it brought forth a howl of protest. Even though it was Baines's idea to 'symbolise the sacrifice of the Empire by a vast monument of simple design' *The Times* was not impressed: 'We will not ask whether another national war memorial is to be desired; but as the Cenotaph is already one, and has met with the most auspicious reception, we may perhaps inquire whether a second, on a site so near, is necessary.'

The Cenotaph of Sigismunda in Gertrude Jekyll's garden at Munstead Wood
(a copy based upon the original, which has disappeared)

By 20 July Mond had to report to the House of Commons that Baines had prepared the scheme in a personal capacity and that it was 'quite dead'. The Cenotaph had well and truly cemented its position as the nation's war memorial.

On 1 September it was reported that unveiling would take place on 11 November, which had been the obvious date from the outset. Wood was still involved because he was carving the wreaths and had been also been asked to provide the silk flags, and was clearly concerned about the deadline. He was working on a war memorial at Ditchingham in Norfolk and wrote to his sponsors, the Carr Family, that Lutyens and Baines were putting him under pressure.

The ceremony around the unveiling in November had been given added poignancy by the decision, at a relatively late stage, to exhume the body of an 'Unknown Warrior' from the Western Front and inter him in Westminster Abbey. The two events formed a natural pair and both were undertaken with great ceremony, the King unveiling the Cenotaph at 11.00 a.m. in the mellow sunshine of a perfect November day before proceeding to the Abbey. This time, the ceremony at the Cenotaph took place in the presence of its architect.

Popular as it had been in its temporary state, nobody could have foreseen the reaction to the Cenotaph once it had become permanent. As soon as the ceremonies were over people began to gravitate towards it and, within five days, it was estimated that over 1,000,000 people had filed past it and that 100,000 wreaths had been laid (the nearest contrast in modern times would be the 320,000 who were estimated to have filed past Churchill's coffin during the three days in which his body lay in state). Even the reopening of Whitehall to traffic did not deter people and, by the end of the first week, the total was 1,250,000 and the memorial was 10ft deep in flowers. The ephemeral structure that had been designed almost as an afterthought had cemented itself in the hearts of the nation and elevated the status of its architect to that of the most prominent in the land.

FIVE
SPALDING

WHILST IT WAS COMMON to commemorate commanders who had fallen in battle, recognition of the individual troops who had died did not occur until the building of memorials to the Boer War, but such memorials are not particularly commonplace. The Great War led to a substantial change in approach prompted by the scale of the numbers of dead and the fact that they came from all sections of the community. As a result there became a clear wish that every individual who had died should be commemorated by name. Small-scale street memorials had begun to appear soon after the start of the conflict, giving names of local residents who had died, but the matter was brought into sharp focus by the ending of hostilities.

There was concern about the type of memorials that could arise from the potent mix of grief and committees of well-intentioned citizens with no experience of commissioning public works. The Royal Academy took the artistic lead and organised an exhibition at the Victoria & Albert Museum in 1919 'for the purpose of assisting the promoters of War Memorials and others who may be interested in the subject, by providing them with a useful survey of modern work by competent artists, and by suggesting the various forms which Memorials might take'.[1] On display were designs of various proposed memorials as well as theoretical examples prepared by architects hoping for a commission e.g. 'War Memorial to be placed in a public garden in a small town' by Robert W.S. Weir and 'Memorial to a Soldier-Architect' by T. Raffles Davison. The exhibition also contained a section on appropriate building stones and a Bureau of Reference, which gave further information on the architects whose drawings were on show. Lutyens was well represented and there were also models of both the Cenotaph and the War Stone.

Spalding War Memorial

In general, the way in which war memorials were commissioned followed a fairly standard pattern. The first step was a public meeting at which a 'War Memorial Committee' would be formed – such committees being independent of the local councils but, for reasons of practicality, usually having either councillors or senior officers from the council amongst their members. The committee would then select an architect and commence fundraising but, for reasons of propriety, building work would not commence until all of the money had been raised. The success of the fundraising therefore governed the speed with which the memorial could be built and, as will be seen, this could in turn cause a change in the design of the memorial if insufficient money was raised. The commissioning of many of the memorials proceeded smoothly, as at Southampton. However, on occasions, local passions ran high and people exercised their voices either through the pages of the local newspapers or at public meetings.

The amount of archive material about Lutyens's war memorials is variable. In some cases there are detailed sets of committee minutes; but usually there are not and it is necessary to try to knit together the various strands of the story from other sources such as newspapers and the catalogue of Lutyens drawings in the library of the Royal Institute of British Architects (RIBA). Frustratingly, even though they number nearly 5,000, there are few references to the memorials in the letters between Lutyens and Emily, which tend to concentrate on family life and personalities rather than the buildings that he was designing. In some cases there are therefore frustrating gaps in the stories for which there is no apparent explanation.

There is compensation because, where full records exist, they show the role of Lutyens, not in his romantic role as the designer of houses, but fulfilling the day-to-day life that would be recognised by an architect in the twenty-first century —

THE LINCOLNSHIRE, BOSTON, AND SPALDING FREE PRESS, JULY 22, 1919.

THE PROPOSED SPALDING WAR MEMORIAL.

FRONT VIEW FROM THE LAKE.

VIEW OF THE INTERIOR.

THE above sketches of the proposed War Memorial in Ayscoughfee Gardens, Spalding, are from designs of Sir Edwin L. Lutyens, A.R.A., the eminent architect and artist, of London. The scheme is estimated to cost £7,000.

Lutyens's initial proposal for the Spalding War Memorial was illustrated in the local press

liaising with clients and suffering their vicissitudes, as well as producing designs that were too expensive and had to be altered to fit the available budget and, on occasion, losing the commission altogether.

The work on the war memorials also brought to the fore the role played by Albert (A.J.) Thomas, Lutyens's Office Manager, as he deputised for him during Lutyens's annual trips to India that continued until 1930.

Thomas had joined the office as an eighteen-year-old and, even at that tender age, had become Lutyens's right hand man. He was not universally popular within the office but proved adept at organising the workload and dealing with clients in Lutyens's absence, skills that were clearly valued by his employer, whom he resembled in many ways – dressing similarly and smoking the same type of pipe. The pair clearly had a close, if occasionally strained, relationship ('I met A.J. Thomas at the station and I had harsh words with him' Lutyens wrote to Emily on 21 September 1929).[2] Thomas was not particularly popular with the women in Lutyens's life, falling foul of both Emily and Lady Sackville. During his absences in India, Lutyens had

given him Power of Attorney over his affairs, which led to the somewhat surreal situation that Emily had to go to Thomas whenever she needed money. This became particularly awkward when accusations were made against Thomas in 1913 by the client during the construction of the Theosophical Society headquarters (which had been designed by Lutyens) although on this occasion Lutyens sided with Thomas against Emily. He also backed him against Lady Sackville when, in 1919, she accused Thomas of stealing £2,000 worth of bonds from her that she needed to buy a new car. Even though Lutyens diplomatically changed his mind to her face, his initial judgement was proved to be sound when Lady Sackville discovered that she had forgotten that she had sold them.

One of the reasons for the lingering mistrust was that Thomas was an architect in his own right and allowed to supplement his income by undertaking work on his own account,[3] a situation that led to concern about whether he was genuinely working in Lutyens's best interests or using the office for his own purposes. Matters eventually came to a head in 1935 over Thomas's work on the Institut Français du Royaume-Uni on Cromwell Road and led to his dismissal after thirty-three years at Lutyens's side.

Lutyens's work on the war memorials also reveals the role played by the quantity surveyor, E.C. Desch. The quantity surveyor is a key person in the construction process and prepares a detailed schedule (known as the 'Bill of Quantity') of the materials that are needed for the project to enable the contractors to assess the costs and submit their tender price. There is no correspondence between Lutyens and Desch of any particularly relevant interest in the various files but it is clear, because of the frequency with which Desch was used and the fact that he is the only quantity surveyor whose name appears, that he and Lutyens must have enjoyed a close working relationship.

There is no better place to commence this overall survey of Lutyens's war memorials than in the fenland town of Spalding in Lincolnshire – not so much because of the knowledge of the detail of Lutyens's involvement but because it illustrates the local passions that could be roused when war memorials were being discussed. Many of the arguments that were raised elsewhere in the country surfaced at a public meeting that was reported in extraordinary detail in the local newspaper, the *Lincolnshire, Boston, and Spalding Free Press*.

The war memorial at Spalding has been overlooked in the consideration of Lutyens's work: it did not make the pages of the three large format Memorial Volumes that were published after his death and has never appeared in any book about him and his work. Like many of the war memorials, it only receives the barest of mentions in his letters to Emily – one telling her that he is meeting the client the next day and another to tell her that 'My Spalding scheme is carried by the Spalding folk, so that is all right'.[4]

The commission for the memorial arose, indirectly, from Gertrude Jekyll. Spalding's MP, Francis McLaren, was the husband of Gertrude's niece, Barbara, for whom Lutyens had built the Corner House in Cowley Street, London,[5] in 1911. An officer in the Royal Flying Corps, McLaren had died in a flying accident on 30 August 1917 when his Avro 504J suddenly lost power over the North Sea near Montrose. Although rescued, he died of his injuries and his body was taken back to Busbridge in Surrey to be buried in the churchyard, where he rests under an oak headboard designed by Lutyens. Barbara McLaren was keen to retain her connection with Spalding and wrote to the local Urban Council as early as 26 January 1918 to propose the erection of a cloister garden at Ayscoughfee Hall, a house dating back to the mid-1400s, which had been bought by the Council along with its grounds to commemorate Queen Victoria's Diamond Jubilee in 1897. Her original thought was to have a memorial that would record the name of each soldier, and have sufficient room for families to add their own epitaphs, but she realised that this would occupy far too much space. McLaren was most emphatic that there should not be a specific memorial to her husband – he was to take his place in alphabetical order with the other casualties of the War – and she informed the Council that she had engaged Lutyens to produce some designs. Her proposal stimulated local debate and other alternative schemes then emerged which, in an echo of the disquiet felt by Charles Aitken when considering the IWGC's cemetery proposals, ranged from the commemorative, such as a clock on the town's Corn Exchange, to the utilitarian and practical – an amusement hall 'where the public could engage in all healthy pastimes'; public baths and the acquisition of a local field coupled with converting Ayscoughfee Hall itself into a recreation centre for the youth of the town. The latter had particular appeal and a committee was formed to consider the idea of developing it as a YMCA. The matter was raised at a meeting of the Urban Council on 1 July 1919 and again, ten days later, when it held a special meeting with a view to making a recommendation about which of the competing schemes it favoured. It was a somewhat testy meeting that was compromised by the unexplained absence of the Council's Chairman, J.J. Chilvers, who was the only person who had critical information about the relative costs of the proposals. There was much discussion about the YMCA in particular and the difficulties caused by transferring Ayscoughfee Hall, which was a public building, into one that could only be used by paid members. After one and a half hours it was agreed that both Mrs McLaren's scheme and the YMCA should be put forward jointly to a public meting to be held on a date convenient to Mrs McLaren.

Local passions ran high and there was much discussion about the memorial in the 'Letters' pages of the *Free Press*, with various correspondents writing in under their own names or adopting

The wooden headboard that Lutyens designed for the grave of Francis McLaren in Busbridge

pseudonyms such as 'Excelsior', 'Ajax' and 'A Lover of Punctuality', the latter naturally supporting a clock. 'Forward' proposed that there should be a combination of the 'McLaren' and 'Chiming Clock' schemes.

The *Free Press* published details of both of the two main proposals – the 'McLaren' scheme appeared on 22 July, showing a cloistered building around a central garden containing a Great War Stone, and plans of the YMCA were printed a week later. The public meeting was arranged for 1 August and three hundred people packed into the Corn Exchange for a three-hour meeting under the chairmanship of Mr Chilvers. A lively time had been predicted and thus it proved.

In addition to the two schemes favoured by the Council, it had been agreed that there could be a presentation of the chiming clock proposal, perhaps due in no small part to the fact that Mr Chilvers had recently been elected chairman of a committee to promote such a clock as a war memorial. Each proponent was to be allowed fifteen minutes in which to present his or her proposal, following which there would be questions and answers before a general summing up and conclusions. Barbara McLaren

spoke first, the meeting having been reminded that she had recently undergone an operation. She said that she had engaged Lutyens because she thought that the best way of commemorating the dead was with a building and she had therefore approached the best architect that she knew. To applause she reminded the meeting about Lutyens's involvement with the Cenotaph, which had only recently been unveiled. McLaren appreciated that the proposed site was a secluded one but she thought that this was appropriate for such a memorial. She estimated the cost as being £7,000 and pointed out that the neighbouring village of Pinchbeck had raised £1,000 for their memorial so she was sure that Spalding was not going to be out-done! To further applause McLaren (who had already revealed that she would be contributing £1,000 to the memorial) said that her father-in-law, Lord Aberconway (who was unable to attend the meeting), would give a substantial donation to ensure that the memorial was carried out in a worthy manner. Questions were invited from the floor. There was particular concern about the likely cost and whether the memorial would be funded by the rates. 'Voluntary subscription, sir; no rates will be raised for this purpose — not while I am in the chair. The whole cost of the proposed scheme will have to be raised before a penny is expended'[6] replied the Chairman emphatically, to applause. It was confirmed that the memorial would be funded via voluntary contributions and that work would not start until all of the funding was in place. A previous Chairman of the Council asked for McLaren's opinion on the YMCA scheme and she diplomatically replied that it, together with her proposal, would provide a complete memorial for the town — the war memorial being an 'artistic treasure' whilst the YMCA would be a peace memorial.

The next presenter was Mr Howitt of the YMCA, who outlined his scheme to convert Ayscoughfee Hall to provide a mixture of facilities to include a concert hall, billiard room, library and reading room amongst others. He began what became a heated presentation by stating that the soldiers had fought for the future and not the past and that the YMCA would be the best way of representing this. He then responded to what the *Free Press* described as a 'fusillade of questions' raised by the audience. It began gently enough with a local vicar asking 'What on earth has the proposal to do with a memorial to the fallen?' before moving on to the issues of subscriptions and whether they would be sufficient to cover the running expenses. To loud applause (with which the Chairman betrayed his impartiality by joining in) a Mr Barker queried why they were contemplating such a proposal given that it would involve taking Ayscoughfee Hall from the

The setting of Spalding War Memorial, at the head of a formal pool, recalls Bodnant, the family home of Francis McLaren

ABOVE AND OPPOSITE Spalding War Memorial

town. A Mr Gooch stoked the fires even further when stating, to applause, 'I think that we have had enough of this gentleman. He is a stranger to this town. We want to get on with business.' Mr Chilvers, remembering his function as chairman, warned the audience not to stray into personalities. Mr Howitt continued to receive a battering before a Mr Cooper rose to his defence to remind the meeting that it was their wish to consider those who had died and what they might have wanted. The Chairman then accused him of making a speech rather than asking a question but Mr Cooper asserted his right to continue, as other people had also made speeches. The meeting then took a distinctive turn for the worse when a councillor in the audience asked whether the Council had ever been asked to give Ayscoughfee Hall to the YMCA. 'Certainly not, to my knowledge,' replied Mr Chilvers but this was not good enough for the questioner, who asserted that the Council had been asked such a question in the past and had very deliberately stated that they would not give it away. The questions continued and Mr Chilvers' impartiality was called into question, with the result that he was asked to stand aside and,

according to the newspaper report 'amid some excitement' the Clerk took the chair although, as soon as he did, there was a motion that Mr Chilvers should be allowed to resume, which he duly did, to 'loud and continued applause'. The questioning then resumed but the excitement had all become too much for Mrs Chilvers, the Chairman's wife who, sitting near the front, proceeded to faint. Her husband rushed from the stage to her assistance, asking the Council's vice-chairman to deputise for him on the stage. The questions continued before Mr Chilvers reappeared and, to the relief of those present, closed the presentation.

By contrast, Dr Farrow, the instigator of the scheme for a chiming clock, received a much warmer reception. He said that he felt that a clock was a suitable item to commemorate a great victory and that, being a carillon, it would be available to be played by anyone who was familiar with a keyboard. He also considered that it would be particularly suitable for being played on festive occasions as well as being able to function as a firebell.

The meeting then degenerated into a general discussion as various members of the audience advanced their own proposals. A Mr

Shotliff raised the issue of whether it would be better to use the money to provide houses for the returning troops, arguing that it would be better to do this and put inscriptions of those who had died upon them rather than spend the money on a building which was only visited by a minority of the townsfolk. The remainder of his speech was drowned in the general rising disquiet when Shotliff was asked if he had any specific proposals and replied that it was the function of the Council to find suitable sites for housing. The next proposal was made by a Mr Bates who suggested that the money should be used to provide playgrounds in the various wards throughout the town so that children would not have to play on the roads. Mr Chilvers responded by welcoming this idea but raised the problem of how the necessary land would be acquired.

The meeting then swung back to considering whether there should be a war memorial rather than a utilitarian scheme. Rev. Ash, who had been making comments from the floor throughout the meeting, referred to Mrs McLaren's 'delightful speech' and said that her plan for the memorial was 'absolutely delightful' and that all the other plans had their own merits 'nevertheless, I think that the nation has shown by the feeling that it exhibited towards the Cenotaph that what we should have is a simple monument "To Our Glorious Dead". My idea is that the site in Spalding for this is the Market Place.' His proposal received applause and he continued 'I don't care what the memorial is — a granite obelisk, a bronze representation of the Lincs. Territorials on the top, and the names of the boys — as long as everybody who came to Spalding could see it: and it would remain there for years and years. I know nothing about the expense but my feeling is we don't want anything utilitarian at all.' He sat down to applause.

The meeting then moved to consider formal proposals and, after a flurry of proposals and amendments, six schemes emerged:

1. Mrs McLaren's Scheme and the YMCA
2. Mrs McLaren's Scheme and the Clock
3. Memorial in the Market Place and Clock
4. Cenotaph in the Market Place
5. Fund for the Widows and Children of the Fallen
6. YMCA and Cenotaph in the Market Place

The Spalding Memorial contained two stone flags, paid for by Francis McLaren's brother Henry. The lower parts of the flagpoles have since been removed

have the vote?' Unfortunately, as the Chairman pointed out, that was the reality of the situation.

Alternative suggestions were made as to how the preferred scheme should be chosen and whether it should be some form of proportional representation (e.g. putting a '6' against the best, '5' against the second best and so on and counting the total); putting '1' against the best, '2' against the second best and counting the number of '1's or whether each person should be given a single vote. The Chairman put the matter to the floor but the meeting descended into confusion and, with the cries of 'one man, one vote' from the rear of the hall, Mr Chilvers closed an exciting meeting before a decision could be made.

It is clear that there must have been further discussions amongst the key people in Spalding after the meeting because, as will be apparent, in the confusion of the meeting the six schemes that were chosen did not include the controversial one put forward by the YMCA in isolation from the others. Some sort of consensus seems to have emerged because, when the voting forms were produced, they included an option that had not been discussed at the meeting – a reduced form of the Lutyens memorial together with the clock.

The poll was duly taken three weeks, on 23 August, on the basis of the Electoral Roll and with each voter being given a single vote, with the result:

Mrs McLaren's Scheme (modified) and the Clock ... 459
Mrs McLaren's Scheme in its original form 286
Obelisk in Market Place and Clock 214
Mrs McLaren's Scheme and the YMCA 139
Cenotaph in the Market Place 40
Fund for the Widows and Children of the Fallen 29
YMCA alone 16

The one surprise, given the mood of the meeting, was the low turnout in the vote – only 17 per cent, compared with figures of under 60 per cent and 50 per cent at the previous General and Local Elections respectively. The *Free Press* raised its concerns about the number who voted in its Leader, which welcomed the result of the poll, and speculated that the extension of the franchise was responsible. Perhaps the local residents were bored with both the War and the whole memorial debate.

The Urban Council held a special meeting on 10 September 1919, at which the 'Spalding War and Victory Memorials Committee' was formed in order to raise funds for the memorial. Lutyens produced an amended design, omitting the cloister, which takes the form of a white rendered Doric temple with a clay pantile roof in front of which is a War Stone. The setting, at the head of a long reflecting pool, is very reminiscent of the well known view of Pin Mill at Lord Aberconway's home at Bodnant in North Wales.

Clearly the budget was not an issue at this stage but the meeting was far from over, as it then had to decide how a choice was to be made between the various alternatives. Needless to say, given the way in which the meeting had developed, this part of it did not pass without debate either. The initial proposal was that the vote should be based on the Electoral Roll and Mr Gooch (who had earlier shown his opposition to the YMCA scheme) offered to contribute £20 towards the costs. However, there was then a discussion about whether such a vote would include the returning soldiers before it was clarified that it would include everyone who was on the register on 15 April 1919. A Miss Crampton then stood up to point out that she was not entitled to vote (voting for women was introduced in 1918 but was restricted to those who were over thirty and either householders or the wives of householders). It was then suggested that the vote should be open to everybody over in the town over eighteen. To loud applause a Mr Frost stated 'Boys of eighteen are old enough to be shot at and the girls old enough to let their sweethearts go – why shouldn't they

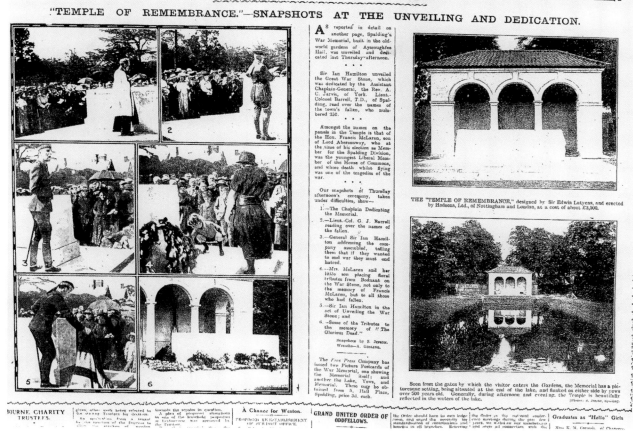

Having recorded the inception of Spalding War Memorial in such detail, the *Free Press* dutifully recorded its unveiling

Despite the optimism shown by Barbara McLaren at the meeting on 1 August 1919 the Committee raised only £400 more than the residents of Pinchbeck. Lutyens's modified scheme cost £3,500, of which Barbara and her father-in-law contributed £1,000 each and Sir Herbert and Lady Jekyll £100 whilst the Hon. Henry McLaren (Barbara's brother-in-law) donated the two stone flags that are inside the building.

The memorial was built by Hodson Ltd of Nottingham and was unveiled by General Sir Ian Hamilton on 8 June 1922 accompanied by stirring speeches from both him and Rev. A.C.E. Jarvis, the Assistant Chaplain General. Barbara McLaren was accompanied by her sons, sister (Pamela McKenna), her parents, Lord Aberconway and her sister-in-law. Bouquets of flowers were provided from the gardens at Bodnant, the boyhood home of her husband. In words that echo down the years to today, the General referred to the fact that the dead had died to end wars: 'The result has been so different. Just think what the results are. Europe is a seething cauldron of racial hatred; Ireland . . . is linked in our minds with the idea of murder; Mesopotamia, India and Egypt are straining at the leash of civilisation and kept in only by the utmost efforts of the exhausted British taxpayer . . . if you want to end war, you must end hatred; if you want to end hatred, you must not be too hard on the vanquished, or grind them down. In that way, I believe we shall be working towards peace, doing our best in our own small way each of us – and Spalding minds united are a big force – and in that way we shall perpetually honour the memory of those whose untimely death we have come here to commemorate.'[7]

The Rev. Jarvis, illustrating the way that values change over time, referred to the dead 'amidst the Poppies of Flanders, but, unfortunately, the Poppy is a heathen symbol, and speaks of oblivion'.[8]

The speeches concluded, a lone bugler played the Last Post, the National Anthem was sung and led by Councillor Banks (who had succeeded Mr Chilvers as Chairman of Spalding Urban Council) wreaths and flowers were laid around the War Stone.

SIX
CIVIC PRIDE

SOUTHAMPTON AND SPALDING were amongst the first of fifty-two war memorials in the UK that were to be designed by Lutyens. The grandest were those that were designed for the major towns and cities and which, with one exception, form the subject of this chapter.

The exception is at York, where the City Memorial is separated from the North Eastern Railway Memorial – Pyramus and Thisbe style – by the city's medieval walls. Because their stories are intertwined, it is appropriate to consider them both together.

It was at a meeting on 5 May 1919 that York Council's Finance Committee first considered the possibility of a local war memorial that would take the form of a public utility. Two public meetings resulted in a series of suggestions that varied widely in aspiration from the grand to the mundane and it was decided that those for a new City Hall and a convalescent home should be carried forward.

A War Memorial Committee was then established, consisting of twelve members including the Lord Mayor and the Dean of York but, rather than clarify matters, it only served to generate new ideas that were equally grandiose, such as a new bridge over the River Ouse, a new maternity hospital, homes for war widows and various educational schemes.

The Committee opened a memorial fund on 1 August and, perhaps because the public was confused by the lack of a single clear proposal, only a few hundred pounds was donated. Further meetings resulted in even more suggestions being made before the matter was brought to a head at a public meeting on 14 January 1920, when it was agreed that the money raised should be used for a permanent memorial rather than a utilitarian scheme. A proposal for a memorial garden with archway and cenotaph was then mooted and the City Engineer was asked to

produce some rough plans, which he estimated construction costs being about £7,000.

In the meantime the North Eastern Railway Company (NERC) was contemplating the site for its own memorial. It had considered Newcastle and Darlington as potential locations because, like York, they were both on the East Coast line that formed the backbone of the company's railway network. However, York was the logical choice given that it was the company's headquarters, and a site was chosen outside the company's offices in the shadow of the city walls. Having abandoned its initial idea of asking employees to contribute towards the cost of the memorial, the company's AGM on 20 February 1920 decided to spend £20,000 on a suitable scheme and also to approach Lutyens, whose formal appointment, at a fee of £700 plus out-of-pocket expenses, was agreed in October 1921. The company clearly considered that, by appointing Lutyens, they had secured a safe pair of hands because he was described by R. Bell, the NERC's Deputy General Manager as 'the fashionable architect and therefore he could do no wrong'.[1]

The city's War Memorial Committee decided to follow the NERC's lead and also appoint Lutyens to design their memorial, although the committee gave him a somewhat smaller budget of £2,000. The architect visited York on 12 August and, together with the Lord Mayor and the City Engineer, inspected no fewer than nine potential sites, reporting back within a month to recommend two alternative locations close to each other alongside the city walls – his preference was a site outside the walls on a former cholera burial ground near the station, whilst his second choice was one inside the walls, in the moat alongside Lendal Bridge that crossed the River Ouse. The Committee preferred the latter, which was 100 yards from the site of the proposed NERC Memorial and, on 2 November Lutyens was asked to prepare a formal proposal. His design, which was submitted eleven

Rochdale War Memorial

weeks later, was a unique treatment for his War Stone that saw it, complete with its base of three steps, raised on a giant podium to have an overall height of 18ft. It was a dramatic change that removed the ability of the Stone to act in its role as a quasi-altar and saw it treated as an object of veneration rather than something with a practical purpose, albeit that it was largely symbolic. It referred back to the way in which he had designed the War Shrine in Hyde Park. It was an approach that Lutyens did not repeat.

The design was approved by the Committee at a meeting on 24 June 1920 subject to minor amendments in connection with the inscriptions. A proposal to put some flower beds on the ramparts near the memorial was defeated because it was felt that the design of such details should be left to Lutyens. The meeting heard that the collection had raised about £1,380.

Lutyens's drawings were put on display in the windows of the *Yorkshire Herald* and approved at a public meeting on 25 November, despite opposition from the Yorkshire Architectural and York Archaeological Society (YAYAS), which felt that the memorial would obstruct the view when walking from the railway station into the city.

Meanwhile the design of the North Eastern Railway Company's memorial was running into problems of its own. Lutyens had used his generous budget to design a memorial with a 54ft-high obelisk at its centre raised upon a U-shaped wall that accommodated the names of the 2,236 fallen and which wrapped around a War Stone. However, the restricted nature of the site meant that the wall would have to be cut into the ramparts of the adjacent city wall. Despite this, the proposal was approved by the Council subject to the wall being underpinned to ensure its stability. This brought forth objections, with both the YAYAS and the York Archaeological Society being particularly vociferous. The NERC's own architect suggested that the memorial could be moved 10ft away from the wall but his proposal was rejected by Lutyens in a cable from India.

Matters came to a head in February 1922 when the secretary of the YAYAS, the redoubtable Dr William Evelyn, used the opportunity of one of his regular lectures to society members to attack the proposals for the two memorials. Having finished his prepared presentation on the subject of the abbey walls he proceeded to attack the NERC Memorial. Referring to the the fact that the coming of the railway to York had lead to the breaching of the city walls, he argued 'I for one think that the old fortification of York is a sacred emblem commemorative of the prestige, skill, daring and bravery of the soldier in times medieval. . . . That being so I deprecate any interference with that sacred emblem . . . I think it is an enormous pity that they can find room in which to place a sacred emblem commemorative of the patriotism, bravery and self-sacrifice of our own soldiers of the

twentieth century and that it should be considered necessary to deface and despoil another sacred emblem.'[2] Evelyn did not spare the City Memorial either when, somewhat strangely in view of his attendance at the public meeting the previous November, he stated 'none of us knows what shape or size this is to be'.[3]

There were also rumblings in the local press about the proximity of the two sites and the disparity in the heights of the two memorials. Councillor Geoffrey Jalland, writing to the Yorkshire Herald said 'But to have two memorials within so short a distance of each other, always remembering that strangers coming into York for the first time will meet the North Eastern Railway one first, is not only sheer waste of money, but a great lack of good taste as well'[4] and he suggested that the City Memorial should be repositioned on the cholera burial ground, which had been Lutyens's first choice of site.

The *Yorkshire Herald*, although not wishing 'to dissent from what is recommended by Sir Edwin Lutyens', argued for consideration of Jalland's letter:

The sites of the two memorials to be erected in York on the ramparts within the City Wall, practically in line at a distance of 300 ft. The city memorial is to be placed on a slope near the archway through the Wall, while the North Eastern Railway memorial is to occupy a position on the site of the Old Station premises. The disparity in the height of the two memorials is the point to which Councillor Jalland directs attention. The height of the city memorial is to be 18ft., while the railway memorial rises to a height of 53ft., both will be visible from the level of Lendal Bridge, and we take it as Mr. Jalland's view that the city memorial, though massive and imposing, will be dwarfed by the towering and impressive outline of the N.E.R. structure 100 yards further on in the same line of vision. There are certainly obvious objections to the site that has been chosen. It is situated at the lowest point of the Lendal slope, which would further emphasise the smallness of the city memorial compared with the railway monument. The city memorial is only to cost £2,000 while the Directors of the North Eastern Railway have voted £20,000 for their structure, so that it is necessarily on a much bigger scale besides occupying a higher and more prominent site. We do not think the citizens have had sufficient information about the matter of their memorial. . . . With every respect for the distinguished architect, we think the matter requires further consideration. So far as we are aware no one has yet seen a complete drawing of the city memorial.[5]

Lutyens, however, did not see the proximity of the two memorials as a problem and expressed the view that the two memorials would compliment each other, showing a common purpose.

PROPOSED WAR MEMORIAL
CITY OF YORK

Lutyens's initial proposal for the York War Memorial featured a War Stone
raised on a podium

The issues on both sites were brought to a head at a meeting convened by the Ancient Monuments Board at the NERC offices on 8 July 1922. The city walls had been formally recognised as an ancient monument and the consent of the Board would therefore be necessary for any work that affected them. To help inform the decision, the NERC had gone to the expense of erecting a full-sized wooden replica of its memorial. The Chief Inspector of Ancient Monuments, C.R. Peers, heard representations from proponents and their architect as well as from the objectors including the inevitable Dr Evelyn. Lutyens was asked if he could modify the design of the NERC Memorial to move it away from the walls and, whilst he agreed to prepare an alternative plan, he commented that it would be to the detriment of the overall scheme and that the reduced wall space that would result would mean that he would have to reduce the size of the carvings of the names. Peers had no concerns about the location of the City Memorial because he noted that its proposed site was not part of the original mound for the City Walls but had been constructed later, when the approach was made to Lendal Bridge.

Lutyens's revised plans for the NERC Memorial were approved by the Corporation of York in October and construction work started the following year, by which time the NERC no longer existed as an independent company as it had been incorporated into the London and North Eastern Railway. The memorial was unveiled by Lord Plumer on 14 June 1924. In his speech at the ceremony Lord Grey of Falloden,[6] one of the NERC's directors, referred to the losses suffered by the company's Board: 'The old North Eastern Board and its General Manager numbered about twenty persons. Out of those twenty, four lost sons in the war and three of them lost only sons. There is no reason to suppose that this proportion is exceptional.'[7] Dr Evelyn pithily commented that he considered the memorial to be a 'pagan erection'.[8]

Peers's decision did not, however, dampen the growing public opposition to the City Memorial. An anonymous letter published in the *Yorkshire Herald* on 8 March 1923 even suggested that the Statue of George Leeman in Station Road should be moved in order to make way for the new war memorial, a suggestion given added piquancy by the fact that Leeman was a former Chairman of the North Eastern Railway Company. The

North Eastern Railway Company War Memorial in the shadow of York's
City Walls

York War Memorial

correspondent made the point that the King had recently allowed the statue of Prince Albert to be moved for the memorial in Manchester (which was also to be designed by Lutyens). By 30 April 1923 Lutyens had submitted a costing which came to £2,400 and it was hoped that the memorial could be ready by Armistice Day, 11 November.

Even though the proposed site had been endorsed at every public meeting that had been called by the War Memorial Committee to discuss the matter, when it learnt that Dr Evelyn had called a public meeting on 3 May 1923, the Committee announced that it was prepared to reconsider the matter. Evelyn's meeting went ahead in any event and seems to have aroused passions similar to those at Spalding. He used lantern slides to suggest potential alternative sites for the memorial, whilst Lutyens's role was defended by Edwin Gray who took a sideswipe at Evelyn and his supporters: 'I prefer to follow the taste of Sir Edwin Lutyens to that of the handful of self constituted guardians of the aesthetic beauties of York.'[9] The meeting's chairman, C.E. Elmhirst, reminded the audience that the site by the city walls was not even Lutyens's first choice and that he had,

apparently, suggested that the memorial should be placed in the middle of the River Ouse.

A.J. Thomas visited York on Lutyens's behalf in order to try and resolve the conflict once and for all and by 3 August a new site, part of a piece of land called Walkers Paddock, was proposed. It had been first suggested by an Arthur Gladwin in a letter to the *Yorkshire Herald* nearly two years earlier on 3 December 1921:

There is a large triangular piece of ground close to the 'Leeman' statue, bounded by the Station Hotel Gardens on one side, by Leeman Road on another, and by Station Avenue on the third. At present it is enclosed and planted with trees and shrubbery, but if it were cleared and laid out as an ornamental garden, with turf, gravel paths, and flower beds, with the memorial in the centre, it suggests itself to me as being as suitable as any site yet proposed. Seats could be placed here and there, and the result would combine what I judge to be the two most desirable features, viz.:

1) That the memorial should be in a public place, on view of both citizens and visitors; and

2) That there should nevertheless be facilities for these relatives who will regard this as a place apart where they may rest in quiet thought in the peaceful 'Garden of the Unforgotten'.

By coincidence, the land was owned by the NERC who decided to present it to the City as a gesture of thanks for the good relations between the two bodies, following their amalgamation into the London and North Eastern Railway.

By mid-November, full permission was given for the use of the Paddock. Lutyens had redesigned the memorial completely and proposed a large scale version of his War Cross standing alongside a War Stone, at an estimated cost of £1,627. Tenders were then invited and, six months later, one of Lutyens's regular contractors, Nine Elms Stone Mason Company, was chosen, having bid £2,446/11/8. However, as this was considerably in excess of the £1,100 in the Memorial Fund, the War Stone was omitted and the Council rather than Nine Elms undertook the layout of the grounds and associated works direct.

Two weeks before the unveiling of the memorial by the Duke and Duchess of York on 25 June 1925 Thomas, *en route* to Manchester, met the Town Clerk together with Mr Petre of Nine Elms to check on the visual impact of the memorial. As a memento a bottle was included in the structure together with coins and a copy of a current newspaper.

After the memorial had been unveiled Thomas advised that a yew hedge should be planted, starting at 3ft and being allowed to grow to 4ft 6in. He also much hoped that the trees in the triangular piece of ground opposite the memorial gardens would not be taken down although some of the ground would be cleared in order to open up a view of the memorial. Thomas also advised the Parks Committee 'When the memorial is completed it should be hosed down once a week, but not washed'.[10]

Despite concerns over the costs, when the account was finally reconciled in April 1926 there was £400 left in the Fund, which was spent on a pair of iron entrance gates to the Gardens. Thomas and Petre met the Town Clerk at the Memorial on 1 June 1926 and subsequently submitted a rough design of gates and pillars together with estimates, and the gates were duly installed in December. Even so there was still £17/6/2 left in the Fund which was then used to pay for three wooden benches. Lutyens's fees for the long drawn out saga were £122/5/3 together with out-of-pocket expenses of £20/8/2.

Things went a lot more smoothly in Rochdale, which followed in the footsteps of Southampton as a commission with a generous budget that went well. A public meeting was held at the Town Hall on 10 February 1919, following which it was decided that there should be a physical memorial as well as a fund to provide for the dependents of servicemen who had been disabled or killed during the conflict. Lutyens was approached to be the designer and prepared a scheme for a bridge over the River Roch

that contained a low-level recumbent figure, which would have been barely above eye level, together with a War Stone as the centrepiece of the bridge deck. However this was not preferred and it was decided to build a more conventional memorial in the form of a cenotaph accompanied by a War Stone, on a site of Manor House, an eighteenth-century house on the Esplanade that had formerly been owned by Lord Byron. The building had an added significance because it was close to the Town Hall and had been the enlisting point for many of the local soldiers before they went off to war. It was purchased as a site for the memorial and given to the town by a former mayor William Cunliffe, who had been made a Freeman of the Borough in 1919. Lutyens prepared a number of designs for the cenotaph, which are contained in the RIBA and the final version, complete with painted stone flags, a recumbent soldier and a War Stone was approved on 18 November 1921, with the tender from Hodson's Ltd of Nottingham being accepted on 31 March 1922.

The large sum of £29,443/10/- was collected of which £12,611 was spent on the memorial, which was unveiled by the Earl of Derby on 26 November 1922. The Earl was the scion of a local political dynasty and served in the War in various capacities as Director of Recruiting, Secretary of State for War and, at the War's end, was the British Ambassador to France.

He also unveiled the memorial in Manchester, two years later on 12 July 1924, when he was accompanied by a Mrs Dingle, from the city's working class suburb of Ancoats, who had lost three sons in the War.

In contrast to Rochdale, the citizens of Manchester were somewhat lethargic in organising their memorial and it was not until 1922, after pressure was brought to bear by the British Legion, that a War Memorial Committee was formed under the chairmanship of the mayor. It agreed to set a budget of £10,000, which was quickly raised. Despite this promising start the scheme quickly ran into trouble over the key issues of, firstly, where the memorial should be located and, secondly, who was to design it. Three sites were suggested – Albert Square, St Peter's Square and Piccadilly. The former was the logical choice, being the city's main civic space in front of the Waterhouse's powerful Town Hall and was recommended to the City Council.

However, there was considerable opposition to this choice from the public and the city's artistic community led by the Manchester Art Federation (which included the Manchester Society of Architects and the Manchester School of Art) and the Royal Manchester Institution. The main reason for the concern was the need to move some existing statues within the square to create an appropriate setting for the new memorial. The fact that the King had already given approval to the relocation of the statue of his grandfather, Prince Albert, cut no ice (this was the statue referred to in the discussions regarding the York City Memorial). The matter was therefore debated by the City

ABOVE Rochdale War Memorial with the Town Hall designed by
W.H. Crossland in the background
BELOW Lutyens's initial proposal for Rochdale featured a war memorial bridge

Council. The logical solution of relocating the statue of Prince
Albert only and leaving the others *in situ* was defeated and a vote
between Piccadilly (the second choice of site) and St Peter's Square
went 71–30 in favour of the former. However the overall planning
of the Piccadilly area was unclear so, with a wish not to delay
things further, the third option of St Peter's Square became, by
default, the memorial's location.

The choice of a suitable architect then arose. The Manchester
Art Federation, supported by the Royal Society of British
Sculptors, had advocated an open competition and the the War
Memorial Committee had appointed local architect Percy
Worthington as the assessor (by coincidence his brother Hubert
had briefly worked with Lutyens in 1912). However, Worthington's
independence was compromised because the committee wished to
reserve the right to overrule his decision, which brought much
criticism in the local press. The continuous haggling worked in
Lutyens's favour because he was awarded the commission after a

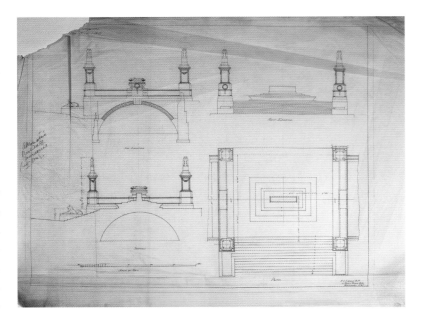

Manchester War Memorial's setting is compromised by the proximity of the cross designed by Temple Moore

sub-committee was delegated to appoint an architect 'who can be trusted to prepare a suitable design'. Given all the infighting and controversy, the design process for the memorial received a relatively smooth passage and the unveiling was to take place little more than a year after the site had been agreed. Lutyens's design comprised two obelisks, a War Stone and a cenotaph with a draped figure. It was built by Nine Elms Stone Masonry Works of London, the committee having either forgotten or ignored its original wish to use the construction of the memorial to benefit local firms and the unemployed within Manchester. The cost came to £6,490, the balance of the fund being used to provide hospital beds for the families of servicemen.

The choice of St Peter's Square had not been without its own problems though as it had its own existing monument to be accommodated – a cross by the Late Gothic Revival architect, Temple Moore, commemorating the demolished St Peter's Church. Although the Bishop of Manchester and the church

trustees had given their consent for the cross to be moved, the work did not take place and, by the time that the memorial came to be built, the trustees had changed their minds. The location of the cross was unfortunate because it severely impinged on the setting of the memorial and appears to be an integral part of it. In the end it was Lutyens who had the last word, saying that he did not object to the cross remaining, owing to the 'susceptibilities of the donors'. The heated discussions regarding the memorial site resulted in a compromise that clearly shows.

The city of Leicester raised a similar sum to Rochdale but, unlike their Northern counterparts, decided to spend it all on the memorial itself. As a result, Leicester has the most imposing of all of Lutyens's war memorials in the United Kingdom and yet, had matters progressed differently, it could have been more imposing still. The process by which the memorial was built was a tortured one that involved a major change of design philosophy and a critical shortage of funds that resulted in key members of the War

Leicester War Memorial

Memorial Committee putting their hands in their own pockets to cover the deficit.

A public meeting to consider the advisability of having a war memorial was held on 14 May 1919 and a twenty-three-man War Memorial Committee was formed a week later, with the Duke of Rutland as Chairman and the Mayor, Sir Jonathan North MP, as his Vice-Chairman. Separate sub-committees were established to deal with design and finance. A suggestion from the Duke that the memorial should be sited in front of the Town Hall was unanimously rejected by the Council and the Committee arranged site visits on 24 September to consider alternatives at Leicester Castle and in the town's Victoria Park, a 69-acre park on the south-eastern edge of the city centre that had been laid out in 1883. It was agreed that a design by a Mr Stevens should be referred to the Design Sub-Committee. There is no further reference to Stevens's design and at meetings in October Victoria Park was confirmed as the preferred choice of location and it was agreed to appoint Lutyens as architect.

Lutyens visited Leicester on 20 October, meeting the Duke and others, and visited the Park. It is clear that the Council also had other plans because when Lutyens submitted his plans for the memorial he referred to 'the future development of the locality of Victoria Park as a civic centre which had been suggested to him'.[11] The plans that he submitted for the memorial were unique within

his canon and, had they been implemented as he designed, would have formed one of the country's most unusual and impressive war memorials. Responding to the park setting he proposed:

The planting of avenues of lime in the plan of a Cathedral Church, consisting of a nave, aisles and transepts with an apse at the east end. At the west end looking east will be the Cenotaph, the same as the one erected to the Glorious Dead in London. At the crossing, in a circle of stone walling on which will be inscribed the names of those brave men who gave their lives will be the Great War Stone, a monolith Altar, similar to those in our military cemeteries abroad and with the same phrase 'Their Name Liveth for Evermore'. Paved paths will accentuate the plan and lead to the monuments and trees will provide dignity and give the atmosphere that should pervade a building devoted to sacred purpose, and this without offence to any of the many creeds within the Empire for which the men of Leicester fought.[12]

The plans were accepted and a model of the site was made by Mr Nott of the Leicester School of Art and placed on display in the City Museum. A Committee meeting on 8 June 1920 reported that a cost estimate of £8,050 had been received from A.J. Thomas. There was obviously some concern about the site because Lutyens

The approach to Leicester War Memorial from Lancaster Road

was asked to visit Leicester again and met the Committee a fort-night later. He reiterated his reason for choosing the particular site on the London Road side of the park because it was on high ground and would get plenty of sun, as it faced south. His decision was endorsed by the Committee and it was agreed to hold a meeting on 25 October at the Town Hall to seek public confirmation of the design. This was received albeit that the cost was reported to being £20,000. The reason for the increase was not known but perhaps it was because Thomas's first figures were preliminary estimates rather than detailed costings. In any event, tenders were sought from six building contractors and the Finance Sub-committee on 4 March 1921 heard that bids had been received ranging from £15,139/11/7 (Thrall and Son) to £24,999 (Cubitt and Co). In contrast, the funds raised amounted to £4,282/0/3.

The lack of money was of concern and at its meeting on 10 June the Committee decided that 'Having regard to the financial position and to the present state of trade in the city it is desirable that the consideration of the matter of procedure with the memorial be adjourned to October'.[13] The Site and Design Sub-committee was asked to look at the design to see if cost savings could be made.

The matter was discussed with Thrall's and Thomas reported back in October that they could reduce their price to £12,382/15/3 through general reductions and the omission of the carved

names on the circular wall. In return, Lutyens was given a reduced budget of £8,000. This resulted in further design omissions, including the wall, but nevertheless the architect responded to the challenges and Thomas was able to write to the client on 14 March 1922 to report how the figure could be met. It was agreed to call a meeting of the full Committee on 29 March because 'It had been found impracticable from a financial point of view to carry out the original design'.[14]

By now eighteen months that had elapsed since the public meeting it seems as though the intervening period had brought a rising level of opposition to the memorial, some of which is hinted at in the minutes of the meeting on 29 March at which, after considerable discussion, it was decided 'that the original scheme of Sir Edwin Lutyens be not proceeded with, and that a memorial worthy of the city be erected on the ground near the main entrance gates'.[15] Reading between the lines it would seem that it was felt that a tree cathedral would not be impressive enough for the citizens of Leicester. Tree cathedrals are rare and there is nothing within Lutyens's background to hint at where his idea originated. The most well-known one in the United Kingdom is at Whipsnade and was created in 'faith, hope and reconciliation' after the War but it did not owe its genesis to Lutyens: it was inspired by a visit by its creator, E.K. Blyth to Liverpool

Anglican Cathedral in the autumn of 1930. In modern times, a tree cathedral has also been built as one of the features of the park network within Milton Keynes.

Happily for Lutyens, although his idea had been dismissed, the Committee wished to retain him as their architect. It deliberated on site in Victoria Park two days later and agreed he should be asked design the memorial in the form of an archway. Lutyens was clearly conscious that there was potentially a wide gap between the committee's aspirations and its budget because, when he met the members in the Park once more on 4 May he warned them that an arch would cost £20,000–25,000, whereas an obelisk would cost only about half that amount. Nevertheless, the same committee that had not been able to raise £20,000 for a tree cathedral now decided to proceed with an archway that could cost £5,000 more.

Lutyens's design for an arch was approved in July and Thomas provided a cost of £24,600 in September. Funds at the end of the year totalled £10,000 and it was the intention to increase this to £15,000 before calling a second public meeting. The Town Clerk and two members of the Committee met Lutyens in London on 18 January 1923 to discuss the finer details of the design, which included Lutyens's favoured device of a flare on top of the arch activated by petrol that would produce smoke by day and a flame at night. It was intended that the arch would form the entrance to the Park from London Road, which would necessitate the removal of the existing gates and a lodge.

However, despite all of the deliberations in the Park there were concerns within Leicester City Council about the precise location of the memorial and its Estates Committee suggested a site away from the entrance in line with Regent Road. The Committee agreed to consult with Lutyens but, before it could do so, the meeting on 23 April decided 'having now heard an explanation of the Town Planning Scheme'[16] that the site should be changed, yet again, to one at the head of Lancaster Road and that 'subject to any observations of Sir Edwin Lutyens's'[17] the proposal should be submitted to a public meeting. The same meeting heard that eight tenders had been received from potential builders, with the cheapest being The Nine Elms Stone and Masonry Works at £24,450 and the most expensive Messrs Palmer and Plumb at £43,704. Thrall's, who had won the original tender, bid £25,550/11/2. Acceptance of the tender was left 'until certain enquiries have been made with regard to local labour as far as possible participating in the erection of the memorial'.[18]

The second public meeting at which the citizens of Leicester had the opportunity to see their memorial took place on 16 May at the County Rooms and 50–60 people attended along with Lutyens himself, who had been shown the new site by the Committee ear-

lier in the day. The Duke of Rutland was unable to attend but sent a letter expressing his confidence that, although the sum required was a large one, he was confident that it would be raised. In his stead the meeting was chaired by Sir Jonathan North, who praised Lutyens for his patience and spoke about the difficulties of raising money for a large memorial during a trade slump. He was aware that there were concerns that the memorial could be seen by some as a triumphal arch but he suggested that it was possible to think of it representing a spiritual triumph, which is why it was to be known as the 'Arch of Remembrance'. The meeting approved the proposals and, a fortnight later, the Committee agreed to accept the tender submitted by Nine Elms – there was no reference to the use of local labour. There was, however, a fundamental problem in that the Committee was at least £10,000 short of the amount that it needed to complete the memorial.

The general matter of the construction of war memorials was a sensitive subject. Although, for practical reasons, many of the people involved on the committees also had functions with the local council, either as officers or members, there had to be a clear separation so that donors could be see that their money was going directly to the memorial and not into the general Council coffers. At the same time, the committee members had to display the utmost probity in raising money and not enter into financial commitments that were not adequately secured. The War Memorial Committee now had a problem. Whilst North blamed the economic climate, 'Here and There' in the *Leicester Advertiser* was in a less conciliatory mood, suggesting that 'dilatoriness on the part of those who had control and a lack of tact in dealing with the public, caused the whole thing to fall flat. I attended all the public meetings called (none too early) to decide upon a suitable memorial, and the impression I got, in common with others, was of an attempt to keep the decision entirely in a few hands'.[19] In any event, the Committee had to do something and it was caught on the horns of a dilemma. Having rejected one scheme it had deliberately chosen another that was more extravagant. If it now decided to delay things further it risked widespread criticism from a public that was already growing impatient for its memorial. It was therefore decided 'That the Town Clerk be asked to interview the Manager of Parr's Bank[20] and ascertain whether the Bank will undertake to honour the Orders of the Treasurer of the War Memorial Fund to the extent of the contract with Nine Elms after a full explanation of the circumstances.'[21] In other words, the Committee was seeking a bank overdraft.

The facility was duly granted and construction work started. Further fundraising was not particularly successful, even though it had been agreed that Committee members would make personal visits to the leading companies in the city. By October 1924 the total donated stood at £16,438/18/8. Somewhere along the line, without explanation but probably because of a takeover, the

Norwich War Memorial

building contractor changed to Messrs Holloway, who built the Southampton Cenotaph.

Finally, on 4 July 1925 and with Lutyens in attendance, the memorial was unveiled. The problems that had dogged the scheme since the first meeting over six years previously continued when Lord Beatty, who had agreed to do the unveiling, was unable to attend. In his place, the Committee approached two local widows, Elizabeth Butler and Annie Glover who, between them, had lost six sons in the War. A crowd of 30,000 attended to see Mrs Butler perform the actual unveiling but, as reported, in the *Illustrated Leicester Chronicle*, the event did not pass without mishap – the flags for the unveiling fell down four times (once during the prayers and once during the hymns) and were finally held in place by some Boy Scouts; more Scouts had to chase dogs from the enclosure during the service and the Minute's Silence

was interrupted by the distant cries of souvenir sellers. Once the formal ceremony had concluded there was a surge of people to the memorial. 'The appeal of some ex-servicemen to "have a bit of respect" strengthened by the forcible ejection of two cads who were dancing on the plinth, went for the best part unheeded.'[22]

Despite the fact that the memorial had been completed it was, one suspects, a relatively sombre meeting that took place between various members of the War Memorial Committee on 21 December. One of the conditions of the bank overdraft was that various individuals had to offer personal guarantees as security in the event of a default. The overdraft had to be repaid by the end of the year and the Committee was still £5,531/19/10 short of its target. As a consequence the five guarantors (Sir Jonathan North, F.S. Brice JP, T. Fielding Johnson JP, Sir Arthur Wheeler Bart and Sir Samuel Faire) all had to make good the shortfall between them. The Committee held its final meeting on 30 June 1926 and the closing accounts revealed that the total cost of the memorial was £27,209/1/7, of which Holloway's had received £23,558/18/2 and Lutyens £1,635/0/2. Somewhat strangely, in view of the actions of Sir Jonathan and the other guarantors, there was a surplus of £1,529/5/1 that was passed to the City Treasurer (on behalf of the Parks Committee) 'for purposes of making more permanent inscriptions on the memorial and for other purposes connected with the surroundings of the arch subject to Lutyens's approval'.[23]

Lutyens and Sir Jonathan had clearly struck up a close friendship because, when North's wife Kate died in 1930 he commissioned Lutyens to design two pairs of gates to Victoria Park in her honour – one, leads to the memorial from Lancaster Road and the other, with a pair of distinctive lodge cottages, is at the entrance from London Road, in the location originally proposed by Lutyens for the war memorial.

At Leicester the seven-year delay between the end of the War and the memorial's completion was due to fundraising and the committee changing their mind about the design, whereas the delay with the Norwich City War Memorial, which was finally unveiled in 1927, resulted from indecision about the nature of the memorial itself. Several schemes had been considered but all had failed either as a result of too much negative criticism or because they were too ambitious: in one case (an enlightened scheme to set up a university college to specialise in agricultural subjects) the donations even had to be returned because it was considered that the project did not appear to unite all social classes.

The situation took a turn for the better when councillor Charles Bignold, a member of the founding family of Norwich Union insurance company, was elected Lord Mayor of the city in 1926. Bignold was an ex-serviceman and, aided the Town Clerk Archie Rice (who had also served in the War) he decided to take the initiative to secure the construction of the memorial before he left office. He was 'utterly opposed to spending a large sum of money on a monument unless it is associated with something benefiting the living, particularly at a time when many excellent benevolent institutions are in sore need of funds'[24] and therefore decided that there should be two forms of commemoration – a civic war memorial and improvements to two local hospitals – the Norfolk & Norwich and the Jenny Lind (because the latter had taken children from the former during the War to provide bed-spaces for injured troops). The fund was called the 'Joint Hospitals and War Memorial Appeal' and a target of £35,000 was set with £4,000 to be allocated for a physical memorial. Lutyens was approached to prepare the design and wrote to Emily about his visit on 13 June 1927: 'Had a quick successful lunch in Norwich. The Lord Mayor is a nice looking sympathetic young man of 34! and holds his rum and talks remarkably well in public.'[25] Bignold took Lutyens to his house ten miles outside Norwich causing Lutyens to comment 'O! the garden he has made'.[26] As elsewhere, Lutyens walked around the town with his client to find the best spot for the memorial and, after taking the best part of a day, chose a position in front of the east wall of the fifteenth-century Guildhall, overlooking the Market Place. As the memorial would not be big enough to contain the names of the 3,544 fallen it was decided that Lutyens should design a Roll of Honour to be made of oak panels on which the names would be painted and for which, in time, a figure of £800–£1,000 was to be allocated.

The design of the memorial itself, which the architect described as 'a jolly monument'[27] was an interesting variation on what had gone before as being the only occasion on which Lutyens designed the Great War Stone to be an integral part of the memorial, forming a projection of a taller wall at the back on the top of which lay a typical Lutyens chest tomb bearing the city's coat of arms. Four flags were to be fixed to the wall of the Guildhall and, in a novel touch Lutyens incorporated bronze gilt flambeaux at either end of the memorial that 'on days of commemoration can blaze with flares'.[28] An inscription on the back of the memorial would record 'The cost of this Memorial was raised by public subscription in association with an appeal for the Hospitals'.

There were objections to both the design of the memorial and its site but Bignold pressed ahead, sure in his mind that he had the support of the majority of ex-servicemen and by early August 1927 criticism in the press had finally subsided. However, despite his apparent confidence, he was sufficiently concerned to ask a colleague, Major Berney Ficklin, to prepare a draft letter that could be issued to the local newspapers in the event that the memorial was criticised after it had been unveiled:

> Destructive criticism has been put aside in the way that it always should be. Constructive criticism has been carefully noted, but in most cases it has been the criticism of the individual rather

Norwich Roll of Honour

than that of the majority of citizens, on whose behalf the Committee has worked.

There are many employed in the City who on Armistice Day may wish to pause for a moment at the memorial, prefer-ably at 11am. In five minutes the memorial can be reached from all the shopping centres of Norwich, and those employed in shop or office may thus be afforded an opportunity of congre-gating at the memorial at the time that they should wish. Secondly most visitors to our city come to see the Guildhall. They will in future see our War Memorial as well. Are we not sufficiently proud of our dead to make our memorial one of those things which everybody who visits the city will see? Thirdly the life of our city is typified by our market place. We have placed the memorial as a perpetual reminder that we live because of those who died for us.

Northampton War Memorial

With regard to the form of the memorial. The form of any War Memorial depends entirely on the money available for its erection. Knowing what this sum was we consulted Sir Edwin Lutyens as to the best means of expending it. We are assured by this eminent architect that in no way will the design finally approved mar or detract from the beauty of the Guildhall. Many members of the public would seem to differ from this opinion. This is to be expected. If everybody agreed to the same form of memorial all towns in England would have the same design. Since it is impossible to satisfy all, we felt that all reasonable persons would be satisfied by the expert opinion of the man who gave London its Cenotaph. Those who place their own opinion before that of the expert will still cavil, but we feel that one cannot do more than abide by expert opinion, once this has been taken. . . .

In conclusion; if we have satisfied those who mourn lost ones and those who are bound together in the great comradeship of the ex-service man and if the average Norwich citizen is satisfied that the stigma to the city has been removed, then perhaps the critics will remember that we have, at least tried our best for the city to which it is our privilege to belong.[29]

The memorial was built in remarkably quick time and Lutyens was present when it was unveiled on Sunday 9 October. The chief dignitary was General Sir Ian Hamilton, who had performed the honours at Spalding five years' earlier. In replying to his invitation the General agreed to attend if a car was sent to fetch him from his London home and then take him back immediately after the ceremony. He also requested a strong cup of coffee on arrival or, failing that, a whisky and soda. In a populist touch, however, the actual unveiling was performed by a local ex-serviceman, Bertie Alfred Withers. Withers's name had been drawn from a hat after Bignold had invited applications from ex-servicemen who fulfilled four criteria: they had to be natives of Norwich who had enlisted before 2 March 1916, had seen service overseas and had been permanently disabled. Withers was an ideal candidate: he had enlisted in the Norwich Drill Hall on 1 September 1914 and, like many other volunteers, lied about his age, saying that he was nineteen rather than eighteen. He did most of his training in East Anglia prior to leaving for Gallipoli in July 1915. After suffering from dysentery and typhoid he rejoined his unit in the Sinai Peninsula and was injured in a Battle of Gaza, in which his battalion was almost wiped out. He was removed in a sand cart, enduring a very rough journey across the desert. Once in hospital he became unconscious and on waking found his left leg had been amputated below the knee. After having made steady progress, he arrived back in England on 19 September 1917 and had further operations in hospital in Liverpool before being sent to the Norfolk & Norwich Hospital, where he remained for a year. He was then transferred to the hospital at Roehampton, where he was fitted with an artificial leg before being discharged on Armistice Day.

Hamilton said a few words at the beginning of the unveiling ceremony before introducing Withers, requesting him to pull the chord that would reveal the memorial. Withers read the few words allocated to him which were also printed in the programme for the day's events. The gas supply was turned on and the two flares were lit and were to remain alight until 10 p.m.. The idea of the war memorial emitting smoke and fire was a recurring theme in many of the proposals that Lutyens made, from the Cenotaph onwards, but Norwich is the only place in Britain where it was achieved.

The final cost of the memorial came to £2,700 compared with the original quotation of £2,222/10/0 and Lutyens received his usual fee of 10 per cent of the building costs.

Although the war memorial had been finally completed work on the Roll of Honour ran into difficulties. Lutyens wrote to Bignold on 6 October 1927 informing him that the cost had risen above the £1,000 estimate to £1,077/7/6, of which £375 was to be spent on painting the letters. Bignold responded by reducing the budget to £600 and then £500 and to make matters worse the Committee that ran the Museum on Norwich Castle (the proposed location for the Roll) felt that it would be an inappropriate place for it to be kept. It subsequently changed its mind but, when the Roll finally arrived in June 1929 not only was its quality deemed too poor to put on permanent display but it was also over the budget, although Lutyens generously offered to pay the £23/10/- difference. Alterations were made to improve the quality of the panels and the Roll was put on permanent display in the castle on 13 January 1931, a final end to a sorry tale.

The citizens of Northampton also experienced a long wait for their memorial. Even though the basic design work had been completed by Lutyens in 1920 it was not unveiled until six years later. However, this was not for the reasons that have been experienced elsewhere but for something far more mundane: the legal process involved in buying the site. Usually this was the least of the problems and tended to be straightforward either because the site was already in public ownership or, as with Rochdale, because there was a willing donor to make it available. Northampton was different though because it was considered that the best site for the memorial would be to carve off part of the churchyard of the seventeenth century All Saints Church in the heart of the town centre. The procedure in such circumstances is to apply to the

Northampton War Memorial

local diocese (in Northampton's case, Peterborough) for a Faculty to allow the land to be sold. The original application was made on 11 July 1922 by the vicar, Rev. Geoffrey Lunt, supported by two churchwardens and three parishioners, who jointly wrote to seek consent to erect a war memorial 'to the men of the Town and County of Northampton who fell in the Great War'.[30] The memorial was to take the form of a War Stone either side of which were particularly fine obelisks raised on coved bases. The obelisks each had deep niches and painted flags. Unusually the War Stone would feature two inscriptions – the familiar 'Their Name Liveth For Evermore' on the side facing the town and the somewhat more cumbersome 'The Souls Of The Righteous Are In The Hands Of God' from the Wisdom of Solomon[31] on the side facing the church.

Matters proceeded slowly, although construction was finally underway when the *Northampton Independent* wrote on 17 July 1926:

Tomorrow the Northamptonshire War Memorial Committee meet again to expedite arrangements for the completion of their task, which has been beset with disheartening difficulties for which they are not really responsible. Delays have arisen through technical, legal and ecclesiastical obstacles, which hap-

pily have now been surmounted. The design is at last appearing to take definite shape, with the result that the censorious attitude of certain critics is abating. The carving of the obelisks is complete and awaiting the correct colourings of the draped stone flags by the staff of the architect, Sir Edwin Lutyens, with a special durable preparation. It is too early yet to state when the memorial will be unveiled, but probably it will be some time in the late autumn, although the Mayor is somewhat sadly dubious whether it will be done during his year of office.'

The memorial was unveiled on 11 November 1926 by General Lord Horne, the commander of the British First Army for the second half of the War. The approximate cost was £5,000.

Needless to say though, not every town experienced the problems at places such as Norwich, Manchester and Northampton. The war memorial at Hove in Sussex, for example, went very smoothly with barely eleven months elapsing between the first suggestion for a memorial in 'Vestry Notes' in a local newspaper and the unveiling of a 20ft-high circular column surmounted by a bronze figure of St George holding a sword, somewhat dangerously, by the blade and sculpted by Sir George Frampton. The unveiling was performed by Lord Leconfield, the Lord Lieutenant of Sussex on 27 February 1921. Lutyens was in India and Thomas attended in his stead.

The memorial in Southend also seems to have had no problems. The original design for a cenotaph was superceded by one for a slender obelisk with painted flags that stands on a generous raised platform on the cliffs, west of the pier. It cost £5,521/15/0 and was unveiled by Lord Lambourne, the Lord Lieutenant of Essex, on 27 November 1921.

The Devon County Memorial outside Exeter Cathedral was similarly straightforward, once a shortage of funds had led to the abandonment of a proposal that completion of the cloisters in the city's cathedral would commemoriate the war dead. The memorial takes the form of a large War Cross hewn from granite from a quarry on Haytor on Dartmoor and was unveiled on 16 May 1921 by the Prince of Wales.

The story of the Lutyens memorials in cities and towns in Britain ends with the curious tale of Edinburgh and the question of whether the City War Memorial, in front of the City Chambers on the High Street, should be considered as part of the Lutyens architectural oeuvre or not.

As the capital of Scotland, Edinburgh was the natural choice of location for the Scottish National War Memorial and the decision to site it within Edinburgh Castle had caused some local controversy. The plans, which had been prepared by the Scottish architect Sir Robert Lorimer, were finally approved in November

1923 and good progress on construction had been made by the time that Earl Haig visited Edinburgh on the Remembrance Day 1925. His comment about the lack of a cenotaph for the city's own dead (which had been put to one side until the national memorial was resolved) acted as a catalyst and, on 19 March 1926, a public meeting was called to discuss the matter under the chairmanship of the Lord Provost of Edinburgh, Lord Sleigh.

The outcome was the formation of the Edinburgh Citizens' Cenotaph Committee with Colonel William Robertson VC as Convenor supported by Lieutenant-Colonel A.S. Blair as secretary and forty-three of the great and the good of Edinburgh as committee members. There was a specific desire that the memorial should be a cenotaph and that it should be the subject of an architectural competition for which Sir George Washington Browne, President of the Royal Scottish Academy had agreed to be the assessor. It was felt that a sum of £5,000 would be an appropriate budget and the Committee agreed a number of key criteria to help them with their eventual choice of memorial: suitability; accessibility; non-interference with traffic; non-removal of existing statues; non-interference with private property; amenity; simplicity and moderate cost. To applause, the Lord Provost closed the meeting by saying that he thought that, with such a committee, the success of the scheme would be assured.

The idea of an architectural competition was soon put to one side because, less than a month later, Blair wrote to Sir Fabian Ware at the Imperial War Graves Commission to ask about the use of a War Stone ('Nothing better would, I think, meet our requirements both as regards beauty of design and cost')[32] for the likely site in Princes Street Gardens. A briefing note to inform Ware's reply was prepared by H.F. Robinson, the Commission's Deputy Director of Works, indicating that such a Stone would cost £400–£700 depending upon whether it was made from local sandstone (which was felt to be more appropriate than Portland stone) or granite. Robinson pointed out that it would be necessary for Lutyens, as the designer of the War Stone, to give his consent to the proposal. He added 'I rather feel that it would be taken as a lack of ordinary courtesy if a Great War Stone became the War Memorial for Edinburgh in such a prominent position as Princes Street Gardens, and Sir Edwin Lutyens was not employed to supervise it.'[33] Suitably briefed, Ware replied accordingly pointing out that the IWGC could not give consent for use of the stone outside its own cemeteries and that Blair should contact Lutyens, although he did not think that Lutyens would object. Blair duly replied the next day, confirming that he would approach Lutyens and that it would 'indeed be a great satisfaction if the necessary work was carried out under his superintendence'.[34] Somewhat darkly he then added 'The only difficulty is that we Scotsmen are a very clannish race, and although I do not hold with most of my countrymen's narrow views in such matters, some of the Committee — possibly more of the public – may criticise the appointment of an Englishman for work of this kind in Scotland, but I think with some tact Colonel Robertson and I might get over this.'[35]

The subject of the city memorial had clearly been the subject of much discussion in Edinburgh and Lorimer (who was also the IWGC's Principal Architect for Italy, Macedonia and Egypt) felt sufficiently concerned to write to Ware about the matter. He sent him cuttings from the local press and was particularly concerned about the Committee's revised proposal to site the memorial in the restricted space in the arcade at the front of the City Chambers (the home of the Council) where it adjoined the High Street. Lorimer condemned the fact that the Committee had made 'every kind of futile proposal'[36] before reaching their decision and enclosed a drawing showing that the available space of 9ft between the piers was not enough to accommodate the Stone and its steps. He suggested that Ware write to the Committee to say that the Commission could not give its consent to the proposal, because the War Stone had been specially designed for the war cemeteries and that, 'in practically every case besides being set on three steps it has been set up on a terrace'.[37] Lorimer was conscious of his role as architect of the National War Memorial and asked Ware to keep his name out of the affair, as there was a widespread feeling that the National Memorial should serve Edinburgh as well and that a separate memorial for the city was unnecessary.

Ware replied, thanking Lorimer for his letter, but regretting that he had no power to take such action.

The restricted space available meant that the Committee had no alternative but to reduce the size of the War Stone and there then followed a flurry of correspondence in which the Cenotaph Committee tried to twist Lutyens's arm into giving consent for a reduced copy to be erected. Lutyens wrote to Blair on 30 May giving consent for the use of the Stone at its original size, asking to see the layout drawings and advising that the IWGC should be contacted for the detailed drawings. Blair responded on 1 June saying that he had asked the City Architect to let him have a sketch and regarding the constricted site, noted that the City Architect had suggested chaining off two adjoining arches 'so as to give a little more space round the stone itself'.[38] He acknowledged that the provision of the steps up to the Stone would be difficult owing to the piers of the arcade but added optimistically 'the City Architect is endeavouring to get over that as best he can'. He reiterated the problems in finding a suitable site: 'site after site having been turned down by the Town Council and others interested' and said that his committee had readily accepted the proposed site due to its proximity to St Giles Cathedral and 'many other historical associations, notably in connection with the early life of Mary Queen of Scots'.

The plans arrived at Lutyens's office shortly before he was due to leave for a week on business. He had the chance to look at them before he left and, after he had done so, got in touch with A.J. Thomas with his thoughts, which were duly passed to Blair:

I have received a communication from Sir Edwin asking me with all courtesy to point out if he is correct in reading the Drawing that the Stone is proposed to be made 9' long instead of the 12'0', that the proportion will be so different that it will not be the Great War Stone as placed in the Cemeteries in the War areas, and elsewhere to commemorate those who fell in the War; and Sir Edwin says, although he is very willing to help all he can, he could not be so interested with the War Stone built to the wrong proportion in the confined position, and also where the steps would have to be truncated – consequently having no relationship to the Great War Stone where the steps are designed in relation to the Stone itself.[39]

Blair responded, referring to 'Herbert' Thomas's letter, thanking Lutyens for his 'kind criticism'[40] but pointing out that they had thought that a 9ft-long version of the Stone had been used by the IWGC. He was pleading for the smaller Stone, as it was 'the simplicity and dignity of the original design which so strongly appealed to us'.

Lutyens had clearly had enough, replying to Blair 'I can only say quite frankly, I do not approve of the reduced War Stone, and I have only allowed the Stone to be reduced where it was impossible to get the larger Stone on account of transport and difficulties of access to the site, and the size of stone procurable – none of which reasons seem to me to apply in Edinburgh. Is it not possible to find another suitable site?'[41] The exasperated Blair replied: 'We have tried everywhere and everyhow; but we have always been up against vested interests and even active opposition to having a War Memorial in Edinburgh at all'.[42] He then ominously added

Still, we have so far surmounted all opposition and have enough money in hand to place a suitable War Stone under the Arch'. In a clear attempt to butter up Lutyens, he concluded 'My Committee fully recognise that in the circumstances, our War Stone can never be an exact replica of your beautiful design. The fons originis of the "Stone of Remembrance" is due to your genius, and my Committee in full appreciation of this have thought it right to lay the whole circumstances before you. We all wish we could have obtained an open site with plenty of room all round; but we have had to make the best use of the site offered; and so may we assume that we have your "blessing" and good wishes?'[43] In an attempt to seek a resolution Lutyens suggested a potential solution by return 'If I were asked the question of how to place a War Monument under the arches, I should advise that it consist of

The truncated War Stone that forms the Edinburgh War Memorial is squeezed into the arcade at the front of the City Chambers

a monolithic Slab of Granite to show five inches or so in depth, carved and moulded, with a fine inscription, and on the inner faces of the four piers, adorn with flags.'[44] Blair agreed to submit Lutyens's comments to his committee and concluded his next letter 'With many thanks for your trouble and interest believe me.[45]

It is clear that Lutyens's concern was shared by the IWGC, whose F.C. Gilter wrote to Ebenezer James Macrae, the City Architect for Edinburgh who was charged with implementing the memorial, to pass on Fabian Ware's understanding that Lutyens 'feels a little perturbed'[46] at the proposal and to set out Ware's own view of the proposed memorial: 'Sir Fabian feels sure that as an architect you will fully appreciate this view of the matter. Sir Edwin's design, one of extraordinary dignity, depends for its effect on its exact proportions and dimensions and on the arrangement of the steps on which it is set. To alter these would be, Sir Fabian feels, to destroy entirely the character of the Monument.'[47] It was clear though that the Commission was not aware that the Committee had been in touch with Lutyens

throughout, and Blair wrote to Gilter on 4 August enclosing copies of the correspondence with Lutyens, before concluding 'I do not know if Sir Fabian would wish me to talk again to Sir Edwin in the matter, but I will do so if he desires although I do not feel that I can add very much to my previous letters to him on the subject'.[48] The matter was effectively concluded when Blair and Gilter met in early September. Blair outlined the whole story and said that they did not want Lutyens to think that they had not taken account of his views but that their hands had been tied by the choice of site. Despite Lutyens's obvious unease, the Committee decided to press ahead with their reduced War Stone hewn from Scottish granite, which was unveiled by Prince Henry on 11 November 1927.

It is clear that, even though ten years had elapsed since Lutyens had designed the War Stone, his passion for it had not diminished. The cramped site of the memorial makes one wish that the Committee had swallowed its pride and asked him to design that type of memorial that he had suggested. Edinburgh cannot, therefore, be considered a true Lutyens memorial.

SEVEN
VILLAGE VOICES

NLIKE THE COMPLICATED STORIES of many of the memorials in the towns and cities, the erection of Lutyens's village war memorials tended to be a lot more straightforward. In many cases it would seem that the main reason for such places to have a Lutyens memorial was that he had already had a client in the area for whom he had built a house or undertaken other work. Such clients were, by their very nature, self-made men who, playing active roles in village life, would be expected to take a major part in providing the local war memorial – both by serving on a committee and, when appropriate, helping out with the funding. Unfortunately, as a consequence, the exploits of the committees are less well documented.

Tyringham, where this book began, is a case in point. Tyringham House was the centre of local life and, in 1913 its owner, Frederick König, had established the Tyringham House Club as a social club for the male estate workers. The club closed down during the War when the house was used for wounded soldiers, but it reopened in 1917, with its membership widened to include female members and also non-estate workers, and it raised £105 for war charities in the final eighteen months of the War. König also chaired the Tyringham War Savings Association that, by June 1918, had raised £1,334 for the purchase of War Bonds from the 40 households in the parish. He was exceptionally proud of the record of his local area in supporting the War to the extent that he had a letter published in the *New York Times* on 30 September 1917 to refute the impression that the Americans thought that 'the English are shirkers, and that their battles are fought by the Scottish, Welsh, Canadians and others'. He then gave figures for the area of Newport Pagnell, the nearby town that included Tyringham within its catchment area:

The figure of St George on the top of the Fordham War Memorial was sculpted by Sir George Frampton

Killed in action	75
Missing, feared killed	5
Prisoners of War	4
Wounded	86
Discharged seriously wounded or medically unfit for further service	16
At present serving	521

Between them the men had earned:

Mentioned in despatches	3
Risen from the ranks	5
Military Cross	1
Distinguished Conduct Medal	3
Military Medal	4
Distinguished Conduct Medal, Military Medal and St George's Medal (Triple Award)	1

It is known that Tyringham had a War Memorial Committee because it was referred to the article in the *Bucks Standard* about the memorial's unveiling but no more is known about it – there seem to be no Parish or local records and the same paper, which had so assiduously reported the deaths and injuries to the local soldiers, makes no mention of any committee meetings or any fundraising activities. Apart from the report of the unveiling, all that is known about the memorial is that there is a drawing in the RIBA Drawings Collection of an earlier version of it, showing a larger tablet either side of which were flags.[1]

In contrast, much more is known about the two war memorials that arose from the influence of another of Lutyens's clients, Herbert Johnson.

Johnson was the kind of self-made Edwardian individual who was attracted to Lutyens. Described by Hussey (Lutyens's biog-

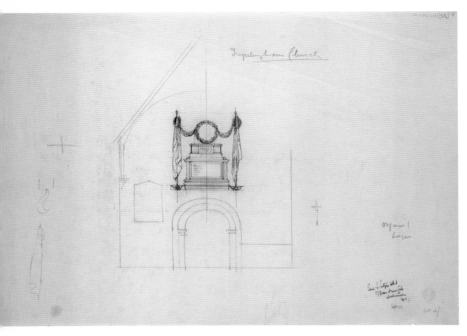

ABOVE Lutyens's initial proposal for Tyringham War Memorial
RIGHT Lower Swell War Memorial

rapher) as an '"adventurer", stockjobber and sportsman'[2] he made his fortune on the stock market, using his own form of ready reckoner to assess potential returns more quickly than had been hitherto possible. He had purchased a large farm alongside the River Test at Stockbridge, in Hampshire in 1891 and, having seen pictures of Lutyens's first house, Crooksbury, in *Country Life* he sought out its architect to build what might otherwise be called today the ultimate 'bachelor pad', in which to indulge his lifestyle. The resultant house, Marshcourt (1901–4), is one of Lutyens's finest, being built out of the local chalk inset with flints and complete with its own Jekyll garden. However Johnson's bachelor existence came to an end when he met Violet Bertram, a local widow, whom he married in 1912. The couple both became heavily involved in supporting the local war effort and, at their own expense, ran Marshcourt as a sixty-bed hospital for wounded soldiers.

At the end of the War Johnson was determined that his village as well as the neighbouring village of King's Somborne should both have their own war memorials designed by Lutyens. A meeting to discuss the King's Somborne memorial was held in the local schoolroom in February 1919 with Johnson in the chair, assisted by the local vicar. Letters containing suggestions were read out and several more ideas emerged from the audience including that of a

wayside cross and Parish Hall. After discussions it was decided to consult the villagers regarding their preference and also to find out how much they would be willing to contribute towards the cost of the memorial. A large representative committee was formed and a fund was started with promises of £100 including a contribution from Herbert Johnson. At the end of the meeting a vote of thanks was given to Johnson for presiding over the meeting and in response he said that 'it always gave him great pleasure to do anything he possibly could for the village and its inhabitants'.[3]

In due course the decision was taken to have a Lutyens War Cross with the names of the fallen being commemorated on a bronze tablet in the nearby Church of St Peter and St Paul. The cross was built and later unveiled on Easter Sunday, 27 March 1921. Writing about the event Johnson stated that he

and the Committee considered the cross they had chosen to be chaste and simple in character, dignified in appearance, while its proportions were beautiful and perfect, and of great artistic merit. It was durable, being of Portland stone, and, therefore, likely to last a very long time to come. If anyone did not agree with this opinion, which was the opinion of the Committee, I am sure they would eventually, as the cross would grow on

ABOVE Mells War Memorial
LEFT Miserden War Memorial

them, and they would be glad to think that they hand a hand in the erecting of it. It was designed by Sir E. Lutyens, and was a replica of those to be erected in the British cemeteries in France.[4]

Johnson also chaired the memorial committee at nearby Stockbridge, which also chose to have a War Cross that, like the one at King's Somborne, stands on a coved base although it is distinguished from its neighbour by having a circular bottom step rather than a square one. Johnson gave the land upon which the memorial stands and was reported by the *Hampshire Chronicle* as having 'subscribed very largely to the funds' and used his influence through the County Council to widen the road to improve the memorial's setting.

In a poignant postscript Violet Johnson died in 1923, aged fifty-two, and her memorial cross in the cemetery at Stockbridge refers 'to her solicitude during the Great War for the wounded soldiers in her hospitals at Marshcourt and Stockbridge contributed to her untimely end'. The cross and her nearby gravestone were both designed by Lutyens.

If there was one village above all others that would have a war memorial designed by Lutyens it would be the village Mells, tucked away in the Mendip Hills in North Somerset. Lutyens had first visited the village in 1896 at the request of Frances Horner, the wife of

Sir John, (a descendant of the nursery rhyme's 'Little Jack Horner' whose 'plum' was the substantial land holdings in the area that he had secured at the Dissolution of the monasteries). Frances's sister Agnes was married to Herbert Jekyll, Gertrude's brother, and Lutyens was a natural choice of architect when she subsequently wanted some building work done to her house, Mells Manor, in the shadow of St Andrew's church in the heart of the village. Writing to Emily on 4 August 1919, on a train back from a visit to the village Lutyens described how he chose the site for the village's memorial:

> Jack and Lady Horner and Katherine met the villagers and walked round all the morning inspecting sites for the War Memorial at Mells, a funny procession. I walked miles Sunday morning with Katherine Asquith to have a preliminary survey. Found a perfect site in the centre of the village, which no one else found, or thought of, and with a little tact and patience it was carried by the villagers with acclamation.[5]

The memorial consists of a figure of St George slaying a dragon on top of a simple Tuscan column, similar to the memorials at Fordham and Hove but given added dignity by adjoining flank walls with undercut benches for the placement of wreaths.

Ashwell War Memorial

The war memorial to the 'Men of Muncaster', a grave and a private memorial were all that Lutyens had to show for his trip to Muncaster Castle, on the western edge of the Lake District. His, discussions with Sir John Ramsden about carrying out alterations to the Castle at a potential cost of around £100,000 came to nothing. However in April 1919 Ramsden decided to commission a war memorial that would take the form of a cross, symbolic of the sacrifice made by the troops. It was in a train on his way to Muncaster that Lutyens wrote excitedly to Emily about possible inscriptions for the War Stone (see page 32).[6]

One village where there was no apparent previous Lutyens connection, but where the memorial was driven forward by the type of person that typified a Lutyens client, was Ashwell in north Hertfordshire. Wolverley Attwood Fordham was one of the directors of the local Fordham Brewery and a group of the villagers met at his house towards the end of 1919 to discuss a war memorial for the village. A War Memorial Committee was duly formed with Wolverley and his wife Phyllis being elected Chairman and Secretary respectively. The villagers had grand plans for their memorial and when the committee met again on 23 December 1919 it had before it proposals for a cross designed by Sir Reginald Blomfield, alternatives of a cross, obelisk or War Stone from Lutyens and a cenotaph from Tappers, a local builder. The Lutyens cross was the preferred option by a vote of six to one and, at a meeting on 5 January 1920, the committee decided to display the design in local shops and to call a public meeting for eight days later in order to discuss the matter. The meeting endorsed the recommendation of the committee and, in Lutyens's absence in India, the committee liaised with A.J. Thomas about the detailed design of the memorial and how it fitted on the chosen site near the village's recreation ground. The building contract was awarded to Messrs Holland, Hannen and Cubitt Ltd, the contractor for the Cenotaph, and the memorial was unveiled by Lord Hampden, the Lord Lieutenant of Hertfordshire on 4 December 1921. The memorial committee met for the last time on 27 April 1922 and, shortly thereafter, Phyllis presented the committee minutes, all dutifully recorded in school exercise books, and accompanying records to the Parish Council, including a full set of accounts detailing the total cost of the whole project at £655/16/10 with the construction cost of the memorial itself at £557 and Lutyens's fee of £42/19/10. She had also recorded a full set of the contributions, which ranged from as little as one shilling up to £150 contributed by Fordham himself. Another local brewer, Mr Page, contributed £25 and Phyllis Fordham, in echoes of the situation in Leicester, had made good the shortfall of £15/14/2.

Unfortunately, Wolverley Fordham did not live to see the unveiling of the memorial, having died in February 1921 and he rests in the local cemetery under a chunky rectangular tomb-

Fordham War Memorial

Hartburn War Memorial

stone with Ionic pilasters designed by Lutyens. The architect had clearly impressed Phyllis Fordham and he was engaged by her to undertake alterations to Ashwell Bury, when she returned to the house that she and Wolverley had left in 1916 when they offered it for use as a convalescent home.[7]

There is also no apparent Lutyens connection with the memorial in Fordham, the Cambridgeshire village north of Newmarket, for which he designed a column with St George, similar to the one at Hove. It superceded the village War Memorial Committee's earlier proposal for a portico with mural tablets listing the fallen to be erected at the entrance to the local cemetery.

Other memorials that would seem to have resulted from direct connections with Lutyens clients were the War Crosses at Busbridge (home of the the Jekyll family), Hartburn in Northumberland (he designed the garden at Angerton Hall for F. Straker in 1904), Holy Island (Edward Hudson and Lindisfarne Castle), Miserden in Gloucestershire (contemporaneous with alterations for Noel Wills at Misarden Park following a fire) and the splendid flaming urn atop a square pedestal on a triangular green

in the middle of Lower Swell, where Lutyens did work for Mark Fenwick in the early 1900s.[8] Although not a Lutyens client herself, it is likely that Margaret Lewin, who paid for the War Cross in the churchyard at Abinger Common, was known to Lutyens as she lived close to Goddards, the house that he had designed for Sir Frederick Mirrielees. She paid for the cross as a memorial to her son, Charles McLean Lewin, who had died in 1919.

The reason for the Lutyens designed cross in Wargrave in Berkshire is also unknown but it probably arose from the architect's connection with the Hannen family. Nicholas 'Beau' Hannen had worked in Lutyens's office from 1902–5 and Lutyens had designed the faintly Byzantine Hannen Columbarium that nestles in the corner of the local churchyard for the family in 1905. The war memorial cross here is the most distinguished of all of Lutyens's War Crosses because the lower part of the shaft is hexagonal rather than oblong or square, as was the norm, and the shape is taken down to a generous four stepped lozenge shaped plinth. A public meeting to discuss a memorial for the village was held on 13 October 1919 and in due course it was

Abinger Common War Memorial

Wargrave War Memorial

decided that it should take the shape of a cross and that, if sufficient funds were available, a bed would be endowed at the Royal Berkshire Hospital. It was agreed that Lutyens should be approached to prepare the design: a fundraising target of £600 was set and £500 was raised in the first eight months. Lutyens visited the village and agreed that the prospective site, which was on the village green and had been donated by a Henry Bond, was the best available and had been well chosen. Lutyens's design was recommended to the villagers in August 1920 and the decision to go ahead was given in November. The memorial was unveiled on 28 May 1922 and, even though it contains the names of the fallen, the same names are also included on two wooden panels within the nearby church.

The War Cross at Sandhurst in Kent is similarly distinguished, although not because of the cross itself, which sits on a single step rather than the traditional three, but because of the way in which the cross sits within a larger ground pattern of a cross formed by parallel strips of Portland stone set into the grass. Unfortunately nothing at all is known about its commissioning.

In the same area of Kent is the wooden memorial board in the church at Wittersham which is attributed to Lutyens in a church guide written in the 1920s by Rev. Watson. Whilst Watson was not the incumbent at the time that the memorial was unveiled in 1921, it is reasonable to assume that this is good enough evidence for it to be included as a Lutyens design.

The question of whether war memorials should be purely symbolic or should serve a utilitarian purpose had been with Lutyens since his first discussions with Herbert Baker and Charles Aitken on the Western Front in 1917. It had, on occasions, surfaced in connection with the memorials that he designed although usually prior to his appointement as architect. The only occasion on which he was given a specific commission for a building to serve a community purpose was at Gerrards Cross. The local vicar, Reverend John Matthew Glubb conceived the idea of a living monument to be used by ex-servicemen and the parish at large and proposed that it be based around the vicarage's North Lodge and its stables. Rather than establish a War Memorial Committee, the project was managed

Gerrards Cross: The only utilitarian war memorial designed by Lutyens

by a newly formed community association with the objective 'To establish, maintain and manage a Community Centre which shall be a War Memorial for activities promoted by the Association and its constituent members in furtherance of the above objects or any of them, the Centre to be called the Gerrards Cross Centre'. The buildings were converted by Lutyens into an elegant single storey building with portico in antis containing billiard rooms, a club room and kitchen with tennis courts outside at a total cost of around £3,500. It was opened on 14 October 1922 by the Lord Lieutenant of Buckinghamshire.

The strangest tale of all, though, occurs in connection with the village of Rolvenden in Kent's Romney Marsh.

To the casual visitor familiar with the works of Lutyens the war memorial at Rolvenden is a puzzle. The slender shaft with its thin arms is completely different from the 'War Cross' that he used elsewhere and, even though it sits on the traditional three steps that one expects of a Lutyens cross, the treads are evenly spaced, unlike the proportions of 2:1:2 that he normally used. The

closest design link with the architect's other work is the wooden cross that he built on top of the bridge that he designed in 1931 at Compton to carry the Guildford Bypass over the Pilgrims' Way, but even that has a tenuous similarity. The attribution is, however, secure, no matter how unusual the design.

On 10 January 1919 the Rolvenden War Memorial Committee met for the first time in the village school and Harold 'Jack' Tennant (for whom Lutyens had designed his nearby house Great Maytham) was elected chairman. One of the committee members, Colonel Arthur Saxby Barham,[9] suggested that the most suitable site was one close to the churchyard occupied by an ancient carpenter's shop that would have to be purchased and demolished. Although this was a more expensive option than building the memorial on a vacant site, the decision was supported by the committee.

The Committee's proposals were endorsed at a public meeting in February, having initially been discussed at a private meeting with the relatives of the fallen: £604/7/6 had already been raised, including donations of £250 from Tennant £200 from Barham.

The question of who should design the memorial was not discussed until a meeting on 3 August and there was a further delay until the meeting on 15 December agreed to appoint Lutyens, who at that time was on one of his regular visits to India.

The architect visited the village six months later, inspected the proposed site accompanied by members of the Committee and undertook to submit a drawing and provide rough costings. However by this time the Fund had dropped to £200[10] and, when Lutyens provided an estimated cost of £465 for his suggested design, he was asked to produce something cheaper. This he duly did, assuring the Committee that the cost would not exceed £200. Unfortunately they did not like the style of the cross on top of Lutyens's revised design and sent their architect a tracing of their suggested alternative. They had not received a reply from Lutyens by the time that they met on 12 December although, at the next meeting on 8 January 1921, Barham was able to present a drawing that he had collected from Lutyens's office that depicted the type of cross that they had in mind. He suggested that a wooden mock-up of the memorial should be made, as suggested by Lutyens, and erected on the proposed site.

The Committee discussed the site once again at its meeting on 19 February and, by a majority of five to one, reaffirmed its decision to proceed with the site that it had originally chosen. It was noted that the wooden replica that had been made was not an exact copy of the proposed memorial as it was 2ft taller than it should have been and the base was hexagonal rather than square. The different shapes of the base were discussed and it was decided that the hexagonal shape was preferable as it better suited the irregular shape of the site and the cross's position upon it.

The meeting voted in favour of the design being accepted subject to the change to the base and that Lutyens should be asked to modify his design accordingly. The Committee also received a cost estimate for the memorial of £215 from Messrs Wallis of Maidstone, which was accepted subject to any cost change as a result of the different base.

On 3 April Lutyens visited the site again to inspect the mock-up and made suggestions regarding the position of the cross and the laying out of the surrounding area, which he promised to incorporate into the latest version of the design. He also thought the height of the memorial should be increased from 16ft to 18ft, i.e. to the size of the mock-up.

It was apparent that not everyone in the village agreed with the Committee's chosen site and during the following night the mock-up was removed from the site and placed on the green not far from the village pump. It was not known who was responsible for this but it can be presumed that he, she or they shared the views of an anonymous correspondent to the *Kentish Express:*

A model has been placed at two different situations in or near the churchyard, but neither seem to be a favourable spot with the general public. The first was, to my mind, unsuitable, as it would block the entrance to the church gates; the second is even worse as it is somewhat in the background and not at all in a prominent position, and further it would have behind it a grey stone wall, against which it could not be seen to advantage. Let us have it free from the precincts of the church, so that it may appear a memorial erected by the public and not by a chosen few.[11]

The Committee responded to this by publishing a letter of its own on 7 April: 'The present proposed site was unanimously approved by the next of kin and by a public meeting held on 19 February 1919. Will anyone desirous of making suggestions on this matter see the Secretary. The suggestions will be considered at a meeting of the Committee on Saturday next.'

Only one reply (which was anonymous) was received, which purported to reflect the views of the ex-servicemen in the village and proposed a site close to a milestone on the road to Newenden. The Committee decided to test the support for this idea by sending a letter to the villagers acknowledging that the site by the Church 'was opposed by a great majority on the ground that all who lost their lives were not Churchmen, and also that the men had not sufficient evidence as to the unanimous agreement arrived at the Public Meeting on 19 Feb 1919, and that they believed not one quarter of the village was present owing to the lack of knowledge of the meeting taking place'.[12] It suggested two possible alternative sites for the memorial – one by the milestone and one on the village green. The committee had also received a letter from Jack Tennant's wife May in which she advocated calling another public meeting.

Passions were rising and, on 16 April 1921, the Committee met sixty ex-servicemen from the village to discuss the matter with them in the hope that two of their number would join the Committee. The ex-servicemen were concerned about the religious connotation that was inferred by having the memorial close to the church and preferred that the memorial should be placed on the village green instead. However, without taking a vote on the matter, the Committee decided to ignore their views and proceed with the site that they had originally chosen.

Henry Tennant had indicated in April that he wished to stand down because his work kept him away from the village and, two weeks later Colonel Barham replaced him as Chairman. The Committee was keen to retain a connection with the Tennants though, and it was agreed to ask May if she would agree to be co-opted to join them, which she did on condition that a public meeting would be held to allow everyone in the village to air their views on the memorial.

Matters returned to the calmer subject of the memorial itself and Lutyens's plans were approved and he was instructed to seek tenders for the building work.

The minutes of the Committee meeting on 12 November record a rising dissatisfaction at lack of Lutyens's responses to them and it was reported that, despite repeated applications to his office and a personal visit from Colonel Barham, they had only recently received the tender prices for the memorial – Messrs Wallis having bid £230 for it to be built from Clipsham stone (a hard limestone from the borders of Lincolnshire and Rutland) whilst a local builder, Mr A. Hilder from Tenterden, bid £338 for a memorial in Clipsham stone and £371 for one in Portland stone. The Committee was concerned that the prices only covered the construction of the memorial itself and there was no allowance for the treatment of the surrounding grounds. It was therefore decided to give Lutyens a fourteen day deadline to submit plans failing which, if they had not received a reply, they would make their own arrangements.

The bid from Wallis of £230 was accepted at the Committee's December meeting subject to seeking expert advice about the choice of stone from the Diocesan Architect (he recommended Clipsham). The same meeting also saw the resignation of May Tennant because the Committee had not held the public meeting that she had made a pre-condition when she joined it in April.

By this time the available funds had dwindled to £69 and Colonel Barham agree to donate a further £500 to add to his initial £200.

Work on the memorial was finally begun in mid-1922 and it was unveiled by the Archbishop of Canterbury on 8 November. The final bill from Wallis amounted to £255 and Lutyens received his hard earned fee of 10 per cent of the costs plus out-of-pocket expenses of £6.

Rolvenden War Memorial

THE MEMORIAL DESIGNED BY SIR EDWIN LUTYENS
WAS UNVEILED ON THE HORSE GUARDS PARADE AT THE
CORNER OF THE ADMIRALTY ON
APRIL 25TH 1925 THE TENTH ANNIVERSARY OF
THE LANDING ON GALLIPOLI
REMOVED IN 1940 ERECTED AT GREENWICH IN 1951 AND REINSTATED ON THIS SITE IN 2005

EIGHT

SOLDIERS, SAILORS, SCHOLARS AND COMPANY MEN

IN CONTRAST TO THE PROBLEMS associated with the war memorials erected in the cities, towns and villages throughout the country, there was a significant group of memorials that seem to have been erected without much fuss – site finding does not seem to have been a problem, funds were readily available and there were no reports of controversies aired through the pages of the local press. This was the group of memorials erected by private individuals and groups that had a clear special interest – army regiments, schools and companies.

It was, of course, highly appropriate that Lutyens should be asked to design a memorial for his father's regiment, the Lancashire Fusiliers, at the regimental headquarters in Bury, and it is typical of him that he was to offer his services for nothing.

A plaque by the memorial records that Lutyens actually had two connections with the regiment – not only was he the son of an officer but he was also the great nephew of Major Englebert Lutyens, Napoleon's Orderly Officer on St Helena. Lutyens considered Bury to be a 'desolate spot' and his visit to the town in early September 1920 is one of the few occasions on which he wrote about his memorials to Emily. He was hosted by the 'very gay and debonair' Colonel Whike and a group of 'wool making colonels'.[1] He was entertained to dinner by a group of officers and there was 'lots of champagne and a lot of English food and many stories told and capped'.[2] Perhaps he dined too well as he woke from a bad dream in the middle of the night. The 'wool making colonels' agreed with Lutyens's suggestion for the site and were rewarded with a particularly fine design for their memorial – a tapering obelisk with apsidal ends, the latter perhaps being a nod towards the nearby cenotaph at Rochdale, which Lutyens was designing at the same time. It also contains coloured flags, in this case the Regimental colours and the King's colours. As with

Royal Naval Division War Memorial, London

memorials elsewhere, there was a strong wish that the living should benefit as well and money was spent on a set of drums and silver bugles for the regiment and a donation was made to the regimental Compassionate Fund.

The memorial was unveiled on 25 April 1922 by Lieutenant-General Sir Beauvoir de Lisle, Commander in Chief, Western Command by the novel method of pressing an electric button. The date of the unveiling had special significance for the regiment because it commemorated the day, seven years before, that members of the regiment had earned 'six VCs before breakfast' during the landings at Gallipoli. Lutyens could not attend the ceremony but sent a cable instead.

The Oxford and Bucks Light Infantry chose a much plainer obelisk for their memorial, which stands on the corner of a road in Cowley, Oxford. The site was donated by Christchurch College and was chosen with special care to enable the memorial to be seen against the sky. The memorial is notable for its heavy relief carving of the regimental badge and was unveiled by the Regimental Colonel, Major-General Sir John Hanbury-Williams, on Remembrance Day, 1923.

Two regiments specifically decided that they wanted reduced versions of the Whitehall Cenotaph. The Queen's Own (Royal West Kent) Regiment's memorial in Brenchley Gardens, Maidstone was unveiled on 30 July 1921 and differs from the Whitehall original as there is no provision for flags.

By way of contrast, the Royal Berkshire Regiment memorial outside the regimental barracks in Reading contains stone flags of the type that Lutyens wanted for the original Cenotaph although there are only two here (the King's colour and the Regimental Standard) compared with six on the original. A stone bowl on top of the memorial is reminiscent of the smoking cauldron that appeared on one of the early sketches of the original in Whitehall. The carving was undertaken by the sculptor, Eric Broadbent

(Derwent Wood having been the sculptor for Whitehall) and a Roll of Honour was placed inside the memorial at the unveiling ceremony on 13 September 1921.

The Welch Regiment had originally commissioned Lutyens to design a memorial for them at Gheluvelt on the Western Front in 1921, the principle of which had been approved by the Battlefield Exploits Committee on 17 October 1922. However, six months later Lutyens wrote to the Secretary of the War Office to tell him that it had been decided to erect it in Cardiff instead. It was subsequently placed outside the Maindy Barracks in Cardiff, where it was unveiled on 11 November 1924. It takes the form of a squat cenotaph, the tomb on top being similar to the one that Lutyens subsequently designed for the graves of James Hackett, Sidney Myer and the Beddington Brothers.[3]

The memorial for the Royal Naval Division is an obelisk standing in a fountain basin raised on a high plinth alongside the Admiralty building overlooking Horse Guards Parade in central London. The Division was an anomaly: commonly known as 'Winston's Little Army', it was founded by Winston Churchill when it was realised that the Navy had a surplus of enlisted men with no ships for them to crew. Although the Division fought on land its members were controlled by the Admiralty and therefore subject to naval traditions, including, at a more prosaic level, being able to grow beards and remain seated during the Loyal Toast. This led to inevitable tensions, with the result that the Division was transferred to Army control shortly after landing in France in 1916, although the names of the battalions retained their naval heritage – Hood, Benbow, Drake, etc. One of the regiment's most distinguished members was Lieutenant-Colonel Bernard Freyberg, who won a VC at Beaucourt in November 1916 and who was the second husband of Barbara McLaren (of Spalding fame) and it might be through this connection that Lutyens was awarded the commission to design the memorial. The Division had fought with distinction alongside the Australians during the Gallipoli landings and it was on Gallipoli Day (25 April) 1925 that the memorial was unveiled by Major-General Sir Archibald Paris, the Division's commander at the defence of Antwerp in 1914. It was also appropriate that Churchill should speak some words:

Everyone, I think, must admire the grace and simplicity of this Fountain, which the genius of Lutyens has designed. The site is also well chosen. Here, under the shadow of the Admiralty building, where, eleven years ago, the Royal Naval Division was called into martial life, this monument now records their fame and preserves their memory. Doubts and disillusions may be answered by the sure assertion that the sacrifice of these men

was not made in vain. And this Fountain to the memory of the Royal Naval Division will give forth not only the waters of honour, but the waters of healing and the waters of hope.

Further east in central London, in the square in the middle of Somerset House that had been used as their parade and drill ground, the Civil Service Rifles (or, to give it its full name, the 15th (County of London) Battalion, the London Regiment (Prince of Wales Own Civil Service Rifles)) erected their memorial. The regiment was raised from the ranks of the Civil Service, for whom Somerset House had originally been built. The memorial is a Lutyens 'one-off' – a square column surmounted by an urn with flags (the King's colours and the Union Flag) either side but made of copper rather than stone. Unveiled by the Regiment's Honorary Colonel, the Prince of Wales on 27 January 1924, the memorial was partially funded by the sale of a history of the regiment.

The Leeds Rifles (the Leeds Rifles Battalions The Prince of Wales's Own (West Yorkshire) Regiment) was the only regiment to choose a Lutyens War Cross when commissioning their memorial for a site on the edge of the churchyard of St Peter Kirkgate in the centre of Leeds. It was unveiled on 13 November 1921 by Captain G. Sanders VC MC of the regiment.

As well as designing regimental memorials Lutyens also designed memorials and graves for the sons of friends and clients who died during the War – six memorials for those who were buried abroad and two graves for those who were buried in England.

The most notable is the memorial to Edward Horner, the eldest son of Frances and her husband Sir John, in the Church of St Andrew in Mells. Horner had been killed in the Battle of Cambrai on 21 November 1917 and his memorial is a rare example of the work of two Presidents of the Royal Academy, being an equestrian statue of Horner, sculpted by the painter Sir Alfred Munnings (for whom this was his first sculpture), on a plinth by Lutyens, and it is widely held to be one of the most moving of personal memorials to the War. It had been originally intended to site it in its own mausoleum, then under the West Tower, before being eventually placed in the Horner or Lady Chapel. Also in the church is Lutyens's memorial to the Prime Minister's son, Raymond Asquith, the Horners' son-in-law, who was killed on the Somme on 15 September 1916, which consists of a bronze wreath above a Latin inscription carved directly into the wall by Eric Gill.[4] In the letter quoted above (page 81) Lutyens recalled that he had take Horner's tablet with him and had spent the evening in the church repainting Asquith's inscription 'All their young men are killed' he told Emily.

By the time that Sir Saxton Noble, a director of the armaments manufacturer, Armstrong Whitworth, fell under Lutyens's spell he had already commissioned Reginald Blomfield to undertake alterations to his house in London and Wretham Hall in Norfolk. As a result, despite plans for a grandiose 'green house' made out

Lancashire Fusiliers War Memorial, Bury

LEFT TO RIGHT Leeds Rifles War Memorial, Leeds; Billy Congreve memorial,
Stowe-by-Chartley; Edward Horner Memorial, Mells

of yew hedges that would have been bigger than the Viceroy's
House in New Delhi, all that resulted from their friendship was
Noble's own grave at Batheaston in Somerset[5] and the fine marble
wall plaque to his son Marc Noble in the Church of St Ethelbert
in East Wretham. Marc was named after his maternal great great
grandfather, the Victorian engineer Sir Marc Brunel, and, aged
ten, had been a member of the first Boy Scouts' camp on
Brownsea Island in August 1907 (an event that ran at a financial
loss that was made good by his father). Marc had left Eton in 1915
and became a Second Lieutenant in the Royal Field Artillery. He
died at Ypres on 1 July 1917, having been wounded whilst rescu-
ing injured colleagues.[6]

The war correspondent Sir Bryan Leighton had married the
sister of Violet Bartram, the wife of Herbert Johnson of
Marshcourt, and it is a family rumour that parts of the interior
of Marshcourt were inspired by Loton Park, the Leighton family
house in Alberbury, Shropshire. Sir Bryan contacted Lutyens to
ask him design a memorial to his son John Leighton, who, having
had a notable military career with the Scots Guards and Royal
Flying Corps, winning the Military Cross and being twice men-
tioned in despatches, had died of his wounds in France on 7 May

1917. The marble tablet, above which is the propeller from his aircraft that had been fashioned into a temporary cross for his
battlefield grave, was fitted around an earlier family memorial in
the Loton Chapel in the Church of St Michael, Alberbury.

Lutyens visited Loton Park in February 1918 and his letter to
Emily about his experience is worth quoting at length:

I reached Shrewsbury in good time and was met at the station by
Sir Bryan Leighton and a parson friend Mr Phillips in a big
American car and off we went. We went straight to Loton
(Alderbury) [sic] church – a funny old church but spoilt with a
very interesting tower, but it was too dark to see anything and
the drive facewards towards a wonderful sunset did not help one
to see in the dark.

However, I got an idea with the help of an electric torch and
darkly visualised the Loton Chapel and came to a conclusion sufficient for my peace of mind that night. Then on to the house
[Loton Park]. An old ramshackle place added to and embellished
by fits and starts. Most of the starts don't fit! And very bad excres-
cences in Victoria's goodly age when Ruskin and hypocrisy
preened its own aprons without the loss of pelican feathers.

Leighton has been at war flying. Apparently he got at cross purposes with the authorities, and they rather he went than probe justice. His job is now felling timber on his estate, for which he gets government labour and his other job is testing parachutes. Did you ever hear of such a job! He is very proud of having jumped out of an aeroplane at 350 feet, 1,200 is nothing if your heart is good enough to stand the change of atmospheric pressure. How I should hate it. He says it is the most delightful of all occupations – ugh! Would you like it?

The house has been untouched and unhousemaided – there were no housemaids and I should think never had been one and it wants twenty – for years, and a litter of every kind of paper and thing – guns, rods, fishing tackle, bows and arrows, old furniture, beds, curtains, pictures and heraldry galore, shields and banners etc. The house shut up, save for his little den, a litter of every sort of thing, very warm, panelled, with a great fire and windows never opened, quite a good dinner of an old fashioned sort and lots of heavy port. Then back to the little room and we talked war monuments and I found it past one before I retired to a terrifying for ghosts bedroom. However I slept very well and woke to a stormy morning and the rooks ablaze with noise and clamour, thoroughly rattled.

Breakfast at 8 then to the church and out to another – a train to Stafford, where I met Hudson. A taxi driver here [to Chartley], an excellent lunch, then to Chartley Church to see how the monument fitted – Billy Congreve – the model behaved quite nicely and satisfactorily. A walk back, tea, talk, dinner, and now this letter to you.[7]

Edward Hudson, who had been so instrumental in helping Lutyens's early career through featuring his articles in his magazine, *Country Life*, was a close friend of Billy Congreve and had published some of his writings sent from France during the War in his magazine. He had also decided to give to Lindisfarne Castle (which had been remodelled for him by Lutyens) to Congreve after the War, but Billy's life was cut short in the Battle of the Somme on 20 July 1916, when he was killed by a sniper's bullet. He was posthumously awarded the Victoria Cross, one of only three cases where it has been awarded to someone whose father also held it. Billy's citation read:

This officer constantly performed acts of gallantry, and showed the greatest devotion to duty, and by his personal example inspired all those around him with confidence at critical periods of the operations. During preliminary preparations for the attack he carried out personal reconnaissances of the enemy lines, taking out parties of officers and non-commissioned officers for over 1,000 yards in front of our line, in order to acquaint them with the ground. Major Congreve conducted a battalion to its position of employment, afterwards returning to it to ascertain the situation after the assault. He established himself in an exposed forward position from whence he successfully observed the enemy, and gave orders necessary to drive them from their position. Two days later, when Brigade Headquarters was heavily shelled and many casualties resulted, he went out and assisted the medical officer to remove the wounded to places of safety, although he himself was suffering severely from gas and other shell effects. He again on a subsequent occasion showed a supreme courage in tending wounded under heavy shell-fire. He finally returned to the front line to ascertain the situation after an unsuccessful attack, and whilst in the act of writing his report was shot and killed instantly.

In addition to the VC Congreve had been awarded the Distinguished Service Order, the Military Cross and the Légion d'Honneur and was the first person to hold all three awards for bravery. Congreve is buried in the Corbie Communal Cemetery Extension and has the unique distinction of two Lutyens memorial tablets: a grand one with a triangular pediment close to one for his father (also designed by Lutyens) in the Church of St John

The grave of Derek Lutyens, Thursley

the Baptist in Stowe-by-Chartley in Staffordshire and an altogether simpler affair in the Church of St Etienne in Corbie.[8]

Henry Tennant was the eldest son of Harold Tennant of Rolvenden, by his second wife. He joined the 2nd Dragoons (Royal Scots Greys) before transferring to the Royal Flying Corps. He was injured when his aeroplane nosedived into the ground in Kent in 1916, and broke an ankle and suffered severe shock in the process. He returned to active duty in France in due course and died on 27 May 1917, being buried in La Chapelette British and Indian Cemetery. His double-sided memorial at the head of the arch to the North Chapel of the Church of St Mary the Virgin in Rolvenden contains his original grave marker. The memorial used to contain his sword too, until it was stolen.

Derek Lutyens, the son of Lutyens's older brother Lionel, was the last of the architect's five nephews to die in the War and is the only one to have a grave or memorial designed by him. A member the Royal Air Force, Derek served on the observation staff at the Royal Aircraft Establishment at Farnborough. His aircraft crashed in flames at Mytchett Heath, Surrey on 8 May 1918, killing him as well as his civilian observer, whose body was discovered a few days later floating in the Basingstoke Canal. Derek was buried in the churchyard of St Michael's Church, Thursley beneath an elegant cross, close to the graves of his grandparents.

Leicester apart, the largest Lutyens war memorial in the UK is the Mercantile Marine Memorial, which commemorates the men of the Merchant Navy and the fishing fleets who had died in the War and had no grave but the sea. The memorial was commissioned by the Imperial War Graves Commission and, like Leicester, had a chequered history. H.F. Robinson, the IWGC's Commissioner of Works had originally chosen a site at Temple Steps, overlooking the River Thames in London, and Lutyens had been appointed architect in September 1925. Lutyens's proposal was for a 54ft-high structure consisting of two massive piers with alternating arches linked by a deep beam resting on Doric columns. It readily received consent from London County Council but it also required the approval of the Commissioner for Works, Sir Lionel Earle, who was advised by the fledgling Royal Fine Arts Commission (one of whose founders had been Lutyens himself). The RFAC was unhappy with the Commission's proposal and, to the horror of Fabian Ware and Lutyens, rejected it in a letter sent on 7 June 1926. They cited two reasons – firstly, they were unhappy that it would require the demolition of an arch built in 1868 by the Embankment's creator, Sir Joseph Bazalgette, and secondly, they felt that it was an inappropriate location for the memorial as they considered that it should be east rather than west of Tower Bridge, where it would be seen by ocean going vessels who were unable to reach this part of the River Thames.

Lutyens railed against the decision to Ware:

Lutyens's initial proposal for the Mercantile Marine Memorial on the banks of the River Thames, rejected because it occupied the site of an existing arch

It is all too silly and too small for words. Are Earls only to be commemorated in the House of Lords, Kings in Buckingham Palace . . . The Bryalgettes [sic] composition is nothing, simply a grandiose and impossible scheme to attract an innocent public in the Victorian Era. That arch a terrible affair and an encumbrance quite senseless . . . We want a civic center [sic] where men who have served the Empire are commemorated and the Embankment would be such a place- not hole and corner brave men because they happen to have been low in status.[9]

He even darkly suggested that there was a loophole in the legislation that would enable the Commission to proceed without Earle's consent ('Let's begin and leave it to the Office of Works to stop us with the odium of as threatening injunction. I yet hope you will be able to convince the Office of Works that the Fine Art Commission's advice is bosh')[10] but Ware preferred a more conciliatory approach and sought, unsuccessfully, to persuade Earle and the RAFC to change their minds. There was no option but to look elsewhere and, shortly thereafter, a site was chosen on Tower Green in the shadow of the Tower of London. It was a poorer site that, although visible from the river, loses the intimate connection that was given by the original location. Lutyens's

The Mercantile Marine Memorial as built

architectural response was less dramatic than his earlier scheme and, borrowing heavily from the ideas for the shelter buildings in the war cemeteries, he designed a Doric temple, with the names of the Missing cast on bronze panels. It was the closest that the architect came to a 'structure full of bronze columns bearing the names of the dead' to which he referred in his letter of 3 August 1917 to Fabian Ware (see page 30). However, even this site was not straightforward as it was discovered that a Statute dating back to the time of King George III protected the rights of the owners of adjoining land. It meant that the Trustees of the garden upon which the memorial was to be built could not give full and unambiguous approval to the Commission's proposals. The matter could only be resolved by an Act of Parliament and the Mercantile

Marine Memorial Act received Royal Assent on 29 June 1927. The builder was Holloway Brothers (London) Ltd and the memorial was unveiled by Queen Mary (in the absence of the King, who was ill) on 12 December 1928. The ceremony was transmitted live on the radio and was the Queen's first broadcast.

The final memorial in this particular group, although not strictly a regimental one, is the stark South Africa war memorial in Richmond Cemetery in London, often wrongly described as being in Richmond, South Africa. It was erected to commemorate the thirty-nine South African soldiers who had died of their wounds in the nearby hospital and was commissioned by the South African Hospital and Comforts Fund Committee. A 15ft-high granite monolith with a pointed, angular top, the severity of which is only

London Assurance War Memorial

City, Lloyd's had an altogether grander design of green and white marble for their panels that were sited near the Underwriting Room. Their memorial was unveiled on 31 January 1922 and was the only Lutyens memorial unveiled by Field-Marshal Haig.

Marble was also used for the Imperial Tobacco Company memorial tablets that lined the entrance hall of their headquarters in Bristol.

The British Medical Association memorial would have had a special resonance for Lutyens because it was erected at the building in Tavistock Square that he had designed as the headquarters of Emily's beloved Theosophical Society. Work on the building had begun in September 1911 but was interrupted by the outbreak of war and was unfinished when it was taken over by the Army Pay Office. The Society was in no position to complete the property after the War's end and sold it to the British Medical Association, who decided to commission Lutyens to design a set of memorial gates. King George V and Queen Mary formally opened BMA House itself on 13 July 1925 and, after a short prayer of dedication from the Archbishop of Canterbury, Lutyens presented the keys of the gates to the Archbishop, which he unlocked to the words 'In gratitude and hope we open these gates'.

The final two memorials in this group are those erected in schools. Little is known about the wall plaque at the University College School in Hampstead, which was dedicated in 1921.

The original intention of Wellington College to create a reading room as a suitable war memorial was abandoned due to a lack of funds. Instead Lutyens was commissioned to design a circular column with his favourite motif of St George to fit the semi-circular space at the end of the north transept of the college chapel that had been previously occupied by an organ. The memorial was unveiled by the Duke of Connaught on 24 October 1922.

As well as the Edward Horner memorial Lutyens designed plinths for two other war memorials that featured horses. The Cavalry Club memorial, at what is now the Guards and Cavalry Club on London's Picadilly, is a small bronze statue of a riderless horse, *The Empty Saddle*, sculpted by Herbert Haseltine in 1924. The Club had set up a sub-committee in July 1922 to arrange and commission the memorial and each member contributed 10 shillings towards the £700 cost. The second memorial had a poignant family connection and was a wooden plinth for a sculpture by the architect's own father, Charles, who had died in 1915. It was dedicated at Easter 1926 to the 'grateful and reverent memory of the Empire's horses' and installed in the Church of St Jude that Lutyens had himself designed in Hampstead Garden Suburb.

relieved by two carved wreaths, the starkness of the memorial almost seems to symbolise the breakdown in the relationship between Lutyens and Baker. It does not even sit on a traditional Lutyens base of three steps. It was accepted on behalf of the Government of South Africa by General Smuts on 30 June 1921.[11]

The war memorials commissioned by companies were similarly straightforward, with the notable exception of the North Eastern Railway Memorial in York (see pages 59–63). The Midland Railway also commissioned their own, grand, memorial that was unveiled in 1921 in Derby and which was the model for Rochdale, three years later but without the stone flags.

The British Thomson Houston Company[12] commissioned a War Cross on a large circular plinth containing the names of the company's fallen for a site immediately outside their offices in Rugby in 1921. The unveiling took place on 28 October, only six months after a meeting of the company's Board left the matter of a suitable memorial in the hands of its Chairman, Lord Carmichael.

Three companies decided that the best place for a memorial was within their own head office. In 1922 the London Assurance Company chose a modest brass plaque for entrance porch in their office in London's King William Street whilst, elsewhere in the

British Thomson Houston Company War Memorial, Rugby

NINE
MEANWHILE ABROAD

THE FAME OF THE CENOTAPH in Whitehall ensured that, not only would replicas be built in the United Kingdom, but that there would also be copies elsewhere in the World. The Government of Bermuda had begun to plan for its memorial in the summer of 1919. It took the decision that it should take the form of a cenotaph and a site was chosen in the island's main town of Hamilton. The cornerstone was laid as an expedient by the Prince of Wales on his visit to the island in 1920, even though the design had not been agreed.[1] Lutyens was contacted in order to obtain his permission to use a copy of the Whitehall original and replied to the Crown Agents (who acted on behalf of the Government of Bermuda) on 21 June 1922 'To supply copies of the small scale detail and full size working detail drawings, I propose to make a charge of 100 guineas. The flags should really be executed in stone but I am afraid this may be too expensive for you as a payment will have to be made to Professor Derwent Wood for the use of his models. As a matter of fact, the Whitehall flags are made of bunting with gilt bronze poles, wreaths and crowns.'[2]

The Government of Bermuda vacillated over whether to have a full-size copy or a smaller version, with Lutyens informing them that 'it is possible to erect the Cenotaph to a smaller size than the one in Whitehall, but it cannot be reduced to less than two thirds and for which I have prepared the necessary drawings which of course, had to be worked to ratios'.[3] Having been sent a photograph and plan of the site he felt that a two-thirds scale version would be suitable and his recommendation was followed. The memorial, complete with bunting flags rather than stone ones, was unveiled on 6 May 1925 and Lutyens was sent copies of the completed monument upon which he commented 'From photographs, work appears to have been carried out most excellently'.[4]

All India War Memorial Arch (now known as India Gate), New Delhi

The Cenotaph in London in the Canadian province of Ontario was paid for by the Imperial Order of the Daughters of the Empire (IODE), a Canadian charitable organisation with branches throughout the country which had been founded in 1900 to 'Improve the quality of life for children, youth and those in need through educational, social service and citizenship programs'. The London branch raised C$100,000 after the War, which, together with funds from by others, helped to provide a War Memorial Hospital for the town. They were also keen to have a war memorial and, in 1925 commenced a movement to have a cenotaph built. They committed C$4,000 of their own funds and began to raise the balance from the citizens and other organisations. Rather than approach Lutyens direct they contacted the City of Westminster (the London Borough within which Whitehall is situated) from whom they obtained plans in 1929 (presumably with Lutyens's approval) for 100 guineas. A wooden replica was built to act as a focus for remembrance ceremonies until the permanent memorial (which is a three quarters scale version) was unveiled on 11 November 1934. The provision of war memorials came under the IODE's 'citizenship' category and it has been estimated that it, together with other similar organisations, was responsible for the provision of up to one third of Canada's 1,300 war memorials.

Somewhat less is known about the cenotaph in Hong Kong, which was unveiled in 1928 and there seems to be no documentary evidence of its history, other than that it seems likely that the construction of a full scale replica design from Lutyens's plans was overseen by the local architectural practice of Palmer & Turner.

As well as these 'official' replicas there are at least five versions of the Cenotaph in New Zealand in which Lutyens seems to have played no part. The most well known is in Auckland, which even appears in the list of his work in the 'Memorial Volumes', a set of three folio volumes containing details of his

The unveiling of the Auckland War Memorial, November 1929

buildings which, together with the biography written by Christopher Hussey, was published after the architect's death by *Country Life*.

The Auckland cenotaph was designed by Keith Draffin, a local architect who, with his partners Hugh Grierson and Kenneth Aimer, had beaten sixty-nine other entrants to win the competition to design the city's War Memorial Museum in 1922. They proposed that the centrepiece should be a copy of the Cenotaph but, despite an overall budget for the project in the region of £200,000, the purchase of the original plans from Lutyens was deemed to be too expensive, and Draffin made several visits to a cinema to sketch the Whitehall original from newsreels. He made a credible copy but it differs from the cenotaphs designed by Lutyens in two key ways: firstly, the wreath on top of the sarcophagus is bronze rather than Portland stone or even, as Lutyens had originally proposed for Whitehall, verdite; and secondly, the steps of the base do not have the 2:1:2 proportions used by Lutyens. Therefore, like the war memorial in Edinburgh, Auckland must be considered

as an interesting curiosity but not a Lutyens 'original' and, in a similar vein, one must ignore the poorer copies elsewhere in New Zealand in Hamilton, Napier, New Plymouth and Paeroa.

It was logical that he would be asked to design the war memorial in New Delhi, given his leading role in the design of the city. The idea of having a monument to commemorate the country's war dead was not necessarily a foregone conclusion. Lord Chelmsford, who had been appointed Viceroy in 1916, harboured notions of a memorial serving a practical purpose, causing Lutyens to complain to Emily 'You cannot represent India in any monument of a utilitarian purpose with her multifarious castes, religions and nationalities. A war monument wherein all India can have the services of her great men commemorated would surely help and bind the country to a common service and purpose'.[5] When Chelmsford changed his mind, there was an obvious site for Lutyens's 'war monument' – a *rond point* at the eastern termination of King's Way (the main processional route leading from the Viceroy's House) that Lutyens had originally intended as the location for some form of a commemorative column. However, it was not inevitable that it would commemorate all of the India's war dead as there were plans for a series of memorials throughout India (including one at Attock to commemorate the troops who had perished in the area around the North-West Frontier) but when the Viceroy and the Commander in Chief, Sir Philip Chetwode, were both consulted they favoured a single memorial in New Delhi.

Lutyens's design is the largest of his war memorials apart from Thiepval and has a heroic scale appropriate to its site. Originally called the All India War Memorial but now known as 'India Gate', it takes the form of a triumphal arch 139ft high given extra solidity by the large attic. It is similar in many respects to the arch at Leicester, and uses the interpenetrating cross vaults of different heights that were to feature at both Leicester and the Memorial to the Missing at Thiepval. The design incorporated a device that Lutyens had originally considered for the Cenotaph whereby a bowl at the top would emit a plume of smoke by day and a column of fire at night. It added a dramatic touch to the dedication ceremony in 1931 'The lofty sacred fire that had begun in a dark pillar of cloud assumed a ruddy glow as the angry twilight sky burned crimson and gold. There was, recalled on official, 'something terrible' about the scene, as if Indian soldiers were marching to rejoin the dead in a fiery Imperial Valhalla'.[6]

The construction work had taken ten years from the laying of the foundation stone (which had to be moved when it was found to be in the wrong place) by the Duke of Connaught, the King's uncle, in February 1921 and, because of its function as a memorial to the missing, the IWGC contributed £14,000 towards the cost.

Lutyens also deisnged a marble wall tablet to the members of the Madras Club. It was made in England and sent to Madras, where it was installed in May 1924.

Irish National War Memorial, Dublin

From India it is but a hop across the Palk Strait to Sri Lanka, where Lutyens designed the war memorial (known as the Victory Column) in Colombo, a tall pillar along the lines of the Jaipur Column in front of the Viceroy's House in New Delhi which was also to incorporate smoke and fire. His letter to Emily of 8 April 1920 records that he visited Colombo on 12 March and met Mr Duncum, the secretary to the Chamber of Commerce, and 'settled to my own satisfaction the site for the war monument – and the popular vote being for a column of victory – its form. Instead of the usual angel I have suggested a brazier to burn petrol and make an occasion – a column of smoke by day and of fire by night'.[7] Construction of the memorial took two years and it was unveiled on 27 October 1923. Emily saw the memorial when she stopped at Colombo on her way to Australia in 1925 and was not impressed by what she saw 'It looked like the eye of a needle, and I did not like it very much. I understand that it is meant for a flame but without the light it looks very odd'.[8]

The last of all of Lutyens's war memorials to be built was the Irish National War Memorial in Dublin, which was not completed until 1939. Over 100 interested parties took part in a meeting on 17 July 1919 in Dublin, at which it was decided to form a committee and establish a National War Memorial Fund to cover the cost of

memorials to the Irish troops at home and abroad. One of its first tasks was to commission a set of memorial records that eventually became an eight-volume directory of the 49,400 names of the fallen, one hundred copies of which were made and distributed to the country's principal libraries.

Several sites were suggested for the war memorial itself, including Merrion Square in the heart of Dublin, but all proved inappropriate for a variety of technical and legal reasons. In an attempt to resolve this impasse the Irish Government decided to take the initiative and, in 1929, suggested the memorial could form part of a 150-acre linear park to be laid out in Longmeadows, on the southern bank of the River Liffey opposite Phoenix Park, to which it would be linked by a bridge. Lutyens was engaged to prepare a design and the size of the site, coupled with a significant budget, gave him the opportunity to produce a design that incorporated elements familiar from his memorials elsewhere within a landscaped setting – the closest that he was to come to the abortive green cathedral at Leicester. A War Cross on a raised platform overlooks a War Stone that sits at the centre of the memorial as a symbolic altar. On each side of the Stone are tall obelisk fountains acting as figurative candles and the composition is completed by a pair of flanking sunken rose gardens complete with stone and

timber pergolas and four 'Book Rooms' that represent the four provinces of Ireland and contain records of the dead.

Construction work on the memorial and surrounding gardens began in December 1931 and took seven years. In an interesting adjunct to the fact that the Irish Free State had been declared in 1921, it was undertaken, without any apparent animosity, by a workforce comprised of 50 per cent ex-British servicemen and 50 per cent ex-servicemen from the Irish National Army. Much attention was given to the planting, which was supervised by a committee, one of whose members was Sir Frederick Moore, the former Keeper of the National Botanic Gardens of Ireland.

Lutyens made a number of visits to the site to monitor construction and, on one occasion in August 1935, spent 16/- on a bottle of whiskey that he shared with six masons and three others on the site.

Unfortunately, two bridges that were a key part of the design (one, across the Liffey, and the other, across a railway line at the back of the site and 'designed to carry elaborate colonnades of chiselled granite') were not built. The Liffey bridge was supposed to be the main entrance into the Gardens and, as a result, the site now has to be approached from the rear.[9]

Although the memorial was completed by the spring of 1939, Eamon de Valera, the Taoiseach, decided that, with the prospect of another war on the horizon, the official opening should be deferred and it seeped into public use without a formal opening.

As well as the various war memorials that he designed abroad Lutyens was also commissioned by the Imperial War Graves Commission to design two Memorials to the Missing in Africa — one at Freetown, Sierra Leone and the other at Abercorn (now Mbala) in Zambia. It had originally been suggested that by the Commission that he should call at Port Tewfik on the way back from his trip to India in 1921 with a view to designing a memorial to the Indians who died in Palestine but it was ultimately decided that the memorial should be added to the work in the area being undertaken by Sir John Burnet.[10] Lutyens was however, in 1924, asked to design a general memorial to be erected in cemeteries in East Africa to commemorate the missing Indian troops. It took the form of a truncated pyramid of rubble with four panels for the commemorative inscriptions but there was a concern locally that the native soldiers would not tend to associate with such an abstract form of memorial and that they would prefer something more figurative. Sir Frederic Kenyon was consulted about the matter and the sculptor J.A. Stevenson was commissioned to design bronze statues of native soldiers, known as 'Askaris', in various appropriate poses.

LEFT Irish National War Memorial, Dublin
RIGHT Memorial to the Missing, Freetown, Sierra Leone

The idea of a truncated pyramid was not wasted though as it re-emerged when Lutyens was asked to design a Memorial to the Missing of the Royal West African Frontier Force in Sierra Leone. The Imperial War Graves Commission had been approached by the Officer Commanding, West African Regiment regarding a memorial to recognise the sixty-three troops (the majority of whom were native soldiers) who had died in the Cameroons Expedition of 1914–16 and subsequent fighting. The Officer (whose name in the CWGC records is, unfortunately, indecipherable) made two visits to the Commission's headquarters in 1926 that he followed up with a letter in May 1927, pointing out that West Africa was the only theatre of war that had not been commemorated by the Commission. He noted that 'the marking of their graves with headstones does not appeal to the West African soldier'[11] and, as a result, the graves had either been lost or, where their location was known, it was not known which body lay within which grave. In order to commemorate his troops appropriately he proposed a memorial, such as a smaller version of Cleopatra's Needle, and sought 'special and sympathetic treatment'[12] from the Commission as he had little money available from the Regimental funds. His request clearly struck a chord and the Commission saw that it provided a wider opportunity to commemorate the 1,109 troops who had died in West Africa and who had no known grave. Lutyens was commissioned to prepare a design which, the Director of Public Works in Sierra Leone suggested, should be built of concrete rather than Portland stone with simulated masonry joints being made in the wooden formwork before the concrete was poured. The Commission considered that such an approach would produce an unattractive memorial that would be more expensive than a stone one to maintain in the future. Instead it was decided to appoint a contractor who would assemble the components of the memorial in the UK and then ship it out to Freetown, with the stone being left in a rough state to be given a final dressing once it arrived on site. The process worked

The unveiling of the Freetown Memorial, March 1931

well and the memorial was erected on a site in front of the Governor's House in the colony's capital, Freetown, where it was unveiled by the then Acting Governor in March 1931.

It is appropriate that the last of Lutyens's war memorials to be considered marks the place where, to all intents and purposes, the Great War finished – the small town of Abercorn in Zambia, a place that was as spiritually remote from the Western Front as was our starting point at Tyringham. The occasion is marked by a small square rubble cairn in the middle of a round-about on the road on the southern edge of the town that acts as the memorial to the 433 Northern Rhodesian native carriers who died and have no known gave.

The manner in which the War's hostilities ended is little known and, like the public meeting when the townsfolk of Spalding considered their memorial, it is an event worth telling.

The German troops in East Africa had undertaken a highly effective guerrilla campaign under the adept leadership of General Paul von Lettow-Vorbeck, a little known figure who was the German equivalent of Lawrence of Arabia. He realised at the outset of the War that he stood little chance of defeating the Allied forces in open fighting due to their superior strength and so decided that the best contribution that he could make would be to tie down as many of them as possible to keep them from the Western Front. He thus waged a highly effective guerrilla campaign through Kenya and Mozambique, bringing him, in November 1918, in reach of the undefended small settlement of Kasama, in Northern Rhodesia.[13] The British troops were 150 miles away in Abercorn, having unsuccessfully tried to anticipate von Lettow-Vorbeck's next move, and so the residents had been evacuated under the direction of G.A.M. Alexander, who had been assigned to the task to replace another official who had been killed by a flagpole that he was trying to erect. Alexander takes up the story:

The Memorial to the Missing in Abercorn (now Mbala), Zambia marks the effective conclusion of the Great War

In the factory itself there was a European, I forget his name, who started firing his big game gun from inside the factory which has a corrugated iron roof, the report of each shot was therefore magnified, and we learnt afterwards that the Germans thought we had a big gun and were using it. The eleven North Rhodesian Police, without a word of command, took up their positions under cover along the bank of the Chambeshi and fired at anything they saw. The whole 'Battle' lasted about twenty minutes. Luckily for us, for at this time, the 13th November, 1918, Barraclough called out that word was coming through the single telephone line system something about the war in Germany being over. This telephone line was attached to trees from Broken Hill to the Chambeshi. Then the word armistice was received.

I never learnt why it was we were not told of the armistice earlier. As soon as word came through, Croad[14] told me to put up white flags, so, as we had all fed in Simpson's dining room, I ran in and grabbed some of his table napkins and gave them to natives to tie on sticks to put along the river bank and other places. Meanwhile I had seized the lovely table cloth and got it tied to a pole and sent a native up the roof and had the pole tied to the chimney. Seeing the white flags the Germans stopped firing and eventually arrangements were made to meet the German representatives. . . . Croad asked me to go with him when he went to see the (German) chief of staff to show him the telephone message re the armistice, but as Brigham had had previous service in France I thought he should go and off they went.[15]

The 'telephone message' (i.e. telegram) that Croad handed to German representative read 'Please send the following to General von Lettow-Vorbeck under a white flag – The English

Prime Minister sent notice that on 11th November an Armistice was signed and that the fighting on all fronts should cease on 11th November at 11 o'clock. I order my troops to end hostilities as from now and I expect you to do the same.' It was signed by General Jacob van Deventer, the head of the Allied Forces in East Africa. The Germans laid down their weapons and thus it was that the conflict that had begin with an assassin's bullet in Sarajevo and had encompassed the horrors of the Somme, Passchendaele and Ypres, the tragedies of Gallipoli and the *Lusitania*, the stalemate of Jutland and had left over 8 million people dead, ended with German troops shooting at a factory building in the middle of Africa before surrendering to someone showing a table cloth – it would be difficult to imagine a more banal ending to a global conflict.

The only drawback was that there were no British troops to accept the formal surrender of the German troops and so they were ordered to march to Abercorn where, on 25 November 1918, fourteen days after the end of the War on the Western Front, with due ceremony in front of General W.F.S. Edwards, his staff and the District Commissioner C.R.B. Draper, they officially surrendered. They numbered 30 officers, 125 NCOs and 1,168 Askaris.

Von Lettow-Vorbeck achieved the twin distinctions of never having been beaten in battle and having commanded the only part of the German Army to invade British territory during the War and, on his return home, was the only German general permitted the privilege of being able to march his troops through the Brandenburg Gate. He was clearly respected by the British commanders that he had harried so effectively and, when he later fell on hard times, some of them helped pay for his pension.

When the time came to commemorate the Northern Rhodesian native carriers who had died, the British South Africa Company proposed to erect something suitable in Livingstone, the then capital of the country. However there was strong pressure from the residents of Abercorn that their town would be the most suitable place, not only because of the official surrender but also because it had been the only part of the country to experience serious fighting, when it was shelled during 1914–15. The matter was solved when a local resident, John Henry Venning, became the Provincial Commissioner and he chose the site where the surrender took place. The memorial was paid for by the Imperial War Graves Commission and was similar to the one in Freetown. However, despite the significance of the site, the first cost submitted for the memorial's construction by the Public Works Department of Northern Rhodesia was deemed, at £850, to be too expensive. The memorial was therefore redesigned, with granite rubble walls and the steps were omitted to reduce the cost to £420. Lutyens approved the design changes and it is believed that the memorial was completed in 1930.

TEN
PERMANENT SEPULTURE

THE BACKGROUND

WHILST LUTYENS WAS DEALING with his various war memorials in Britain and abroad he was, of course, heavily involved with the Imperial War Graves Comission as one of their three Principal Architects alongside Herbert Baker and Sir Reginald Blomfield, and working to the lead established by the Commission's artistic advisor, Sir Frederic Kenyon. On the face of it Kenyon would seem to have been a curious choice, because he had no particular architectural or artistic background, and had gained his reputation as a biblical scholar. He had been appointed Director of the British Museum in 1909 and his position was felt to be sufficiently important that, in 1917, the Museum's Trustees were able to recall him from the Western Front, where he was serving. He was recommended to Ware by Charles Holmes, the Director of the National Gallery and, even though Kenyon and Ware had completely different temperaments ('the one [Kenyon] cool, pragmatic, methodical, the other [Ware] highly-strung, immediate, a natural fighter and persuader of men')[1] they formed an immediate and enduring friendship and Ware was perfectly content to give Kenyon complete freedom to act as he thought fit.

Kenyon's report to the Commission in January 1918, 'War Graves: How The Cemeteries Abroad Will Be Designed', set both the architectural and the administrative framework for the subsequent design of the cemeteries. Not only did he support Lutyens's War Stone and propose the introduction of a Cross (which was subsequently designed by Blomfield), but he also endorsed the principle of planting that had already been established under the stewardship of Arthur Hill from the Royal Botanic Gardens at Kew. Critically it seems that Kenyon was given no particular financial brief from Ware and it is apparent that,

Monchy British Cemetery

whilst cost was of general concern, it was not an undue constraint. The Commission was therefore allowed to do the job for which it had been established in the manner that it felt fit, rather than produce a solution for the cheapest possible cost.

This important freedom manifested itself in three particular ways.

Firstly, the Commission could have chosen, wherever necessary, to disinter the bodies of the fallen and concentrate them in a series of 'super cemeteries', a solution that would have minimised both the intial construction and future maintence costs. Had Tyne Cot (the largest Allied cemetery on the Western Front, with nearly 12,000 graves) been adopted as a model, this would have given rise to another sixty-two cemeteries of similar size. However, the Commission decided that, with a few exceptions, any bodies that had to be disinterred would be buried in existing cemeteries. Some new cemeteries were created, but they are the exception rather than the rule. As a consequence there is a ribbon of more than 900 cemeteries, some of which contain less than fifty bodies, stretching from the French border with Switzerland to the North Sea and marking the ebb and flow of the Front Line. Whilst the sheer scale of Tyne Cot ensures that any visit to it is a moving experience, it is through the sheer number of cemeteries and their variation in sizes that one experiences a greater sense of the War's real tragedy.

The second critical decision was to avoid a 'pattern book' approach to the cemetery design. It would have been easy to produce standardised buildings and operate to a strict formula. Instead, each cemetery was to be unique and even though there was a common theme to their designs, it was not a prescriptive one. It is clear that, where it was appropriate, the architects were allowed to treat the cemeteries as serious pieces of design in

A post-War party clearing shells from Hooge Crater Cemetery

their own right and use special treatment for a particular cemetery if they considered it appropriate.

The final choice, and one which was clearly promoted by Kenyon, was that the Commission should not have its own 'in-house' architectural team, but that there should be a combination of junior architects working for the Commission who would carry out the basic design work and report to external architectural consultants. The latter would give guidance and assistance in order to add variety and flair as well as an external perspective, very much in the medieval manner of 'Master and Apprentice'. In time, the 'apprentices' were to become known as the 'Architects in France' (AIFs) and the 'masters' the 'Principal Architects' (PAs). It was Kenyon's intention that the PAs would reserve some cemeteries to be designed solely by themselves whilst the AIFs would carry out the balance in conjunction with the PAs and that both architects would receive the appropriate design credit: 'it is hoped that, by cordial and loyal co-operation on both sides, this will be compatible with allowing full scope to the initiative and genius of the younger man.'[2]

Prior to the involvement of Kenyon, Lutyens had thought that he would have overall responsibility for designs ('Just had a

pleasant talk with Gen. Ware. His idea is that I am made top dog to carry it all out!!! Employing Baker etc!' he wrote to Emily in his 'Ball of Bronze' letter from the battlefield in 1917)[3] and the matter was still under discussion in October 1917 when Ware was sufficiently concerned to ask Lutyens if he could afford to undertake the role. Lutyens confided to Emily 'It may mean that I shall have to give up a lot of private work. I am rather vague about this and must think it out'.[4] However Ware and Kenyon subsequently decided that there should be three PAs: 'the temperamental Reginald Blomfield, the gentler Herbert Baker and the brilliant Edwin Lutyens'[5] who were formally appointed on 5 March 1918 at a salary of £400 per annum (subsequently raised to £600 in 1919). They were *pro bono* appointments that would sit alongside the work that the architects did for other clients and, for Lutyens, the annual salary paid by the Commission would have been the equivalent of the fee for one of his average-sized war memorials.

The AIFs were to be full time employees of the Commission at a salary of £500 per annum and would be based at the Commission's office in St Omer. It was Kenyon's intention that the work would be split into three geographical areas, each with its own PA and AIF, so that each would have its own character.

Hooge Crater Cemetery today

He discussed the matter with the three PAs and wrote to Ware: 'As to the junior architects, Blomfield asks for Berrington, Lutyens for Holden, Baker for Pearson. I think that this will be best, as Holden will be more able to keep Lutyens's vagaries in check than anyone else.'[6] However, it was decided to spread the workload more widely and advertise the AIF's posts. Whilst one or two AIFs came and went, there were six who, to all intents and purposes, saw the task through to completion: William Cowlishaw, George Goldsmith, Arthur Hutton, Noël Rew, John Truelove and Wilfrid von Berg. A seventh, the Charles Holden who was wanted by Lutyens, started as an AIF but was subsequently made a PA in 1920. All had seen some form of active service and Goldsmith and von Berg had served with particular distinction, each having been awarded the Military Cross. Goldsmith and Truelove were both given references by Lutyens, the former having worked in his office from 1907–10. As a group they were not necessarily the type of young architects that Kenyon had envisaged: Cowlishaw (the oldest) having been born in 1870 and von Berg (the youngest) in 1894. In addition, Cowlishaw, Goldsmith and Rew were all experienced architects in their own right who had all operated their own architectural practices prior to the outbreak of the War.

Von Berg later recalled: 'In France in early 1919 . . . I was awaiting demobilisation and wondering rather grimly what were likely to be my prospects of re-entering the profession in England when a notice arrived in the Orderly Room stating that architects were invited to apply for positions in the Imperial War Graves Commission. Without a moment's hesitation I saddled my horse, galloped off to a neighbouring town, was interviewed and accepted.'[7]

The appointments made, the Commission decided to proceed with the design and construction of three experimental cemeteries to test their principles in action and, equally importantly, to gain an idea of the likely construction costs. It had been intended that each PA would be given a cemetery to design but as their work had been allocated on a geographical basis and the areas allotted to Baker and Lutyens were inaccessible, it fell to Blomfield to design all three (at Forceville, Le Tréport and Louvencourt) albeit that it would appear that Holden was heavily involved with Forceville at least, because the shelter building bears the hallmarks of his severe aesthetic. The three cemeteries were completed in 1920 to great acclaim – the correspondent in *The Times* calling them 'The most perfect, the noblest, the most classically beautiful memorial that any loving heart or any proud

The standard headstone designed by the IWGC for its cemeteries

therefore formed a special committee comprising Dugald Sutherland MacColl (Keeper of the Wallace Collection), Charles Holmes (Director of the National Gallery) and Macdonald Gill (artist, illustrator and brother of sculptor Eric) to seek and consider suggestions, which they did before producing a solution of their own – an oblong slab of stone 2ft 8in high, 1ft 3in wide and 3in deep with a gently curving top. The face of the stone would contain suitable wording in a special Roman typeface designed by Macdonald Gill together with a carving of the appropriate regimental badge and a personal inscription at the base, chosen by the family of the deceased soldier.

The design was not greeted with universal acclaim and the debate held by Lutyens, Baker and Aitken in France and back in England about the significance of the cross took place on a wider public platform. The Commission placed a strong emphasis upon the value of equality in death and the subordination of individual choice in favour of a greater common benefit. It fully appreciated that there would be those to whom religious symbolism would be important and considered that the best way that this could be handled would be with an appropriate treatment on the face of the headstone where, for example, a cross or a Star of David could be carved with ease.

There was a significant opposition to this approach that would not be appeased, led by Lady Florence Cecil (wife of the Bishop of Exeter), Lord Balfour, Lord Lansdowne and Sir Edward Carson. They wanted the opportunity for people to have a cross as a headstone instead of the Commission's plain slab and their voices became so vociferous that the matter became a subject of a debate in the House of Commons on 4 May 1920. The main proponent for the Commission's style of headstone was Burdett Coutts, an MP who had sat in the Chamber for thirty-five years without attracting any attention but, for some reason, was inspired by this particular subject. He took a great care to prepare himself with a full background briefing from the Commission before standing in the Chamber to give the speech of his life – one that was described by a reporter as though Coutts's lips had been 'touched by fire'.[9] The contrary view was put with equal passion before the Commission's case was eloquently reinforced by its Chairman, Winston Churchill, who laying out his argument for the choice of headstone also referred to Lutyens's War Stone which, he considered, would still be in existence in 2,000 years' time and would 'preserve the memory of a common purpose pursued by a great nation in the remote past and will undoubtedly excite the wonder and the reverence of future generations'.[10] The matter was the subject a free vote and, to the undoubted relief of Ware and others, the Commission's stance on the headstones was endorsed.

nation could desire to their heroes fallen in a foreign land. . . . It is the simplest, it is the grandest place I ever saw.'[8] The Commission was not completely happy with the result however and felt that there was an element of over design and, in particular that the enclosing walls were too high and should be reduced in height from 5ft to 3ft. However, the combination of architecture and planting had worked well and design work could now start in earnest, the more so because the Commission had finally resolved the controversial issue of the design of the headstones that would mark the individual graves, an issue that had rumbled on for eighteen months after the conclusion of the War.

Both Lutyens and Baker had originally produced designs for the headstones but they were not considered suitable. (Lutyens's design consisted of a rectangular headstone with an inset cross with circles at the end of each arm, in the manner of the face of the Southampton War Memorial – see page 39.) The Commission

At this stage it is now appropriate to return to two key elements of the cemetery design – the Cross and the War Stone.[11]

Etaples Military Cemetery

Kenyon wrote a 'Memorandum on the Cross as Central Monument' in January 1919 as an adjunct to his main Report to the Commission. Whilst he regarded the War Stone as 'the universal mark of a British War Cemetery',[12] he was less prescriptive about Blomfield's Cross, which featured a bronze sword attached to the octagonal shaft and expressed the type of symbolism that Baker admired. He felt that

> Each Principal Architect must be free to follow his own judgement unless the Commission decides otherwise. . . . In asking three eminent architects to undertake the control of architectural design in the theatre of war, the intention was not that these three shall jointly devise a common method of treatment, but that, on the basis of the general scheme permitted by the Commission, each should be free to follow the dictates of his own genius. . . . I would therefore still recommend that

> each Principal Architect shall be free to do as he thinks best in the areas allotted to him. If all agree in all cases to adopt the one pattern, I have nothing more to say; but if any of them feels that in certain circumstances of ground or surroundings a different pattern is desirable, I think he should be free to adopt it.[13]

Despite this flexibility, however, all three PAs decided to adopt the Blomfield Cross and it is appropriate, at this point, to debunk one of the myths that has grown up around the crosses in the cemeteries designed by Lutyens, and which can be dated back to Hussey's biography.[14] In a footnote Hussey stated 'Both Lutyens and Blomfield designed Memorial Crosses, but in order to implement the principle of joint responsibility, the Commission usually placed Blomfield's Cross in cemeteries containing Lutyens's War Stone and Lutyens's Cross in cemeteries designed by other architects'.[15]

The 'Lutyens Cross' to which Hussey referred was the tapering cross that that the architect designed as a war memorial, particularly for villages such as Abinger Common and Stockbridge, but also in a larger version for Exeter and York. There are contrary views upon its design. One holds that, with its short arms, it is verging on being a 'non-cross' and in accordance with Lutyens's own religious beliefs he was trying to design something that gave the merest representation of a cross.[16] Another, contrary, view is that its faceted shaft gives it the appearance of a sheathed sword inside a scabbard. There is no evidence that Lutyens's Cross was designed for use on the Western Front and, despite Hussey's assertion, it does not appear in any of the Commission's cemeteries. One might think that Lutyens would have availed himself of the freedom presented by Kenyon to use his own cross but it seems as though both he and Baker were happy to use Blomfield's design.

There were four versions of the Cross, ranging in height from 14ft 6in to 30ft to suit the size of the particular cemetery. However, Lutyens was not prepared to show the same flexibility over the War Stone although he agreed that it could be reduced in length from 12ft to 10ft (*pace* Edinburgh and 9ft) if circumstances dictated as long as all of the other dimensions were altered in proportion. It is, however, not certain whether such reduced sized War Stones were ever used. The way in which Lutyens was protective of the War Stone was recalled by von Berg 'I remember that Lutyens evolved his own system of calculation where, for example, the curve of the entasis on his Great War Stone was measured in four to five decimal points of an inch, and many of the French and Belgian contractors were dismayed in attempting to carry out such minute accuracy in this work'.[17]

Architecture apart, it is the planting, as much as anything, that gives the cemeteries their unique British flavour. It will be recalled that Arthur Hill had been dispatched to the Western Front to examine soil types and make recommendations regarding the overall horticulture as early as 1916, even before the architecture had been considered. The involvement of Lutyens's long-term collaborator, Gertrude Jekyll, was relatively limited[18] and, although she provided planting plans for the cemeteries that Lutyens designed upon his return from the battlefields in 1917, there is no evidence of any detailed involvement by her in their eventual designs, although she is known to have provided plants for some of them from her own nursery. However, her influence is everywhere, and the overwhelming impression of the cemeteries, particularly in the spring and summer, is of the style of cottage gardening that she popularised. The effect that the flowers can have upon a cemetery can be gauged by comparison with the German cemeteries, where the headstones are set directly into the grass and the lack of colour gives a particularly sombre appearance.

THE PROCESS

THE CONSTRUCTION OF THE CEMETERIES was described by Rudyard Kipling, the IWGC's literary adviser as 'the biggest single bit of work since any of the Pharaohs, and they only worked in their own country'[19] and, whilst this may be a touch over exuberant (the establishment of the canal and railway networks spring to mind as obvious comparisons) it makes the point that the Commission's accomplishment in designing and constructing over 1,000 cemeteries on the Western Front and around the World, (many of which were on shell-ravaged battlefields) in little more than ten years is a substantial achievement by any measure.

Such a task could only have been accomplished within such a short timescale using a well-ordered administrative procedure for the design, costing and approval of plans and the implementation of the subsequent construction process. Unfortunately the detailed records of this hectic period of activity were not retained. It is therefore necessary to use a certain amount of conjecture to derive the way in which the process worked, using such records as do exist coupled with the correspondence between one of the AIFs Wilfred von Berg and Gavin Stamp, written when the latter was preparing the 'Silent Cities' exhibition at the RIBA in 1977 that focussed on the activities of the CWGC.[20]

To a certain extent, until construction work had started in earnest, the potential costs of the cemeteries were unknown, a situation not helped by the fact that the building industry in France and Belgium was still recovering after the end of the War. An initial budget of £10 per grave was set by Colonel Albert Arthur Messer, an architect who served as Ware's second-in-command. However, although it was found to be too low once the three experimental cemeteries had been built, the Commission found that it could redress the balance by increasing the size of the construction contracts to obtain economies of scale. In the end, rather than have an absolute cost per grave, a sliding cost scale was established by Lieutenant-Colonel F.R. Durham, the Commission's Director of Works, to which was added a cost of £5/10/- per headstone.

Despite Kenyon's original intention for the PAs to have their own discrete areas, there seems to have been no particular rationale for the way in which the cemeteries were allocated to them and, as it transpired, over half of the cemeteries (mainly the smaller ones) were designed by the AIFs themselves with no involvement from the PAs.

The backbone of the design process was an Approval Form (AF) for each cemetery that was filled out by the AIF and then circulated, together with architectural and horticultural drawings, to the key members of the IWGC's internal team and its external advisers, all of whom could add their comments, before the form reached the desk of Sir Frederic Kenyon for final approval on

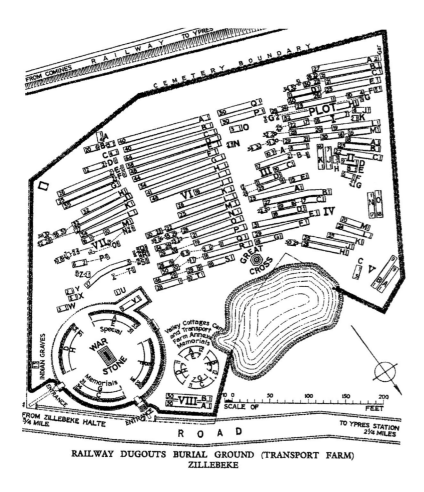

RAILWAY DUGOUTS BURIAL GROUND (TRANSPORT FARM)
ZILLEBEKE

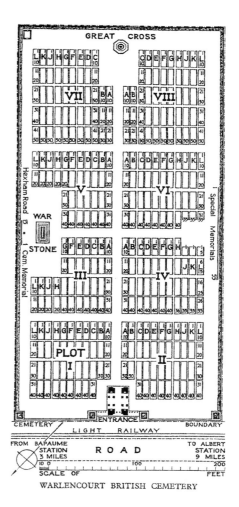

WARLENCOURT BRITISH CEMETERY

The layout of the Railway Dugouts Burial Ground cemetery shows the contrast between the haphazard wartime burials and the post War burials around the War Stone

Warlencourt British Cemetery was made after the War made to accommodate scattered bodies from the local battlefields

behalf of the Commission. From the AIF it would go in turn to the Horticultural Officer, the Deputy Director of Works, the Chief Surveyor, the Financial Adviser, the Principal Architect and the Botanical Adviser before reaching Kenyon.

As well as drawings, a full cost breakdown would be appended to show how the scheme measured up against the Commission's benchmarks. Fortunately some of the AFs still exist and it is they or, rather, the comments upon them, that shine a light upon the process and the minds of those involved. Unfortunately, despite 1,000 cemeteries having been through such a process, fewer than 100 of the AFs seem to have survived but, fortunately for devotees of Lutyens, fifty-one of them are for cemeteries with which he was involved.

Our understanding of which the way in which the PAs and AIFs worked together comes from both these forms and the recollections of von Berg: Lutyens 'showed a lively concern coupled with a delicious sense of humour. I remember how once he introduced an

asymmetrical feature into one of my designs saying with a chuckle "That's cockeye but let's do it",' whereas Blomfield 'took a meagre and superficial interest in my work and rarely had much to contribute'. His preference, was for Holden 'serious and painstaking, . . . a senior architect for whom I had the greatest respect'.[21] He had no recollection of Baker as he did not work with him. Von Berg also revealed a hitherto unknown side to Lutyens when he recalled how 'At a party in the chateau at Longuenesse . . . to everyone's delight he climbed on a table and danced a little jig.'[22]

The pattern that emerges is that, in most cases, Lutyens would visit the site, either in conjunction with the appropriate AIF or with some other official of the IWGC, and then either sketch or discuss his thoughts with them, leaving the AIF to draw up the plans e.g. 'This cemetery was visited in the company of the Principal Architect and the general lines of the design were indicated by him on site. . . . The survey on which Sir Edwin made certain notes is enclosed' (Houchin British Cemetery), 'This cemetery has been visited by the Principal Architect, and the enclosed sketch design is according to his wishes' (Lapugnoy Military Cemetery).

Often Lutyens's comment on the form is, simply, 'Approved' but there are occasional glimpses of the detail with which he would view the drawings 'The stone quoins may be omitted with advantage and a stone plinth substituted on a level with the second step. 2 posts on the gate way instead of one. I regret the blocks on the cornice. The roof might be simplified and it would gain in dignity – with a lower pitch, in stone' (Barlin Communal Cemetery Extension); 'The shelters want further consideration and I prefer one gargoyle if possible. The columns should have a cap to them and entasis to the shaft, the bottom part curving into the step, and the wall on either side should be thicker to work into the width of the covetto of the base. The step also wants widening and a bigger return. I have made a rough sketch on tracing paper, and have enclosed it in the plan' (Klein Vierstraat British Cemetery). He also showed the appreciation of religious sensitivities that recur throughout his work 'I apologise – I did not realise the cross came so close to the Jewish plot and it would be good manners to a central position' (Chocques Military Cemetery).

Lutyens did not necessarily always get his way though: at Lillers Communal Cemetery and Extension the AIF Arthur Hutton had the temerity to relocate the War Stone: 'The War Stone as sited by the PA encroaches on the graves' was the comment on the AF by the IWGC's Deputy Director of Works W. Binnie, following which Lutyens commented: 'I prefer the War Stone in the East position on the river bank. . . . The foundation of the War Stone could stand in the stream if there is difficulty as to its encroachment on graves' – the War Stone stayed where placed by Hutton. On one occasion Lutyens delegated completely to the AIF: 'I know nothing of Chinese Art, I can but express my admiration! Capt. Truelove should go to London and visit the British Museum and the wholesale Chinese warehouses in London' (Noyelles-sur-Mer Chinese Cemetery). Whether Truelove did as he was bid is not recorded but the solution includes a typical Chinese gateway.

It has been assumed that Lutyens did not become involved with the design of cemeteries with fewer than 250 graves but this is not the case: for example, the AF for Fienvillers British Cemetery (124 graves) showed his concern for the way in which the Cross might be obscured from the road. It is reasonable to assume, though, that his involvement with such cemeteries would have been less for the simple reason that there was less architectural work involved as they typically consist of the graves, a Cross and the enclosing walls.

As with his war memorials, Lutyens's detailed involvement in the design of the war cemeteries would have been compromised by his regular visits to India but it would seem, based on the AF for Esquelbecq Military Cemetery (where Hutton's comment as AIF was 'This cemetery was designed by me and superintended by

Major G.H. Goldsmith acting for Sir E. Lutyens RA while the latter was in India') that Goldsmith acted *in loco parentis* on at least one site, so it is reasonable to assume that it would have happened elsewhere. There is also evidence that the drawings were sent to Lutyens's office for comment so it can be presumed that Thomas would have commented on them in his employer's absence as well. The involvement of Goldsmith accords with von Berg's recollection of him as being 'a slavish devotee of Lutyens and allowed his own talents to be submerged in his efforts to copy the master'[23] and someone who was 'rather smug'[24] about being initiated into Lutyens's intricacies of calculating entasis on the War Stone.

Lutyens did not restrict his comments to the architecture and, even though the AF was circulated to both John Parker, the Commission's Horticultural Officer[25] and its external Botanical Adviser, Arthur Hill, he was quite happy to comment upon the horticulture himself, e.g. 'I doubt if cypresses will grow' (Fienvillers British Cemetery); 'Personally I do not care for euonymus in this association' (Beaulencourt British Cemetery); 'Agreed, but why plant privet? Cannot thorn or yew be used?' (Esquelbecq Military Cemetery).

THE ARCHITECTURE

THE RESULT OF ALL OF THESE INFLUENCES – from Kenyon's desire to give the architects their heads to the choice of Principal Architects with differing design styles and the combination of them working with a series of junior architects to do the day to day work – has been the creation of an extraordinary confection of sites and buildings spread across northern France and southern Belgium and, whilst common threads and patterns emerge, each site is unique and, no matter how small, always has something of interest for the visitor. The classical form that was adopted for the shelter buildings that are the key features of many of the cemeteries provided the excuse to exploit the axial design possibilities presented by the main structural components of entrance, Cross, shelter and War Stone and it seems as though every possible combination of arrangements has been used to wonderful effect. It is the logical extension of the English landscape tradition that can be traced back to Stowe and Stourhead.

Lovers of Lutyens will delight in the attention to details and keen students of his work will enjoy spotting features that derive from his buildings away from the Western Front, e.g. the gargoyle from Lindisfarne appears in a number of places (notably Gezaincourt Communal Cemetery Extension AIF Goldsmith) and the paving at Le Touquet-Paris-Plage Communal Cemetery (AIF Cowlishaw) appears to have been lifted from Marshcourt.

Overall the cemetery designs can be analysed as a combination of a number of basic elements:

Vendresse British Cemetery

The Graves

There was an original hope that all of the graves should all face eastwards towards the enemy, the end result is anything but. The way in which the soldiers were buried depends, to a certain extent, on where they died. Battlefield burials tended to be hasty affairs and took place wherever was convenient, e.g. the bodies in the Devonshire Cemetery were buried in the trench from which the troops had advanced on the first day of the Battle of the Somme.

As a result such cemeteries tended to have haphazard layouts with little conscious planning and the direction in which the bodies were buried would be the furthest thing from the minds of the burial party. The further behind the Front Line, the more order was introduced and the cemeteries have a much more regular appearance. However, it would still appear that

there was no conscious decision that the graves should face in one particular direction more than any other. It is certainly true that, where the opportunity afforded it within the new cemeteries that were created after the War, e.g. Warlencourt British Cemetery (AIF Goldsmith) and the symbolic 300 graves of Allied troops and French troops in the shadow of Thiepval, the graves face east. But, by comparison, the graves in the new Villers-Bretonneux Military Cemetery (AIF Goldsmith) face each other north – south across the central axis leading to the Australian Memorial to the Missing. What is apparent, therefore, is that the layout of the graves was treated very much as an architectural element in its own right and if, as at Railway Dugouts Burial Ground (Transport Farm) (AIF Truelove) it suited the architecture to have some of the graves in a circle (see page 113), then so be it.

The Entrance

At its simplest this is just a pair of entrance piers with the cemetery name carved into the stonework but it will often be combined with bronze gates that give a satisfying 'clunk' as they are closed – Jonchery-sur-Vesle British Cemetery (AIF Truelove) being a particularly fine example. Often the entrance offered the architects the opportunity to exploit a change in levels and sometimes even the smallest of flights of steps can create drama – the nine treads at Dernancourt Communal Cemetery Extension (AIF Goldsmith) are part of an entrance sequence that turns the visitor through 270° to face the War Stone. But even the merest change of levels can give delight, such as the twin platforms that rise either side of the entrance at Villers-Bocage Communal Cemetery Extension (AIF Goldsmith). In its grandest form the entrance will be through a shelter building, which is described further detail below.

ABOVE The entrance building at Serre Road Cemetery No. 2
RIGHT Different treatments to cemetery entrances. Clockwise from top left: Pernes British Cemetery; Moeuvres Communal Cemetery Extension; St Martin Calvaire British Cemetery; Jonchery-sur-Vesle British Cemetery; Villers-Bocage Communal Cemetery Extension, H.A.C. Cemetery

ABOVE Dury Mill British Cemetery. The grass track is owned by the CWGC to provide convenient access to the cemetery from the nearest road
BELOW Maple Copse Cemetery is enclosed by a ha-ha

The Enclosure

The cemeteries are enclosed by either a low hedge or wall, in keeping with Lutyens's concern about wanting horizontal rather than vertical lines to respect the nature of the area. The walls are built from either local stone or brick, possibly with a limestone coping. Occasionally, as at Douchy-les-Ayette British Cemetery (AIF Goldsmith) and Mazingarbe Communal Cemetery extension (AIF Cowlishaw) there is extra detailing such as an undercut coping to the wall.

The War Stone

In contrast to the layout of the graves, it would seem that Lutyens's wish that the War Stone should be placed on the eastern side of the cemetery was largely observed. Again, this did not occur if it was to the detriment of the overall layout of the cemetery but, of the eighty-three Lutyens cemeteries that have War Stones, 66 per cent can be broadly counted to have them on the eastern side of the cemetery (i.e. in the quadrant north-east to

The wall around Quarry Cemetery, Marquion represents a church

south-east). Of the balance, 19 per cent have the Stone in a central position and the remainder have it positioned in a variety of directions. In some cemeteries the allegorical function of the War Stone as an altar is given greater significance by it being elevated above the rest of the cemetery – most memorably at Bagneux British Cemetery (AIF Goldsmith) (see page 27) – where it has been raised on a terrace so that it can be seen to great effect against the sky with the falling ground behind it – but Chocques Military Cemetery (AIF von Berg) (see page 31) – where it is on a grass mound – and Bellacourt Military Cemetery (AIF von Berg) (see page 28) – on an intermediate terrace above the graves but below the Cross) – are also significant.

The Cross

As discussed earlier the size of the Cross varied according to the size of cemetery. It was originally intended that it should be placed at the back of the cemetery so that the sword on its front face would face the graves and be seen by passers-by. However this was not carried out, with the result that the Cross is treated as a piece of architecture in its own right and placed appropriately. Critically, and contrary to the views of Lutyens who felt that vertical features should be avoided, it is the Cross that acts as the landmark for the cemetery for visitors and one of the enduring images of the Western Front today is of the smaller cemeteries in the middle of the fields identifiable from a distance by the Cross.

The Shelter Building

It is these buildings, where they are provided, that can give the cemeteries their uniqueness. In general they adopt a classical style but occasionally, as with the works of Holden, they have a more Modernist appearance. It had been the original intention that such buildings would be provided in each cemetery, in order to give visitors a place for quiet contemplation and prayer but, when the costs were being readjusted following the construction of the three experimental cemeteries, it was decided to restrict them to the larger cemeteries. There was no hard and fast rule on this

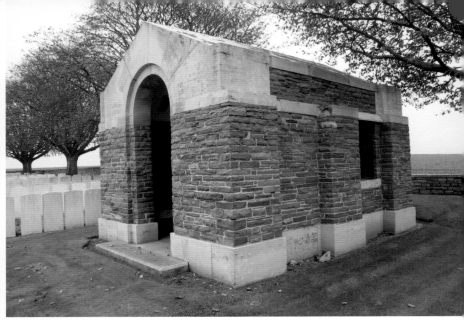

however and sometimes one can find relatively large cemeteries, for example Voormezeele Enclosure No. 3 (1,611 graves) with no building and a relatively small one, for example the nearby Voormezeele Enclosure No. 1 and No. 2 (593 graves) with two. The logical explanation for such inconsistencies, which is supported by examination of some of the Approval Forms, is one that would be familiar to architects the world over. The Commission's budgetary process gave an allocation to each cemetery based on the number of graves but there were sites that, either due to their particular topography or to the whim of the architect, demanded a more expensive treatment. As a result, money was reallocated from another cemetery to leave it short of the facilities that it would otherwise possess. The supreme example of this within the cemeteries designed by Lutyens is the Croisilles British Cemetery, where the entrance terrace, shelter building and flight of stairs are substantially more than one would expect for a cemetery with 1,171 graves.

The variety of designs of the buildings is bewildering and it is only in the east, in the scattered cemeteries around Reims (where Lutyens's AIF was Truelove) there is evidence of a pattern book approach and the same shelter design appears at Buzancy Military Cemetery, La Ville-aux-Bois British Cemetery, Raperie British Cemetery and Vendresse British Cemetery. Otherwise there is complete variety and the buildings can either stand alone, act as the cemetery entrance or be designed in pairs, on occasion being linked together by a screen wall to frame the War Stone or Cross, for example Chauny Communal Cemetery British Extension (AIF Hutton). Simple buildings that they are, the shelter buildings are full of delight and it is especially noteworthy that they were all designed so that they would not be disfigured by external drainage gutters and downpipes. Some buildings, such as those at Brown's Copse Military Cemetery (AIF Goldsmith) and Hooge Crater British Cemetery (AIF Rew), clearly show links back to the garden buildings that Lutyens designed at Heywood and Hestercombe respectively. Others show a clear development away from this and a fusion with what Hussey described as Lutyens' 'Elemental Mode', with the introduction of flat roofs, for example at Favreuil British Cemetery (AIF Cowlishaw) and Klein-Vierstraat British Cemetery (AIF Truelove) or the reduction of detailing to its most subtle level, for example at Grove Town

One of the twin shelter buildings at the Villers-Bretonneux Military
Cemetery that frames the approach to the Australian National War memorial

British Cemetery (AIF Hutton). It was only to be expected, given
their sheer number, that the designs would show common
themes but, just occasionally, there are complete 'one offs' that
have no precedents either from within Lutyens's work on the
Western Front or from anywhere else. One such is the multi-
columned 'temple' in the middle of Béthune Town Cemetery
(AIF Goldsmith) and the other is the pair of modernistic entrance
pavilions at La Neuville British Cemetery (AIF Goldsmith) that
almost seem as if they could have come from the drawing board
of Holden – was this Lutyens's answer to Holden's nearby cemetery in Corbie where Billy Congreve was buried?[26] The supreme
classical set pieces though are the entrance building and open
'temples' with their gently upturned roofs at Serre Road British
Cemetery No. 2 (AIF Rew) and the entrance pavilions at Villers-

Bretonneux Military Cemetery (AIF Goldsmith), which frame
the approach to the Australian Memorial to the Missing and are
reminiscent of the way in which Temple of Music and the Bathing
Pavilion frame the pool at Tyringham.

The materials used for these buildings varies according to the
locality and can either be the local red brick, limestone or other
local stones, with tufa rubble in the area around Reims. Roofs are
either stone or red clay tiles.

The Land Tablet and Cemetery Register
The land for the cemeteries was given by the French and Belgian
nations to Britain and the Empire in perpetuity and this gift is
recorded on a tablet in the cemetery, usually on the wall of the
shelter building or a gate pier. The wording, in Belgian or French

One of the entrance buildings at Dernancourt Communal Cemetery Extension contains the Land Tablet. Perhaps this was what Lutyens had in mind when making his suggestion for the Edinburgh War Memorial

ABOVE Mory Abbey Military Cemetery: Seat with a typical panel erected by the CWGC in recent times to provide information for visitors about the cemeteries and their context

BELOW Héninel-Croisilles Road Cemetery: seat and register box

(as appropriate) and English was devised by Kipling (and modified by Lord Arthur Browne) after suggestions had been sought from the general public and reads: 'The land on which this cemetery stands is the free gift of the French [or Belgian] people for the perpetual resting place of those of the allied armies who fell in the war of 1914–1918 and are honoured here'. At Dernancourt Lutyens chose to make a feature of this and put the wording on a large vertical slab of a design that he used for the tombstones for Barbara and Ernest Chaplin.[27] The Cemetery Register is the list of all of the graves and their occupants that is held inside a box with a bronze door that is usually set within either a gate pier or the shelter building.

The Tool House

Many of the cemeteries have small buildings for the use of the Commission's maintenance staff. They were designed at the same time as the cemetery although, as a rule, they are relatively ordinary and tucked into one corner of the site and do not form part of the overall architectural composition. Whilst they are in keeping with any other buildings on the site they do not carry the same level of detailing. The best one in a Lutyens cemetery is at Béthune Town Cemetery (AIF Goldsmith).

The Pergolas and Paths

To all intents and purposes the cemeteries were gardens and other

Tool Houses at Gézaincourt Communal Cemetery Extension (left); Béthune Town Cemetery (top) and Beaulencourt British Cemetery (bottom)

garden features appeared in them as circumstances dictated. Lutyens did not make much use of pergolas, which is surprising when one thinks of the gardens that he designed, such as Hestercombe and Heywood, where they are major parts of the gardens' designs. They only appear in four of his cemeteries – Achiet le Grand Communal Cemetery Extension, Albert Communal Cemetery Extension, Bagneux British Cemetery and Douchy-les-Ayette British Cemetery where, in all cases, Goldsmith was the AIF. No doubt because of the cost and ongoing maintenance costs, the pergolas in the cemeteries all have concrete cross members instead of the oak which Lutyens used in his gardens. Paths are not a common feature within the cemeteries as there is no particular need to marshal visitors in any one direction and they are left to wander over the grass at will. The most extensive use of paving is to be found at Mazingarbe Communal Cemetery Extension (AIF Cowlishaw) where brick paths with limestone edgings complement the surrounding brick

walls and thus divide the cemetery into four. The limestone path at Favreuil British Cemetery (AIF Cowlishaw), which is inset with panels of the local stone, is particularly fine and forms a dramatic feature linking the gate, Cross and shelter building, and the circular feature inside the entrance at Ontario Cemetery (AIF Goldsmith) in a similar style is also noteworthy. The opportunity is often taken to introduce patterns into the paving beneath the shelter buildings – notably at Sanctuary Wood Cemetery (AIF Rew) and Warlencourt British Cemetery (AIF Goldsmith).

Other Features

Other features appear in the cemeteries as appropriate – usually small bench seats if there are no shelter buildings. The classical arch and matching niche at Monchy British Cemetery (AIF Goldsmith) are particularly distinctive as is the flight of steps insider the entrance at Croisilles British Cemetery (AIF Goldsmith) where a grand, broad flight of twenty-two steps and

Achiet-le-Grand Communal Cemetery Extension (above); Ontario British Cemetery (below); Favreuil British Cemetery (right)

intermittent platforms leads down into the cemetery — it is a masterful sequence in which, as at Dernancourt, the visitor is turned through different directions before reaching the graves.

Planting

It is the planting, more than anything else, that gives the cemeteries their unique flavour so reminiscent of an English garden. The initial plans prepared by Lutyens and Jekyll in 1914 (see page 31) incorporated specific areas of garden design away from the graves (Auchonvillers featured a pool in a screened entrance area with a shelter and War Stone). In the end a simpler solution was adopted with formal planting to give structure (typically around the boundary and key features such as the War Stone and Cross) and herbaceous perennials and floribunda roses at the foot of the headstones to add colour and variety as well as providing a secondary function of preventing wet soil from splashing up on to the personal inscription at the base. The

structural planting consists of both deciduous and coniferous trees, on occasions supplemented by pleached limes (for example at Daours Communal Cemetery Extension and Windmill British Cemetery) as a feature or to hide an unsightly view. The herbaceous planting is usually carried out in groups of twenty plant species repeated along the rows of headstones and, where roses are used, they are planted in blocks of the same colour rather than at random. Larger shrubs are often used at the ends of rows in order to fringe the main pathways.

FOLLOWING PAGES

LEFT Clockwise from top left: Croisilles British Cemetery; Anneux British Cemetery; Serre Road Cemetery No. 2; Grévillers British Cemetery
RIGHT Clockwise from top left: Jonchery-sur-Vesle British Cemetery; Klein-Vierstraat British Cemetery; Le Touquet-Paris-Plage Communal Cemetery; Kemmel Chateau Military Cemetery; Noyelles-sur-Mer Chinese Cemetery; La Clytte Military Cemetery

Clockwise from top left: La Ville-aux-Bois British Cemetery; Cojeul British Cemetery; Croisilles British Cemetery

THE RECORD

BY THE 1930s there arose an increasing demand from visitors to know the names of the architects of the cemeteries and Memorials to the Missing. The matter was considered by the Commission in May 1935, when it was confirmed that the only names that should appear within the cemeteries should be the names of the Fallen. There was an appreciation, however, that knowledge of the designers was a legitimate query and it was decided to prepare detailed lists. This was no easy task and a note from H.F. Robinson, the Commission's Deputy Director of Works, to Fabian Ware contained more than a hint of exasperation, as well as shedding light on the working regime at St Omer in the early 1920s:

> I find that the records . . . are unfortunately not only incomplete, but what exist are inaccurate. The allocations on the files in this office were at the time never corrected after Mr Charles Holden was brought in and, moreover, exchanges were carried out between the Principal Architects which has made the lists hopelessly complicated. The Architects themselves kept no lists and I have been in touch with Colonel Higginson who is now working on it, and is hoping to unearth a list which he believes exists'.[28]

Higginson either found such a list, or managed to create his own version because, three months later, Robinson was able to provide detailed lists of all of the schemes designed by each architect together with the details of the Assistant Architect involved. Thus we have been able to learn that Lutyens and his assistants were responsible for 126 cemeteries. However it is still necessary to enter a note of caution regarding this figure because the Approval Forms show Lutyens as having been the PA for a number of cemeteries that are not on Higginson's lists. Whilst they are mainly small sites and, as a result, his involvement may have been limited, it is still necessary to include them as part of his oeuvre for the sake of accuracy. The total of cemeteries that should therefore be attributed to Lutyens is 137.[29]

The matter surfaced again in 1938 following a request from Sir George Macdonagh, one of the IWGC's Commissioners, who had visited France with members of the Anglo-German-French Committee. He asked that consideration should be given for inscriptions on the Memorials to the Missing giving details of the architect, the unveiling date and the person by whom it was unveiled. The matter was referred by Robinson to Lutyens, whose letter says much about the humility of the man, even towards the end of his career:

> I feel that no names other than those of the dead should be inscribed, save that of The King, to give record of His cognisance in the sacrifice made in His service.

Personally, I consider that to put my name on Monuments in which I have had some part in the construction would be impertinent.

On the other hand, if it is decided that the names of all who took part in the construction should be recorded, then I should regret if mine was omitted. But on general principles, I think no other name should be recorded beyond those to whose honour the Monument was conceived.

There will be records in the archives of the Imperial War Graves Commission of all facts relating to the erection of the Memorial, to which anyone seriously interested in the question would have access.[30]

Robinson's reply, written the next day was succinct: 'Thank you so much – this gives us exactly what was wanted.'[31] The matter was discussed at the Commission's meeting on 14 September 1938 and there was a suggestion that the details would be included within a book of photographs but no action was taken and it was decided to leave the matter in abeyance.[32]

Baker	111
Blomfield	119
Holden	67
Lutyens	137
Cowlishaw	229
Goldsmith	66
Hutton	66
Rew	65
Truelove	16
Von Berg	36
Others	7
Total	919

TABLE 1: Architects for cemeteries on the Western Front

Cowlishaw	27
Goldsmith	58
Hutton	13
Rew	12
Truelove	15
Von Berg	10
No AIF	2
Total	137

TABLE 2: Architects in France for cemeteries where Lutyens was Principal Architect

ELEVEN
KNOWN UNTO GOD

ONE OF THE CARDINAL PRINCIPLES of the IWGC was that the names of all of those who had died during the conflict should be remembered in the appropriate theatre of action. This was relatively straightforward for the bodies that were capable of identification but proper consideration had to be given to the 'Missing' – the 517,000 who were known to have died but whose bodies either could not be found or, if they could be found, could not be identified. The unknown bodies were buried under a headstone inscribed with words chosen by Kipling; 'A Soldier of the Great War Known Unto God' supplemented by any other relevant information that could be gathered from the uniform on the body, for example 'A Captain in the Lincolnshire Regiment', etc.

This left open the question of how to commemorate the names of the Missing. An initial thought, dismissed on the grounds of cost and practicality, was to have each name inscribed on a headstone above an empty grave. However, the idea that eventually emerged, having been initially promoted by Lutyens and Blomfield, was to have the names inscribed on stone walls in the cemeteries – one for each of the eighty-five official 'Actions' of the War. An idea of what this might have looked like can be gauged from the various memorials to commemorate the New Zealand Missing. Alone of the countries of the Empire New Zealand decided that it would not have a single national memorial but that its Missing would be commemorated in cemeteries throughout the battle area. One such, designed by Lutyens, forms the back wall of the Grévillers British Cemetery where it records the name of the 446 New Zealanders who died in the 'Advance to Victory' in 1918 whose bodies could not be found and identified.[1]

Recognising that it would take time to assemble accurate lists of the Missing and reach a conclusion as to which was the appropriate cemetery for each Action, it was suggested that hedges could be planted in the cemeteries as an interim measure until the precise size of each wall was known.

Whilst the Commission was wrestling with this problem, it had been included as a member of the Battle Exploits Memorial Committee (BEMC), which had been established by the Adjutant-General in 1918 to consider the general question of battlefield memorials – both the smaller regimental memorials, for which there was an increasing number of requests, as well as memorials for the major actions of the War.

One of the first items that the BEMC had to consider was the question of some form of memorial at Ypres, the salient around which had seen some of the War's most bitter fighting. One idea, which was supported by Winston Churchill (the IWGC's

LEFT Faubourg d'Amiens Memorial to the Missing
ABOVE New Zealand Memorial to the Missing, Grévillers British Cemetery

Lutyens, top hat in hand, at the dedication of the Memorial to the Missing at Faubourg d'Amiens, 1932

Chairman), was that the town should be left in its war-ravaged state to form an eloquent reminder to future generations of the horrors of war. It was an intriguing idea that, if it been implemented, would have provided a stark contrast between the indiscriminate shelling that had laid waste to the town and the twenty-first-century approach to modern warfare with pinpoint targeting. However, as with the grand schemes to rebuild London after the Great Fire of 1666, it was defeated by practicality and the return of the people who had been dispossessed by the fighting to reclaim their homes. For all of the closeness

between them, Fabian Ware did not think that Lutyens was the right man to design the Ypres Memorial. His name had been suggested by the War Office but, when the Committee met on 7 August 1919, the appointment was opposed by Ware, who subsequently wrote to Kenyon:

However, after considerable discussion (in which, I fear, I did my usual amount of talking) it was decided to ask Blomfield to undertake Ypres and to ask Lutyens to make suggestion as to certain other battle exploit memorials.

MEMORIAL TO THE MISSING.
FAUBOURG D'AMIENS, ARRAS.

ABOVE Lutyens's initial design for Faubourg d'Amiens
RIGHT The Flying Services Memorial at Faubourg d'Amiens. The globe carved
by Sir William Reid Dick is positioned as it appeared on 11 November 1918

I took a rather strong line about the matter as I knew that you would feel that Ypres with its gothic associations etc etc was not the kind of work at which Lutyens would excel. The other memorials will give more scope to the special blend of Lutyens genius'.[2] Kenyon replied that 'Lutyens might very well have the Somme or Cambrai – St Quentin'.[3]

The BEMC meeting on 30 September recorded that Lutyens should be asked to design the various national memorials and it was proposed to invite him to accompany its members to the Western Front in order to select suitable sites, but the trip was cancelled. However, the Committee continued its deliberations and, by the end of 1919, recommended that there should be five major battlefield memorials on the Western Front – Ypres, Mons, the Somme, Arras and the Hindenburg Line. In due recognition of the significance of these major memorials it was decided that the responsibility for their implementation should be handed over to a new committee – the National Battlefields Memorial Committee

Faubourg d'Amiens Cemetery

(NBMC) under the chairmanship of the Earl of Midleton, leaving the BEMC to deal with the more minor memorials.

The NBMC produced a comprehensive set of proposals involving the rebuilding of the Menin Gate at Ypres (to be designed by Blomfield), a memorial at La Ferté-sous-Jouarre (to mark the earliest days in the War) and a cenotaph in Paris, as well as a series of memorial tablets to be placed in the cathedrals in the area of action. However, it became apparent that its proposals were converging with the Commission's own plans for the commemoration of the Missing. Sensitive of the need to avoid duplication and unnecessary cost, and following pressure by Fabian Ware, the Cabinet decided on 5 August 1921 that the NBMC should be wound up and its functions transferred to the IWGC.

The Commission acted quickly and, by October 1921, had drawn up plans for memorials on twelve sites in France and Belgium which were to act as Memorials to the Missing as well as battlefield memorials. Two memorials (Arras and St Quentin) were allocated to Lutyens and one to Baker, whilst the remainder were to be the subject of architectural competitions, one (La Ferté-sous-Jouarre) being limited to the Commission's Architects in France. Progress was slow and compromised by the need to acquire the land and secure consent for the designs from the French Commission des Monuments Historiques. As the Commission developed its plans the French began to be concerned about both the number of the memorials and their size, as they were in danger of overshadowing their own commemorative proposals. These doubts were expressed through the Anglo-French Mixed Committee, which had been established in 1918 as the liaison point between the Commission and the French authorities. The French view was shared by Ware and his colleagues and consequently, in May 1927, the Commission endorsed

Faubourg d'Amiens Cemetery

a new plan that saw one memorial moved over the border into Belgium and the names of the Missing being split between four stand-alone memorials together with appropriate enlargements to a number of existing cemeteries. Three of the sites were already committed (Soissons, Neuve-Chapelle and La Ferté-sous-Jouarre), either because the land had been bought or construction work had started, leaving just one site to be decided. The original list of twelve had included memorials for various phases of the Somme battles, rather than a single memorial, but with no other Somme memorial planned, it was decided that the final site should at Thiepval to commemorate the area that, along with the struggle at Ypres, had become one of the most significant areas of the Western Front.[4]

By the time that the Commission had undertaken its reappraisal Lutyens had already made substantial progress with the two projects allocated to him. The site at Arras was within the town and, as well as being a general Memorial to the Missing, was to commemorate the missing of the Flying Services. It had escaped the cuts because it was based around an existing cemetery rather than being a stand-alone site although the proposals were changed to make the memorial less intrusive. Lutyens had originally designed a tall, slender stepped pyramid belltower as the centrepiece of a cloister which had been subsequently modified into a 124ft-high arch-cum-belltower with three smaller side towers. Under the 1927 rethink a new design was prepared omitting the towers altogether. Instead, the Flying Services Memorial became a 29ft-high square column on top of which is a 4ft 6in-diameter globe weighing nearly three tons girdled with a band of flying stars that was carved by Sir William Reid Dick. The 380ft-long cloister was also designed to take a more complex form with a series of interpenetrating axes and courtyards focused variously on the Cross, War Stone and the Memorial.

ABOVE Some of the 72,099 names carved on the memorial's pillars

RIGHT The Memorial to the Missing of the Somme, Thiepval

The St Quentin design had also been through a number of iterations, having initially been proposed as a memorial to those who had died in the 'Advance to Victory' in 1918. When the local Commune had first been approached about the matter it suggested that the Commission's memorial could be placed in a new square that they were creating in the middle of the town for its own memorial. The Mayor met Lieutenant-Colonel M.P.L. Cart de Lafontaine (the Commission's French speaking architect who had the responsibility for liaising with the local authorities)[5] to discuss the matter and stated that he did not want an obelisk or statues but would prefer a building such as a pantheon or a Hall of Memory within which the names could be inscribed. Lutyens went to France and met Paul Bigot, the architect of the commune's memorial, on 9 July 1923 and concluded that the location was unsuitable because of the difficulty of combining two memorials on the one site especially as the British one would overpower its French counterpart. As a result Lutyens suggested an alternative location, on the road north out of the town towards Cambrai. However, when Lafontaine and Major Ingpen of the Commission subsequently met the Mayor on 14 August it transpired that the site that Lutyens wanted, which was the highest point on the road, was in the neighbouring commune of Fayet. They therefore decided to move it further south to an intermediate ridge 2km north of the town. The mayor welcomed the Commission's proposals as he considered that they would 'considerably add to the historic and artistic interest of St Quentin'.[6] Lutyens was asked to draw up designs for a memorial to contain 60,000 names and he prepared plans for a multi-columned arch to straddle the road. He signed a contract on 17 March 1925 at a fee of 4 per cent of the tender price for the memorial with an additional fee of 2 per cent of the

Details from Thiepval

cost of carving the names, upon which he was required to advise on their disposition alone.[7] The agreement also provided that, in the event of cancellation, Lutyens would receive an abortive fee of either 30 per cent or 75 per cent depending on whether the design was at the sketch stage or whether contract drawings had been issued. The Commission then reduced the number of names to be accommodated to 30,000 and, at about the same time, the French highway authorities objected to the principle of an arch across the road. However the number of names was

then increased back up to 60,000 and Lutyens was asked to 'go into his design with a view to the accommodation of the larger number'.[8]

Although the Commission did not endorse its revised plan for the memorials until May 1927, it had already been attuned to the French concerns and the possibility of relocating the St Quentin memorial to Thiepval to become a memorial for the Missing of the Battles of the Somme had been raised with Lutyens the preceding July. Wasting no time, he inspected the area in August

Thiepval vaulting

The War Stone at Thiepval stands in the void at the centre of the memorial

with E. Pontremoli, the Inspecteur Général des Batîments Civils et des Palais Nationaux. It seems as though the possibility of reverting to the original idea for the memorial spanning the road was considered but a commanding site, away from the roads on a ridge south west of the village was chosen.[9]

Approval of the design was finally received from the Commission des Monuments Historiques on 12 April 1928 and construction work was in progress on the foundations by the following March, albeit that formal consent from the French authorities was not given until 24 April 1929.

The memorial as built is the largest British war memorial in the world and its 'extraordinary pile of red brick and white stone'[10] has been described by Gavin Stamp as 'one of the finest works of British architecture of the twentieth century'.[11] Despite its chequered history the basic design of the memorial remained relatively constant and the main change was to its size, as it was scaled up or down depending upon the number of names that it had to accommodate, whether or not it was to bridge a road and the views of the French authorities. It stands 140ft high and takes the form of a series of interpenetrating arches of four increasing heights, which give rise to sixteen massive pillars on which are carved the 72,099 names of the Missing. The main building material is red brick with limestone being used for the panels that hold the names and to provide cornice lines that wrap around the memorial to link the keystone of an arch on one level with the springing point of the one on the next. It is a masterful composition, made all the more so because the use of differing heights of arches gives it two profiles – from two sides chunky and muscular, from the other two tall and slender. At its heart, in the void created by the two tallest arches sits, reverentially, a Lutyens War Stone on its familiar three stepped plinth, the top and lower treads twice the width of the middle one.

The Memorial to the Missing of the Somme at Thiepval was unveiled on 1 August 1932 by the Prince of Wales, the day after the unveiling of Arras and, even though the ceremony was broadcast live on the radio by the BBC, it was to a world weary of the War. The first day of the battle whose dead Thiepval commemorates was as distant from the unveiling as was from the ending of the Victorian age. The world was a different place. The 'Land fit for heroes' that had been promised to the returning soldiers was not all that they had been led to believe. The first Labour Government had been elected in 1924, the General Strike had occurred in 1926 and the nation was being run by a National Government in the wake of the economic fall-out following the Wall Street Crash. In a replay of the arguments that surfaced at Spalding, where Lutyens's memorial had been preferred to the YMCA, people questioned the wisdom of spending money on a memorial rather than something of a more practical nature. It was a downbeat finale as the completion of Thiepval effectively marked the end of the Imperial War Graves Commission's work in France and Belgium. The total cost of what had been built was in the order of £8.15m: by comparison the cost of one day's shelling in September 1918, as the War was drawing to its conclusion, was £3.75m.

There was, however, to be a coda for both Lutyens and the Commission: the Australian National War Memorial at Villers-Bretonneux. It was the last of Lutyens's work on the Western Front to be completed and there have been criticisms that he had been instrumental in supplanting another architect, which research within the CWGC files shows not to be true. The story behind the memorial also illustrates the dynamic qualities of Fabian Ware at their best – supporting an original proposal but, when it foundered, seeking to do something about it rather than letting it fester for others to resolve.

Villers-Bretonneux had a special resonance for the Australians because it was the place where, on 24 April 1918, that its troops under the skilled leadership of General Monash halted the German Spring Offensive; the turning point that led to the eventual defeat of the German Army.

The idea for a memorial was first suggested in 1919 when a proposal by a Lieutenant Keating to erect an obelisk at a cost of £5,000 was rejected by the Australian Prime Minister as being inadequate. It was considered that a grander solution was required and sketches were made for a U-shaped cloister around a tall obelisk to be erected at the rear of the Commission's Villers-Bretonneux Military Cemetery and a budget of £70,000–£100,000 was suggested. However, amidst wider concerns about levels of Australian public expenditure generally, there were specific concerns that the site was too far from the road to be visible and Malcolm Shepherd, Australia's representative on the IWGC, felt that it should be reconsidered 'on the ground that the money expended on it would be out of all proportion to the results achieved'.[12]

Nothing was happening and, in an attempt to make some progress, Ware wrote to Shepherd in July 1923, offering to help defray part of the cost by contributing £3/10/- for the name of each of the Missing that the memorial was to commemorate, in lieu of the amount that the IWGC would otherwise have spent on adding the same names to its own memorials. He also suggested that the memorial should be the subject of an architectural competition for Australians who had served in France and Belgium. Somewhat conspiratorially he added:

> Writing confidentially, I should like to add that owing to the action of the French and some well-meaning people here with regard to the so-called Somme Battlefield Memorial there is likely to be considerable delay in fixing on the 'Missing' memorial in or near that town for all of the 'Missing' of the Empire and you may feel that public feeling in Australia is not prepared to wait much longer. In the position I hold it is my duty to advise you impartially.[13]

The Australian Government accepted Ware's advice and launched a competition in December 1925 to design 'an enduring material symbol of those ideals which were the bases of participation by Australia in the Great War, and that it shall be a fitting monument to the deeds of every Australian who gave his services for the preservation of those ideals'.[14] Despite Shepherd's misgivings, the original site was retained. It was a requirement that the memorial should have an observation tower from which to survey the surrounding battlefield and that the facing materials should be Australian granite or other such Australian materials as appropriate. The overall project budget was

£100,000, of which £90,000 was reserved for the memorial itself. Entry to the competition was restricted to those who had served in the conflict or their parents (to allow for the participation of those whose sons might have died in the course of the War). The competition was to be run under the auspices of the Royal Institute of British Architects and the eminent architect Sir Giles Gilbert Scott would select the winner. The first prize was £250 and the closing date of 30 April 1926 was subsequently put back by three months to 31 July.

Considering the status of the competition and the available budget, the response was poor and only thirty-three entries were received. Three were shortlisted by the Australian assessors (under the chairmanship of Major General Sir Talbot Hobbs) who commented on their disappointment that a large number of the entrants had seemed to disregard the cost limits. The selected entries were passed to Scott for his adjudication and he chose a scheme prepared by William Lucas, an architect from Melbourne, whose son had died of wounds in 1916 and was buried in the Lahana Military Cemetery in Greece.

Lucas's design was for four massive 56ft-high polished trachyte columns 7ft in diameter standing on a granite plinth, above which were to be observation windows reached by a lift or staircase. Four bronze sculptures at the top were to represent Mercy, Truth, Righteousness and Peace. Having been declared the winner Lucas travelled to Britain to finalise his designs in consultation with the IWGC; the note of a meeting on 21 March 1928 with H.F. Robinson, the Commission's Deputy Director of Works, confirmed that it had been arranged that Lucas should call on Lutyens (who had designed the Villers-Bretonneux Military Cemetery that stood between the memorial site and the road) and also visit the site itself. Robinson privately expressed his reservations about the design and the cost, however the drawings were completed by the end of the year and approved by the French authorities in April 1929.

However there were concerns in Australia about public expenditure due to the general economic climate and, following a change of government, the IWGC was informed in April 1930 that work on the memorial had been formally suspended, albeit that, two months later, they were then given approval to spend £500 to fence the site, acquire a right of way to it and undertake general horticultural work. Lucas had probably seen this coming because, two months earlier, he had received a letter informing him that the Government did 'not desire at present to submit your account for services'.[15]

The delay provided the opportunity for Hobbs (who was himself an architect) to air some general misgivings about the Lucas scheme that he had been clearly harbouring since it was chosen. In a note to his Government colleagues, which was forwarded to Ware in July 1930, he revealed that he and his fellow

assessors had been less than happy about the outcome of the competition. They had been asked to shortlist six schemes and the three that they chose were the only ones that they felt were capable of being built within the available budget. To make matters worse, they had actually placed Lucas third out of the three entries that had been forwarded to Scott. Hobbs felt that the chosen design had two basic flaws — it did not provide enough wall space for the names of the Missing and it did not contain a viewing terrace, albeit that it had 'observation windows'. To save cost, and because he was also concerned with the general weathering ability of the Australian stone, Hobbs suggested that the requirement for native Australian materials should be dropped. Ware's advice was sought on a possible re-design but he tactfully replied that it was a matter that should be left to the Australians, albeit that he gave them a gentle nudge by saying that he thought that it would be possible to erect an appropriate memorial incorporating a viewing platform and using local stone at a cost of £30,000–£40,000 and he offered the IWGC's assistance. When pressed further he said that they would be able to contribute about £20,000 (10,977 names at £1/15/- — a reduction from the £3/10/- originally offered).

The matter continued to drift and, in an attempt to bring it

The competition winning design by William Lucas for the Australian National War Memorial at Villers-Bretonneux. The lower picture shows the entrance buildings designed by Lutyens

Lutyens's initial design for Villers-Bretonneux, without the tower

to a conclusion, Ware wrote to Sir Granville de Laune Ryrie, Australian High Commissioner in London on 14 January 1932, pointing out that the IWGC found itself in a difficult position because it was not able to complete its task of commemorating the Missing. To expedite matters he proposed to use IWGC's contribution to the overall scheme to provide a separate Memorial for the Missing that could then provide a suitable setting for whatever memorial the Australians wanted to erect at a later date when funds became available: 'You may rest assured that this work would be carried out in a way worthy of those we commemorated and of the land from which they came'.[16]

Ware deputed Robinson to discuss the matter with Lutyens who, as well as being the only one of the Principal Architects still involved with the Commission,[17] was a logical choice given that he had designed the adjacent cemetery which would act as a gateway to the memorial. The two shelter buildings that he had designed as exquisite Classical temples are amongst some of his best work on the Western Front.

Lutyens was conscious of Lucas's prior involvement and wondered whether he ought to write to him about it.[18] He said that he would be prepared to accept the commission to produce something at a cost of no more than £20,000 as long as the IWGC obtained confirmation from Australia House that they wished him to produce a design that would not preclude the eventual erection of the Lucas scheme. It was duly confirmed to Ware that the arrangement with Lucas could be ended and that there was no problem about professional etiquette.

Somewhat surprisingly given that, by now, Lucas had been working on the project for nearly six years, he had not been given a formal contract. It was clearly a working relationship that had been based around a considerable degree of trust, on his part if not the Government's. It was entirely predictable, therefore, that when he was informed in May 1932 that his services were no longer required, he was less than happy. His response was to send a rambling twelve-page letter to the Australian Prime Minister railing, amongst other things, about his lack of a contract. It is clear though that his clients had no great love for him: 'Here is another packet from Mr Lucas. . . . which you may care to have in your records' said the letter from Herbert Creedy in the Australian War Office to Ware.[19]

The matter then seemed to lie dormant until, following a trip by Ware to Australia in 1935, it was reactivated and, in June, Lutyens was given a formal brief to produce sketch designs for a memorial with a budget of £19,000. His fee was £285, which would increase to 5 per cent of the building costs if the work ultimately proceeded. Lutyens felt it appropriate to write to Lucas and, whilst there is no copy of his letter on the IWGC files, it was felt sufficiently important for someone within the Commission to write a recollection of what he thought had been written:

> I have just been informed by the IWGC that the Australian Government has terminated their agreement with you as regards the memorial at Villers-Bretonneux. I am so sorry that this means no memorial from your hand. The IWGC have asked me, I think you know I am one of their consulting architects, to prepare the sketches showing how the 11,000 names can be commemorated in a simple and inexpensive manner.[20]

It is difficult to gauge Lutyens's sentiment in writing this letter – whilst he is expressing sympathy for a fellow architect in losing a commission there is no obvious praise for the scheme that was now not to be built. And why seek to detail the requirements to which Lutyens was working? It is also strange that Lutyens should profess a (diplomatic?) ignorance of the decision to dismiss Lucas that had been taken three years previously.

Quite what Lucas would have thought of the letter was another matter, the more so because Lutyens had earlier written to him in May 1932 telling him about the completion of Thiepval and asking 'When do you start your monument?' as both Thiepval and Lucas's proposal for Villers-Bretonneux had been approved by the French authorities at the same time.

Lutyens had had plenty of time to prepare his thoughts for the arrival of the eventual commission and within a month he submitted proposals for a courtyard formed by four loggias on a raised walkway, access to which was gained from a grand flight of stairs, at the top of which was the rising sun emblem of the Australian Imperial Force. His scheme found favour with the Australians with one objection – it did not contain the required observation tower that had formed part of the original brief. It was pointed out that Hobbs had, much earlier, erected his own tower on the site as a result of which he had determined that the required height should be 75ft.

Lutyens wrote to Ware in October 1935 'I think I have to agree, in the light of the letter received from Australia, that it would be well nigh useless to send them a design that does not include a central Tower. I am sorry.'[21] He went on to say that, having looked at the matter carefully, he felt that, because the tower would need to stand above the adjacent walls containing the names of the missing, it would need to be 100ft high to maintain the correct sense of proportion. In doing so it cannot have escaped his attention that the approach to the tower, along a concave slope through his own cemetery, was a miniature version of the situation at Raisina Hill in New Delhi and that the base of the tower was not capable of being seen from the entrance of the cemetery.

Inevitably the requirement for a tower would increase building costs and the Commission, via Robinson, felt that the extra cost would be in the order of £5,000 above the overall budget, which had been increased to £30,000. Ware, in informing his *de facto* clients of the extra cost, adopted a stance familiar to all of those involved in such situations and added a margin of comfort telling them that the overall budget would now be £35,000– £40,000. The Australians replied in a manner typical of clients who receive such news of a potential cost overrun and told Ware that, not only did they require the tower, but also that there were not prepared to increase the budget to take account of it.

Lutyens duly added the tower as per his instructions and there was an exchange of correspondence, made all the more confusing because of a lack of understanding of the drawings, with the Australians thinking there were two towers and then wanting to omit some terrace walls without realising that they were only 2ft 6 in high and would save little money. In any event, in order to reduce costs, Lutyens had to omit a cloister that he had inserted into the scheme and replace it with a wall. In designing the tower, with its stark appearance, Lutyens repeated the motif of classical aedicules standing in voids that he used on the loggias but, for its most arresting device he reached back nearly thirty years into his catalogue of unbuilt work and, from a scheme for a water tower at Milton Abbott, he plucked the idea of a cantilevered staircase that breaks through the upper part of the structure to hang around the top of the tower like a torc.

The design was accepted by the Australian Government in December 1935 and an application was made to the French authorities for formal approval. This was duly given, despite a number of reservations about the external staircase, and a surveyor was instructed to prepare documents to put the proposals out to tender. Again, in a stance that will resonate with design teams today, the IWGC discussed whether they should invite tenders for a scheme that included the omitted cloisters, in case they received a competitive bid that allowed them to be built. However, they did not take this course of action. Ware was reminded that the budget for the scheme was £30,000 of which the Australians would be contributing £10,000.

Bids were invited from ten contractors and, as might be expected with this project, the lowest bid was £36,000 and therefore substantially above the budget. However perhaps the Australian Government were beginning to tire of the affair and was conscious of the fact that the cost of the recent Canadian Memorial at Vimy Ridge was more than £250,000, they agreed to pay the extra £6,000 without demur.

The contract was given to Maple and Co. (Paris) Ltd, and the IWGC re-engaged Louis Shonfield as their Clerk of Works. Shonfield was one of the many unsung heroes within the IWGC and his role, as the client's representative on site, was to ensure that the contractor faithfully followed the architect's plans. Having previously worked with Baker in South Africa he had been the Commission's Chief Clerk of Works until he was laid off following the completion of the Arras Memorial as the Commission's work was drawing to an end. He had struggled to find work and Robinson wrote to all of the Principal Architects to see if they could help him, praising him as 'A most efficient fellow. . . . I know of nobody who gets a better job out of a contractor'.[22] His salary for the supervision of Villers-Bretonneux was £33/6/8 per month. He would have been heavily involved when the building work encountered a major problem with the pouring of the concrete floor in the high level observation room. The work had already been delayed by a day because of cold weather, because concrete cannot be laid if the temperature is too low. Rather than risk further delay, the contractors decided to mix the concrete with warm water and, once it had been poured, fires were lit underneath it to keep it warm overnight to prevent it from freezing, a technique unused by building contractors today.

Needless to say, as completion approached, Lucas was still chipping away in the background and, as well as writing letters to the Australian press complaining about the fact that the memorial was designed by a non-Australian architect, he wrote to the Australian Prime Minister about the unveiling, presuming that 'an official invitation will in due course reach me'.[23] As late as 13 April 1939 he wrote to Lutyens saying that he had taken advice from a solicitor and a King's Counsel, who advised him that he had a claim for breach of contract as a result of which he could sue for damages for a loss of profit and for the opportunity to advance his reputation. Lutyens was advised that there was no need to reply.

The memorial was finally unveiled by King George VI on 22 July 1938.[24] Barely a year later the world was at war once more and the Imperial War Graves Commission was preparing to resume its task.

BELOW AND RIGHT Australian National War Memorial, Villers-Bretonneux

TWELVE
THE UNBUILTS

Lutyens was no different from any other architect in that, alongside his built work, there is a collection of schemes and opportunities that, for one reason or another, did not progress beyond the drawing board.

The first step in any building project is the need to secure the commission and, in early 1921, Lutyens was one of a distinguished shortlist of candidates along with the sculptor Sir George Frampton and architects Sir John Burnet and Sir Robert Lorimer to receive a letter from the Lord Provost of Glasgow inviting them to submit competitive designs for a cenotaph to commemorate the city's war dead. When the city's War Memorial Committee met in May 1921 it heard that Frampton, Burnet and Lorimer had all declined, the latter two citing the reason that the RIBA (Royal Institute of British Architects) rules stated that they could not enter a competition for which there was not a professional assessor. Lutyens had had a bitter experience of competitions as he had been deeply affected by his failure to win the one held in 1908 for the design of the new headquarters of the London County Council and he had replied 'I do not like competitions because the chance of failure destroys my interest'.[1] He was also concerned about the deadline that required the memorial to be ready for unveiling in the following November: 'All I could do would be to submit my original cenotaph in Whitehall with such amendments as your site may demand with wreaths and flags in stone as was my first intention and with such revisions in detail too subtle to show on other than a working drawing'.[2] The architects' responses were discussed and a motion was proposed and seconded that the commission should be offered to Burnet. However, there was clearly a feeling of support for Lutyens and an amendment was passed whereby the Lord Provost and 'any other members of the Committee who may happen to be in London at

an early date'[3] were empowered to meet Lutyens and ascertain whether he was proposing to replicate the Whitehall Cenotaph or whether he would produce a different design altogether. The same people were also required to meet Burnet and seek his views on the potential form of a cenotaph that he would design, were he to be awarded the commission.

The results were duly reported at the committee meeting on 6 June. Lutyens had clarified that his offer of the design of the original cenotaph was only made because of the time constraint but, if this were not an issue, then he would gladly prepare a new scheme. Both Burnet and Lorimer had also been seen and the Lord Provost felt that their excuse for not entering a competition was a red herring and that, in reality, they had declined to take part because they 'did not consider there was any higher Artist than themselves to whom they could submit their designs for adjudication'.[4] It became obvious that the Committee's laudable wish for a competition was a non-starter and following a discussion it was unanimously decided to appoint Burnet. His eventual design, a cenotaph guarded by two watchful lions carved by Ernest Gillick, was unveiled by Sir Douglas Haig on 31 May 1924, somewhat after the date of November 1921 that the Committee had originally wanted. Like Lutyens, Burnet worked for the IWGC and he designed Memorials to the Missing at Port Tewfik, Gallipoli and Jerusalem.

Two proposals that were suggested for Hyde Park by Sir Alfred Mond, the First Commissioner of Works also did not progress beyond sketch stage. His first proposal was the Temporary War Shrine (see page 32) and his second was the National War Museum.

A committee to establish the Museum had been set up in March 1917. Lutyens prepared a series of sketches, now held by the RIBA, which show a substantial building of nearly 300,000 square feet consisting of a central memorial hall around which was a series of colonnaded courtyards. It was intended that the building

Lutyens's proposal for the Temporary War Shrine to be erected in Hyde Park would act as both a museum and a national memorial but the proposal was rejected by the Cabinet in March 1918 as being premature and because it was felt to be inappropriate to combine to two functions into one. In the end the Cenotaph unexpectedly appeared to fulfil the requirement for a memorial whilst the museum (which became the Imperial War Museum) was established at the Crystal Palace, opening on 9 June 1920 before transferring to the former Imperial Institute, South Kensington in 1924, and then reopening at its current site, the former Bethlem Royal Hospital (Bedlam) on Lambeth Road, on 7 July 1936.

One place that might have been expected to have a Lutyens memorial was the village of Shere in Surrey, where the architect had worked for Sir Reginald Bray, one of his earliest clients and for whom he had designed a village shop, three houses and a lych gate at the start of his career.

The *Parish Magazine* of October 1919 noted that 'There is probably some curiosity as to the form which the Shere War Memorial will take, for which designs are being drawn up by Sir E. Lutyens, the famous architect, and we are likely to know within a short period'. The villagers soon had their curiosity satisfied, but not in the manner foreseen by the magazine for, at a meeting on 7 November, the village War Memorial Committee unanimously decided to proceed with an alternative design for a war cross to be based on the design of one at Whitby, in North Yorkshire. The prime mover behind this change was Dr Cory, a local worthy who had carried out various beneficial projects in the parish. It is said that Sir Reginald was dismayed at the decision but, nevertheless, he agreed to unveil the memorial, which stands in front of the Lutyens lych gate and, strangely, looks nothing like the Whitby Cross, on Armistice Day 1921.

Although there are no sketches by Lutyens for the memorial in Shere there are some for a proposed memorial for the Inner and Middle Temple Inns of Court in London that was to be built in Temple Church. Lutyens met the joint committee of the two Inns on 24 June 1919, five days after the Armistice Day parade and, according to the minutes of the meeting, proposed that the memorial should take the form of an obelisk. It is clear that there was some concern about the precise location of the memorial and, upon the casting vote of the chairman, Lutyens was asked to provide the cost of a movable model so that members could gauge the impact of it for themselves. The trail then goes cold because there is no mention of Lutyens at all at the next committee meeting a year later on 21 June 1920, when two options were put before the meeting – a tablet let into the floor and an cross outside the church. The matter was left to the Masters of the Bench of the Inns to decide and they chose to have two tablets – one for each Inn – which were unfortunately later destroyed in 1941 during the London Blitz.

The RIBA Collection has two sketches dated June 19 showing two columns (rather than a single obelisk) in the style of the war memorials at Fordham and Hove, one topped with a lamb with a cross and the other with a winged horse, the symbols of the two Inns. It is not known whether these predated the meeting that Lutyens attended or not.

Another scheme that progressed no further than a sketch was a proposal for a war memorial at Byfleet in Surrey. According to a letter published in *Country Life* on 16 December 1922 Lutyens had suggested a memorial for the town and he designed a small cenotaph on an undercut base with flags on either side, that was to sit on a small three arched bridge (the drawing of which is also in the RIBA). However, nothing came of it and a local resident, Mr F.C. Stoop, designed an unusual memorial in the local church that consists of a plain white marble tablet surrounded by twenty-two wooden crosses that had originally been erected over the graves of the village's dead on the Western Front, the largest such collection in the UK.

There are also nothing but drawings to show for Major James Archibald Morrison's utopian scheme at Basildon in Berkshire to build a War Memorial Church as part of a model village centre along the lines of Hampstead Garden Suburb,[5] complete with vicarage, Men's Institute, almshouses and a communal kitchen. Lutyens's letter of 27 May 1918 to Emily gives a hint as to why the project would not progress beyond the drawing board and offers a bleak picture of the supposed idyllic rural life:

Saturday night I won through with the communal idea. Sunday I lost it. Phillips the parson and self in a minority. Rural conditions difficult. The difficulties they have had even in only semi-detached cottages with the women quarrelling they say makes the scheme impossible. He would like me to bring Barnes and Hyndman too.[6] I am not sure it is wise as they and Lansbury[7] mean to upset any scheme qua buildings by introducing trades union and other questions and it will all get on crooked lines and mixed up endeavour. I shall be able to achieve nothing except trash of unions! There will certainly be a communal kitchen and a communal laundry, but it seems a communal building is impossible in the country. The villager will not be manhandled. As near neighbours the women quarrel.[8]

Lutyens's sketches show a church with a small dome and a series of descending hipped roofs and a tall campanile. Although the scheme did not proceed, Lutyens designed a cottage and a pair of houses for Morrison in the early 1920s.

In an interesting postscript, Basildon did not get its war memorial until around 1931. A public collection was made after the end of the War but, by the time that the village decided to commission a memorial, the vicar (who was the custodian of the funds) could not account for the money raised, a matter of some concern that

Lutyens's abortive design for the War Memorial Church at Basildon

caused the villagers to boycott his church. A second collection was therefore made and and a memorial duly built. It is takes the form of a simple rectangular block of stone with slight setbacks at the top and bottom. The typeface of the inscription matches that used by Lutyens for his memorials and, while there is no evidence at all to link it to him, its distinctive and unusual form makes one wonder whether it might be the result of something that he sketched for Morrison whilst he was working with him.

Unfortunately there are not even drawings to show for two potential schemes for memorials on the Western Front. All that exists are letters in the archives of the Commonwealth War Graves Commission containing tantalising references to sketches that are not present on the files: one for a 'Taj Mahal' type memorial to commemorate the Indian dead and another for a private

memorial at Mons which was promoted by Brigadier General E.L. Spears for which Lutyens prepared a drawing of a column. Lutyens had also been recommended by Fabian Ware for the design of a memorial to mark the twelve men of the 117 Tunnelling Company who died whilst mining at Railway Wood in Hooge, Belgium but a Blomfield cross (as used in the war cemeteries) was erected instead.

There were however two war memorial schemes that Lutyens designed upon which significant progress was made before the decision was taken not to proceed.

Together with the Cenotaph, the most powerful of the country's war memorials is widely considered to be the Royal Artillery Memorial at Hyde Park Corner, the combined work of the sculptor Charles Sergeant Jagger and the architect Lionel

The joint design by Lutyens and Derwent Wood for the Royal Artillery
War Memorial

The Cenotaph was accepted, alike by artists and by ordinary persons such as myself, because it lifted us out of the actual world into an ideal world of sacrifice; I believe that the Royal Artillery memorial will be rejected because it fails to do this. And yet there the monument will remain as long as stone lasts. There that howitzer will sit, squat and yet overpowering, on one of the finest sites in the world, and one which many people pass nearly every day of their lives. I have no pretensions to be an art critic. . . . But I am one of the public, and it is the public who have to look at the monument.[9]

Given the criticism that the memorial drew it is somewhat ironic that, for some time, Lutyens had been the preferred designer.

The Royal Artillery War Commemoration Fund (RAWCF) had been very clear that it wanted a memorial that would depict the regiment in action and would be 'unmistakably recognisable as an Artillery Memorial to any gunner or layman of ordinary intelligence immediately it comes into view'.[10] In February 1920 it had considered a design by Captain Adrian Jones (later to be the sculptor for the Cavalry Memorial) which used the idea of a gun coming into action but, after due consideration, it was rejected and Lutyens, Herbert Baker and Sir Aston Webb were all invited to submit designs.

Webb declined and Baker felt that the regiment should not have its own memorial but should be involved in an 'All Services' memorial instead. This left the commission open to Lutyens who, in May 1920, submitted three proposals based around a 30ft -high pedestal, one containing a recumbent figure in the style of his Southampton Cenotaph. Whilst the drawings do not appear to have survived there are some developmental sketches in the RIBA that show a memorial based on the apsidal form that Lutyens used for his cenotaphs at Derby and Rochdale, with the addition of field guns around the base. The Committee did not feel that the proposals had the required symbolism and, in September, Lutyens was asked to incorporate a howitzer into the design, at which point he asked Derwent Wood, the sculptor with whom he had worked on the Cenotaph, to assist him. Their revised scheme was a stepped pylon with carvings of gun teams at the bottom and a stylised howitzer at the top but the Committee was still unhappy, feeling that the representation of the gunners showed people 'sort of hanging around short of a job'[11] whilst Lutyens and Wood, for their part, felt that the proposal to put a gun at the top of the memorial 'in our opinion would appear ridiculous'.[12] However, not only was there concern about the memorial from the RAWCF, but also doubts were being raised about its proposed location. The Committee had rejected the site that it had been originally offered, close to Marlborough Gate on the north side of Hyde Park, in favour of one at Hyde Park Corner. However, the Commission On Sites For Monuments In The London Area declared, on 6 December 1920,

Pearson. Whereas the Cenotaph succeeds by its abstract form, the Royal Artillery Memorial underlines the stark reality of war – the centrepiece not being the typical field gun that one would associate with the regiment but a stone carving of a 9.2-inch howitzer, a brute of a fieldpiece that had a range of over six miles and which took thirty-six hours to dismantle when it had to be moved from one site to another. Around the base of the memorial are bronze sculpted figures including a highly controversial one of a dead soldier shrouded by his greatcoat. The starkness of the memorial meant that it was not universally popular when it was unveiled in 1925 and a correspondent to *The Times* compared it to the Cenotaph:

that it was not happy with the relationship of the Lutyens/Wood memorial to the nearby Wellington Arch and suggested that the memorial should be circular and lower in height. Whether it was this, or general dissatisfaction with the Lutyens/Wood scheme, is not known but, in February 1921, the RAWCF decided to commission an alternative design and approached Jagger, who had the advantage of having served in the War and could empathise with the everyday life of a soldier that the Committee was trying to capture. His brief was to produce 'a realistic thing'.[13]

Jagger produced a design for sculpted group in bronze on a pedestal (the howitzer was to appear later) and models of it and the Lutyens/Wood proposal were shown to the Office of Works, who approved the former and noted that, if the RAWCF wanted the latter, then a new site would have to be chosen. However this did not prove necessary when, on 28 June 1921, the second annual meeting of the RAWCF decided to proceed with the Jagger scheme.

Lutyens's involvement did not end though and, in May 1924 and acting on behalf of the RIBA and the Royal Fine Arts Commission, he and Sir Reginald Blomfield suggested that the whole memorial should be turned through 180° to face Grosvenor Place rather than Hyde Park. Jagger and Pearson were initially unhappy with the suggestion but accepted that it increased the power of the memorial because it would mean that the profile of the howitzer would then be running against the fall of the land. The memorial was eventually unveiled on 18 October 1925.

Lutyens clearly bore Jagger no ill-will and worked together with him on a number of commissions, notably in New Delhi and upon the Metropolitan Church of Christ the King in Liverpool, for which Jagger sculpted a maquette for the figure of Christ.

The loss of Lutyens's commission for the Royal Artillery memorial is tempered by the knowledge that the Jagger scheme that replaced it is of such high quality. There is no such compensation however at Great Yarmouth, where the war memorial that was abandoned because of its cost would have been amongst Lutyens's finest civic schemes. His commission was an early one and its design was one of those (together with Southampton, Spalding and the Cenotaph) exhibited at the War Memorial Exhibition organised by the Royal Academy in 1919.

The proposed memorial featured not one, but two, arched cenotaphs either side of a War Stone and a War Cross, the arrangement being reminiscent of the designs that were subsequently to appear in cemeteries on the Western Front at Dernancourt and Monchy. Lutyens had been given a budget of £5,000 and, by comparison with the cenotaph at Southampton that he was designing at the same time (the cost of which was £8,500), his design for Yarmouth seems over-extravagant. The Borough's War Memorial Committee asked him for a cost esti-

Lutyens's design for Great Yarmouth War Memorial

mate at their meeting on 5 February 1920 and, when he finally submitted it eight months later, it showed a figure of £6,495, excluding the costs of the water tanks that formed an integral part of the design. In a display of bravado it was decided to press ahead and invite tenders from contractors. This is not an uncommon technique in the construction industry and is used by clients who have fallen in love with their design and hope, optimistically and against all of the odds, that one of the tenders will be within their price range. The Council also might have been hoping that the turbulence around the construction industry at the end of the War would have aided their cause in receiving a competitive bid. It was, however, to no avail, and the figures that they finally received in April 1921 were actually worse than had been anticipated – ranging from £7,750 to £10,267. In such circumstances the client is then faced with two choices. Either he will blame the architect for a woeful misunderstanding of the brief, pay him off and then give the work to someone else, or, if he has a strong relationship with him, seek to develop an alternative scheme that will meet the budget. For once, Lutyens's famous charm does not appear to have worked and the Council took the former course of action. It was a strange course to take because the memorial was a series of component parts that, as at York, could have been trimmed back to match the available funds, but it is indicative of the fact that the Council had lost faith in their architect. The decision to sack Lutyens was taken at a meeting on 26 April 1921 at which the tenders were presented and the work was given to a local architect, F.R.B. Haward, who was present at the same meeting and volunteered to design a simple cross for under £5,000 and to charge no fee apart from out-of-pocket expenses. Lutyens was therefore paid off with £157/10/0 to cover the costs of himself and his quantity surveyor, E. Desch, and £95 was paid separately to Messrs G. Jackson to cover the cost of the model. Haward's memorial was unveiled by Prince Henry on 7 January 1922 having cost £3,836.90.

THIRTEEN
THEIR NAME LIVETH FOR EVERMORE

T HE WAR MEMORIALS THROUGHOUT BRITAIN that commemorate the dead of the Great War were erected on a wave of patriotic enthusiasm and, as we have seen at places such as Spalding and Rolvenden, passions often ran high. Whilst it may indeed have been the intention of the various War Memorial Committees that, to quote the words of the Chairman of Lloyd's, they had 'erected a memorial that should last for generations',[1] how has Lutyens's work fared with the passage of time?

A general overview is very positive: the memorials are well respected and where there have had to be changes they have, with one notable exception, been undertaken with care and sensitivity. Maintenance represents an ongoing challenge and the work of the Commonwealth War Graves Commission (renamed from the Imperial War Graves Commission in 1960) acts as a beacon for all of those involved in maintaining public facilities. Not only is the horticulture immaculately maintained, always giving the impression to visitors that they have arrived at the cemetery just after the gardeners have left, but care is taken over the gravestones to ensure that any damage is quickly repaired.

The one continuing issue affecting both the CWGC and those who look after memorials elsewhere is the choice of the stone that has been used. Many of the memorials, including the Cenotaph, and the majority of the CWGC's headstones, are made from Portland stone, an oolitic limestone from the Isle of Portland in Dorset, which became popular after the Great Fire of London. Its chief characteristic, and the reason that it is chosen for many public buildings, is that it becomes whiter with age due to the act of rainwater. Its fine grain makes it easy to carve but, being a limestone, it is susceptible to weathering and intricate carving, particularly of letters, can become lost with the passage of time. This may not matter so much for the Commission, for whom it is relatively easy to replace a single headstone, but it presents a greater problem with traditional war memorials — especially

LEFT The Visitor Centre at Thiepval
ABOVE The Lloyd's War Memorial – currently in storage

where small letters have been carved to record the names of the fallen. As a result, the restorers of such memorials are faced with the challenge of whether to recut the lettering or allow it to erode naturally. At both Southampton and the North Eastern Railway Memorial at York the decision has now been taken to leave the memorials alone to avoid the risk of damaging them further,[2] whereas the alternative approach was taken at King's Somborne and the letters were recut and filled with black paint to improve legibility, a regrettable step that destroys the purity of the memorial.

Ongoing maintenance has been an issue at Thiepval where the downpipes that Lutyens had designed were not large enough to take the rainwater that collected on the flat roofs within the memorial. The resulting water penetration damaged the brickwork and comprehensive repairs were undertaken in 1952–5 to improve the drainage and reface the memorial with bricks that were more durable. However, it did not solve the problem and it was necessary to reface it for a second time in the early 1970s, this time with a British engineering brick, the Accrington 'Nori.'[3] The brickwork on the walls of the forecourt in front of the memorial had also suffered and, in the 1960s, it was decided that the walls around the rond point should be removed and those leading from it to the memorial should be reduced to a constant height rather than, as they had been previously, stepping down from the memorial. A more positive alteration was to incorporate a monumental staircase to give easy access from the memorial to the cemetery below.

Another alteration to Thiepval, which was also sensitively handled, was the construction of a building type peculiar to the late twentieth century – a Visitor Centre.

Whilst there had been regular battlefield tours in the period upto 1939, aided by a popular series of Michelin guides and handbooks such as *How to See the Battlefields* written by Captain Atherton Fleming (the future husband of Dorothy L. Sayers) interest fell away after the Second World War. By the time that Martin Middlebrook visited the area for the first time in 1967, an experience that led to the publication of his seminal work *The First Day on the Somme* four years later, there were no guidebooks to help him plan his trip and he encountered no other visitors during his tour. His book which, for the first time, looked at the events of one particular day through the eyes of those who had taken part, helped to rewaken interest in the Great War. As a result he and others began to organise regular battlefield tours to satisfy the demand from those who, having experienced one war, felt a natural curiosity to investigate another. At the same time, there has been an increase in interest in the War shown by schools, many of which now visit the battlefields as part of their studies, and by private individuals, who are using the power of the Internet to investigate their family roots. As a consequence battlefield

tourism now forms a significant part of the local economy in northern France and southern Belgium. This has all increased pressure upon the main areas, as visitors are keen to learn more about the War and put the memorials and cemeteries that they see into context.

With visitor centres already having been built at Delville Wood and Vimy Ridge (the South African and Canadian National Memorials respectively) it was logical that there would be pressure to provide one at Thiepval too and a project was instigated in 1998 by Sir Frank Sanderson, a retired Sussex businessman. The £1.8m building was the subject of an open architectural competition won by Plan01, an architectural collective based in Paris, who designed a 5,000sq-ft building skilfully set into the ground out of sight of the memorial. The overall cost was raised from charitable donations together with grant aid from the French and British authorities and the EU, and the building was opened jointly by the Duke of Kent (the President of the CWGC) and Pierre Mirabeau (the Préfet de region) on 27 September 2004, the eighty-eighth anniversary of the day that the Germans were driven from Thiepval village.

The subsequent opening of a Visitor Centre at Tyne Cot, outside Ypres, left Villers-Bretonneux as the only major site on the Western Front without such a facility and, in April 2007, the Australian Government announced plans for a £1m centre here too. The major challenge in providing such buildings is that they will inevitably increase the number of visitors to the particular site and therefore, not only does the architect have to design a building that does intrude upon the memorial's setting, but also has to accommodate the parking of the attendant cars and coaches. Villers-Bretonneux is particularly exposed and, unlike the other main memorial sites, was specifically designed so that visitors could climb the observation tower to see over the battlefield. This third dimension provides its own challenge and demands a solution of the utmost sensitivity if viewers are not to be look out over a sea of parked vehicles.

It is inevitable that some of the memorials would be damaged when war returned to Europe in 1939. The war cemeteries were, by and large, respected by the occupying troops although Villers-Bretonneux was damaged in 1940 when a German tank and a Messerschmitt 109 fired upon a Senegalese observation post that had been established at the top of the tower. Most of the damage has been repaired but a number of bullet marks have been left as a reminder (as can be seen in the photo on page 145).

Two war memorials in England were affected by enemy bombing: the London Assurance offices in King William Street, London were hit on 29 December 1940 although the Lutyens plaque survived, and the Lutyens War Cross in the peaceful churchyard of Abinger Common, deep in the Surrey countryside, was severely damaged along with the adjacent church on 3 August 1944 by a V1

The view from the top of the observation tower at Villers-Bretonneux shows that care will have to be taken to ensure the proposed Visitor Centre and attendant parking do not intrude upon the memorial's setting

flying bomb. Both the church and the war memorial were restored, the latter being re-erected in 1948 in memory of Margaret Lewin, who had paid for the original.

Two other War Crosses have suffered damage – a car hit the one at Stockbridge in the early 1990s and the one at Holy Island was snapped in two during hurricane force winds in the winter of 1983–4, but both have been repaired.

The only other memorial to suffer damage was the one at University College School, which was destroyed in a fire in 1978, but regrettably has not been replaced.

A number of the memorials have been relocated. The Royal Naval Division Memorial on Horse Guards Parade in London has actually been moved twice. It was put into storage prior to the start of the Second World War to make way for the construction of the Citadel as a bombproof centre for the Admiralty, before being re-erected in 1951 at the Royal Naval College at Greenwich.

When the college closed in 1998 the opportunity was taken to return the memorial to its original site and a fund raising appeal was launched under the patronage of the Prince of Wales. Over £200,000 was raised which, together with grants from the War Memorials Trust and the English Heritage Grant Scheme for War Memorial Repair and Conservation, was sufficient to pay for the cost of relocation and to endow a fund for future maintenance. The memorial was rededicated by the Prince on Beaucourt Day (13 November) 2003, the Regimental Day that commemorates the division's successful attack at Beaucourt-sur-l'Ancre in the Battle of the Somme in 1916.

A second relocation is planned for the Lancashire Fusiliers Memorial at Bury, which was moved 100 yards in 1961 to accommodate a road improvement scheme and is due to be moved again when the regimental museum is transferred from the regiment's barracks adjacent to the memorial to Sparrow Park.

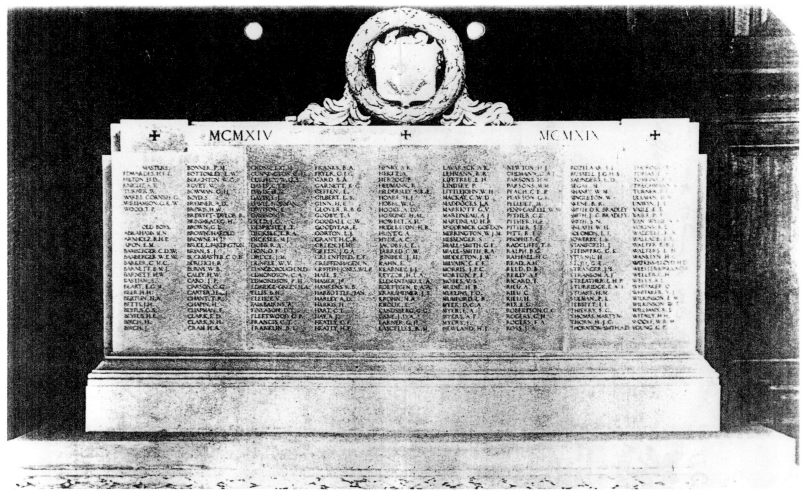

University College School War Memorial – destroyed by fire in 1978

The Civil Service Rifles Memorial has only been moved once. It originally stood in the centre of the courtyard of Somerset House but, by the 1990s, was marooned in a sea of car parking and looking somewhat forlorn. In an inspired piece of thinking it was decided to banish the cars from the courtyard and create a new public space featuring, depending upon the time of year, fountains or an ice rink. Inevitably the war memorial had to be moved and, in 2002, was resited to the nearby riverside terrace overlooking the Thames.

The Colombo war memorial was dismantled during the Second World War because it was in a military area and there was a worry that it made an obvious target for Japanese bombers. It was put into storage and re-erected in a different location in Victoria Park (now Vihara Maha Devi Park) after the War.

The only controversial relocation has been that of the Edward Horner Memorial that dominated the Horner Chapel in St Andrew's Church at Mells. The Church was keen to regain use of the chapel to provide a quiet area for prayer and small meetings

and proposed to move the memorial to the church's north aisle. This was opposed by the Lutyens Trust, which considered that placing the memorial in the body of the church would turn it into the equivalent of a museum piece and that it would therefore lose the significance of being a private memorial in a family chapel. However, the Trust's view was not supported and consent for the relocation was given in Autumn 2006.

One memorial that escaped relocation was the one at Abercorn that marked the end of the War. It had been built alongside the main road out of the town and had been sited with care to take account of any future road improvements. However, when the time came to widen the road forty years later it was alleged that the memorial was in the wrong location and would have to be moved to a site near the Colonial Office in the town. The authorities had reckoned without the redoubtable Mr Venning, a local resident who had been responsible for choosing the memorial's original location. He garnered local support and argued that the proposed new site had no significance and that it

The Civil Service Rifles War Memorial in its original location at Somerset House

was all part of a bureaucratic plot to relocate the memorial, regardless of whether or not it was in the way of construction work. His view prevailed and, when the site was resurveyed, it revealed that the memorial was only four inches from where it should have been. It was therefore allowed to stay and a roundabout built around it. Even in the depths of Southern Africa forty years after the War, a war memorial still had the power to evoke public reaction.

Civic memorials, such as Abercorn, have the benefit of being at the heart of the annual Remembrance Day ceremonies and have a natural constituency of interested residents to watch over them. The same cannot be said for the memorials erected by companies and it is they, more than any other form of memorial, that have suffered most since they were erected being subject to the general vicissitudes of corporate life. It will be recalled that, even before the North Eastern Railway Memorial in York was completed, the company itself had ceased to exist having been swallowed up into the London and North Eastern Railway and since then there have

been two further changes of ownership with first, the nationalisation and then, the privatisation of the railway network. As a result the York memorial and the Midland Railway memorial at Derby are both in the care of BRB Residuary Ltd, which reports to the Department for Transport and is responsible for the liabilities of the former British Rail.

As well as being taken over, companies also move office and those memorials that are an integral part of the building will therefore be at risk. Lloyd's originally erected their memorial in their offices in the Royal Exchange and took it with them when they moved to their new purpose-built headquarters in Leadenhall Street in 1928. However, when in 1986 they moved for a second time into their distinctive building designed by Richard Rogers, they could not find a suitable space for the memorial and it currently lies in storage.

The same care was not, however, taken by Imperial Tobacco when their headquarters in Bristol was demolished in 1986 to make way for an Asda superstore. The company's war memorial in the

The Imperial Tobacco War Memorial – now no more

entrance hall consisted of a marble tablet raised on four pairs of Tuscan columns and, with demolition pending, it was offered to the Bristol Marble Company. The firm was so appalled at the thought of what was to happen that it refused to accept it, one of their workmen commenting that it was 'like ripping out the ceiling of the Sistine Chapel'.[4] It was therefore decided to break it up for scrap, in a move surprisingly sanctioned by Imperial Tobacco's branch of the Royal British Legion, which received the proceeds from the sale. It remains mercifully one of few cases nationwide where a war memorial has been deliberately destroyed.

By contrast, the London Assurance Memorial, being smaller and, therefore, more portable has ended up at the National Memorial Arboretum in Alrewas, Shropshire, having been donated by the Royal and Sun Alliance insurance company into which the company had been subsumed in 1965.

Two memorials suffered particularly from neglect. The South Africa War Memorial at Richmond was simply forgotten. Having been the focus of commemoration in the 1920s and 1930s, it was ignored until the CWGC became aware of its existence in 1981, whereupon it agreed with the South African government to be responsible for its maintenance. The Irish National War Memorial was ignored rather than forgotten as it was caught up in the wider political situation between the Irish and British Governments, there being unease that it commemorated the

Norwich War Memorial awaiting the refurbishment of its setting

dead from both countries. The site fell was shamefully neglected but was restored in the 1980s, being formally dedicated on 10 September 1988.

Inevitably the war memorials are likely to receive their share of graffiti, most famously when the Cenotaph was daubed in the anti-capitalism riots in London of May 2000 but, also equally inevitably, it is usually quickly removed. The most wanton act of vandalism to a Lutyens war memorial occurred in Fordham, where the memorial was pulled down by vandals in June 1991, apparently so that they could steal the bronze figure of St George that stood at its top. The thieves were never caught and the villagers raised £4,750 to re-erect and repair the column and to provide a fibreglass copy of the sculpture, which was recreated from photographs by a local sculptor, Robert Donaldson. Further thefts have occurred from the grave of Derek Lutyens's grave in Thursley (the RFC 'wings'), the memorial to Henry Tennant at Rolvenden (his sword) and the Empire's Horses Memorial in Hampstead (the bronze horse by Lutyens's father Charles).

It is the risk of vandalism that leads to the regrettable but understandable decision, where it is possible, to lock off the memorials to deny access to the public. It is particularly unfortunate at Leicester, where one is not able to walk under the splendid arch and, to a certain extent, such a decision makes sense of the surrounding railings, but it is perverse at Northampton, where it is a straightforward task for any miscreant to avoid the locked gates by climbing over the low wall that surrounds the memorial.

It is, however, the sad case of the Norwich memorial that acts as a parable for our times. It was relocated from its original site outside the Guildhall to stand proudly above the Market Place as an integral part of the Memorial Gardens that were laid out in 1938 alongside the new City Hall. In 2004 maintenance problems were identified in the structure that supports the memorial and it was closed to the public due to concerns about safety, although access was given to the Royal British Legion to lay wreaths on Remembrance Sunday. It was fenced off by a council bereft of money to pay for the repairs, leading the former MP and BBC journalist Martin Bell to comment in October 2007 'To find a war memorial in a state like that you would have to go to Iraq'.[5] Fortunately there seems to be a solution at hand as the Council has been able to find some land to sell to raise the estimated £2.6m to pay for the refurbishment of the memorial and the adjoining gardens. However it makes one wonder what would have been the reaction of Charles Bignold and the others who worked hard to raise funds for the original memorial had they known that, seventy years later, it would be fenced off waiting for land to be sold to pay for its restoration.

FOURTEEN
ENDGAME

THE WAR CHANGED THE NATURE of Lutyens's work completely. Before 1914 he had been, to all intents and purposes, a designer of country houses. After 1918 his fame as a result of both the Cenotaph and the Viceroy's House led to an increasingly wide range of commercial and public projects. Foremost amongst these was a series of four buildings for Midland Bank, who had appointed Reginald McKenna (one of the architect's loyal pre-War clients) as Chairman in 1919. The first building was a small branch in London's Piccadilly ('A very successful hors d'oeuvre' according to Pevsner)[1] in the shadow of St James's Piccadilly by the architect's great hero, Sir Christopher Wren. It was followed by a new headquarters for the bank in Poultry, close to the Bank of England; a branch in nearby Leadenhall Street and a regional office in Manchester. Elesewhere in London he designed headquarters buildings for the Anglo-Iranian Oil Company (now BP) in Finsbury Circus and Reuters and the Press Association in Fleet Street. Further west, in Mayfair, a number of buildings were commissioned by the Grosvenor Estate, notably the Grosvenor House Hotel. Another commission from the same source resulted in Lutyens's largest housing project in Britain – eight blocks of balcony access flats ranged along Page Street in Pimlico, identified by stark chequerboard facades of grey and white brickwork and classical community buildings at the entrance to each courtyard.

However, valuable though the commercial buildings were, they did not offer Lutyens the same challenge as did his pre-War domestic houses and they were usually designed in partnership with other architects, with Lutyens retaining the interesting bits such as the façade and the public areas for himself and leaving his collaborators to carry out the more mundane, bread and butter design work of the private areas.

His fame also brought him the type of public projects that had eluded him before the War including the British Embassy in

LEFT Filgrave Clock Tower, presented to the village by Frederick and Gerda König, and Frederick's brother Henry, to mark the Silver Jubilee in 1935. Lutyens was present at its unveiling.
ABOVE The Midland Bank in Piccadilly (1922) was one of a number of buildings that Lutyens designed for the bank

Washington, Hampton Court Bridge and the post-(Second) War replanning of Hull and London. At the other end of the scale was the building with which, along with the Cenotaph, his name is most fondly associated: the Queen's Dolls House. Architecturally held to be one of his most mundane designs, it was constructed as a present for Queen Mary in the drawing room in Lutyens's house in Mansfield Street, London, before being exhibited at the British Empire Exhibition at Wembley in 1924 and then moved to its permanent home in Windsor Castle.

ABOVE The Western Front comes to the West End – the rooftop plantrooms at the Grosvenor House Hotel recall Lutyens's shelter buildings for the cemeteries in France and Belgium

RIGHT Lutyens designed the fountains in London's Trafalgar Square as memorials to two leading figures from the Great War – Admirals Beatty and Jellicoe

The Viceroy's House, which had financially supported his office for the best part of twenty years was completed in 1930, the same year that saw building work finish on a project that had outrun New Delhi by two years – Castle Drogo, built on the edge of Dartmoor for Julius Drewe, the grocery tycoon.

The architectural historian Nikolaus Pevsner would have it that Lutyens was the 'greatest folly builder that Britain has seen'[2] and if the Viceroy's House and Castle Drogo can both be seen as follies, then so too can the building that was to occupy the final fifteen years of Lutyens's life – the Metropolitan Cathedral of Christ the King in Liverpool. Lutyens had been approached in 1929 by Richard Downey, the Archbishop of Liverpool, who had conceived a plan to build a cathedral to rival the city's Anglican Cathedral designed by Giles Gilbert Scott, the construction of which had been started in 1904. The initial drawings were made public in 1930 and revealed a brick and granite building larger than St Paul's and with a dome second only to St Peter's in Rome. The foundation stone was laid in 1933 and construction work started before being halted during the Second World War, never to progress any further than the foundations and the crypt.

However the saddest part of Lutyens's post-War years was that he became a logical choice of designer for the graves and memorials of many of his friends and clients as they died – Gertrude Jekyll, the Horners and the McKennas amongst others.

Lutyens was to return three times to North Buckinghamshire to carry out work for Frederick König. Firstly, in the mid-1920s, he designed a garden scheme for Tyringham House in which the disposition of two Classical buildings (the Bathing Pavilion and the Temple of Music) either side of a rectangular lake act as a gentle reminder of the arrangement of the two pavilions that frame the approach to the Australian Memorial at Villers-Bretonneux. His second project also had echoes of the Western Front – the brick clock tower in Filgrave that commemorates the Silver Jubilee of 1935 is strongly reminiscent of the side towers of the original scheme at Arras. His third and final scheme, was at the Church of St Peter, where this book began. Frederick König died in 1940 and he and his wife Gerda are buried in a rectangular plot surrounded by a box hedge designed by the architect of the local war memorial. It is visible on the right hand side of the churchyard in the picture on page 12 and was to be one of Lutyens's last commissions.

L'ENVOI

S IR EDWIN LUTYENS[1] died of lung cancer on 1 January 1944, surrounded by drawings of Liverpool Cathedral. His obituary in *The Times*, whilst mentioning the Cenotaph and the War Stone, ignored his work for the Imperial War Graves Commission and Thiepval was not thought sufficiently important to rate a mention. Nineteen days later, at their next meeting, his clients for this supreme memorial passed a resolution:

'The Commission place on record their profound regret in the death of Sir Edwin Lutyens OM KCIE, PRA, one of their Principal Architects from 1918 to 1930, and since 1930 their Honorary Consulting Architect, to whose genius they owe it that so many British dead of the Great War are buried in cemeteries or named on memorials supremely worthy of their sacrifice; and request the Vice-Chairman to convey the expression of their deep sympathy to the members of his family.'[2]

The paper that had been presented to the Committee beforehand noted that the Commission 'Were fortunate in finding a man who, like the small group of men who were his colleagues, could rise to the height of the task which in 1918 faced the Commission; that of dedicating the genius of British architecture to the memory of a million men who died in the supreme struggle for liberty'.[3]

The Cenotaph

APPENDIX 1:
WAR MEMORIALS

Brief details of all of Lutyens's extant war memorials are listed below, together with some details of their locations. The ☆ symbol is a personal ranking system, with a ☆ ☆ ☆ mark meaning that the memorial should not be missed by any serious admirer of Lutyens.

ABINGER COMMON (SURREY) ☆

A War Cross on a circular base – no steps. Sword carved on cross in a manner reminiscent of the sword attached to the Blomfield War Cross for the Imperial War Graves Commission – the only example of this. Presented by Margaret Lewin of Parkhurst, Abinger Common, in memory of her son Charles of the 4th Hussars, who died in 1919. Cost £190 and built by H.T. Jenkins and Sons of Torquay. Destroyed by a Flying Bomb in 1944 and rebuilt in 1948.

Church of St James

ALREWAS (STAFFORDSHIRE) – LONDON ASSURANCE ☆

Bronze plaque relocated from the company's original office in London via the Ledsham (Cheshire) office of the Royal and Sun Alliance (into which the company merged). The memorial sits in an outside cloister of the other memorials that have been similarly relocated.

National Memorial Arboretum

ASHWELL (HERTFORDSHIRE) ☆

War Cross on square base on two circular steps – an unusual arrangement requested by the village's War Memorial Committee. Stands above the road and is reached by flight of six steps. Built by Holland, Hannen and Cubitt, the builders of the Cenotaph. Approximate cost £650. Unveiled on 4 December 1921 by Lord Hampden, the Lord Lieutenant of Hertfordshire.

Junction of Station Road and Lucas Lane

BURY (LANCASHIRE) – LANCASHIRE FUSILIERS ☆ ☆

Portland stone obelisk raised on rectangular pedestal with apsidal ends, standing on two circular steps and large circular base. Painted stone flags with Regimental and King's Colours. Overall height 22ft 6¾in. Built by Messrs John Tinline of Bury. Unveiled on 25 April 1922 by Lieutenant-General Sir Beauvoir de Lisle, Commander in Chief, Western Command. Lutyens did not charge a fee as his father and great uncle had both served in the regiment.

Wellington Barracks, Bolton Road

BUSBRIDGE (SURREY) ☆

War Cross on coved base and three square steps. Unveiled by General Sir Charles Munro Bart on 23 July 1922. The churchyard contains three graves designed by Lutyens – Gertrude Jekyll (together with her brother and sister-in-law), Julia Jekyll (her mother) and Francis McLaren (see Spalding War Memorial). Lutyens also designed the chancel screen inside the Church.

Church of St John the Baptist

CARDIFF – WELCH REGIMENT ☆

Small square cenotaph of Portland stone standing on three steps. Empty tomb of same design as that used for tombs of James Hackett, Sidney Myer and the Beddington brothers. Unveiled on 19 July 1924 by Field Marshal Lord Plumer.

Maindy Barracks, Whitchurch Road

COWLEY (OXFORDSHIRE) – OXFORDSHIRE AND BUCKINGHAMSHIRE LIGHT INFANTRY ☆

Portland stone obelisk 28ft 11in high on three square steps. Regimental badge in bold relief on two sides. Unveiled on 11 November 1923 by the regiment's colonel Major-General Sir J. Hanbury-Williams.

Rose Hill

CROWTHORNE (BERKSHIRE) – WELLINGTON COLLEGE ☆ ☆

Wooden Doric column raised on a marble pedestal atop of which is a statue of St George slaying the dragon. The main part of the column is black but the upper part, including the statue, is white, and is seen to great effect in front of the blue painted ceiling behind. The main inscription is carried on the wall of the apse within which the memorial stands. Similar to Mells but with Union Flag on the front. Marble lectern holding a book with the names of the fallen. A delicate and unknown memorial. Unveiled on 24 October 1922 by the Duke of Connaught.

Chapel, Wellington College (not on public view)

DERBY – MIDLAND RAILWAY ☆ ☆ ☆

31-foot-high cenotaph with recumbent figure, apsidal ends and flanking walls. Built by J. Parnell and Son Ltd at a cost of £10,309. Unveiled on 15 December 1921 by Charles Booth, the company's Chairman.

Midland Road

EXETER ☆

Large War Cross of granite from Dartmoor standing on three steps. Unveiled on 16 May 1921 by the Prince of Wales. The surrounding railings are an unfortunate twenty-first-century addition.

Green in front of Exeter Cathedral

FORDHAM (CAMBRIDGESHIRE) ☆

Statue of St George (from the studio of Sir George Frampton) on top of Doric column. Unveiled on 7 August 1921. Built by Frank Johnson, a local builder. The original statue was stolen and has been replaced by a fibreglass replica.

Carter Street

GERRARDS CROSS (BUCKINGHAMSHIRE) ☆

Extension to former stables to act as a Parish Hall, the only example Lutyens designing a war memorial that served a utilitarian purpose. Single-storey, white painted brickwork with hipped slate roof. Central recessed entrance with four bellied Doric columns. Opened on14 October 1922 by the Lord Lieutenant of Buckinghamshire, Earl Carrington.

East Common

HARTBURN (NORTHUMBERLAND) ☆

War Cross with chunky rectangular base set on stone circle in grass. Paid for by Mr and Mrs H. Straker of Angerton Hall, for whom Lutyens and Gertrude Jekyll had designed the gardens in 1904. Built by H.J. Robinson of Meldon. Unveiled by Colonel E.P.A. Riddell, commander of the Northumberland Infantry Brigade in August 1921.

On triangular green in heart of village

HOLY ISLAND (NORTHUMBERLAND) ☆

War Cross on circular base made of pink ashlar. Unveiled on 4 June 1922 by Major Morley Crossman DSO. Snapped in half by winds during winter of 1983–4. Lutyens' remodelling of the nearby Lindisfarne Castle for Edward Hudson, the proprietor of *Country Life*, is deservedly one of his most famous works.

The Heugh

HOVE (SUSSEX) ☆

16ft-high grey granite Tuscan column topped by figure of St George from the studio of Sir George Frampton. Stands on three steps. Similar to Fordham. Unveiled on 27 February 1921 by Lord Leconfield, the Lord Lieutenant of Sussex.

Grand Avenue

KING'S SOMBORNE (HAMPSHIRE) ☆

War Cross on coved base with three square steps. Unveiled on 27 March 1921 by Rear-Admiral Sir Godfrey Paine.

On triangular green near church in heart of village

LEEDS – LEEDS RIFLES ☆ ☆

Although this War Cross is in the churchyard it faces the adjacent street and, owing to the difference in levels, incorporates a stone seat that doubles as a ledge for wreaths. Unveiled on 13 November 1921 by Captain G. Sanders, VC, MC, formerly of the Regiment.

Church of St Peter Kirkgate

LEICESTER ☆ ☆ ☆

Square Portland stone monumental arch with the familiar Lutyens device of tall openings on the main elevations and smaller openings on the minor ones. Heavy attic with low dome, similar to the original proposal for the Memorial to the Missing of the Somme at Thiepval. Four stone flags inside – the Union Flag and those of the three Armed Services. Surrounded by metal railings with gate piers topped by bowls raised on pillars. Unveiled on 4 July 1925 by Mrs Elizabeth Butler, a local resident. Built by Messrs Holloway (cf Southampton). Cost £22,700.

Victoria Park

LONDON – BRITISH MEDICAL ASSOCIATION ☆ ☆

Screen gates across courtyard of building originally designed by Lutyens for the Theosophical Society. Opened on 13 July 1925 by Archbishop of Canterbury.

Tavistock Square

LONDON – CAVALRY CLUB ☆

Small figure of a bronze horse by Herbert Haseltine on a marble base. Estimated cost £700.

127 Piccadilly (inside – not on public dispay)

LONDON – CIVIL SERVICE RIFLES ☆ ☆

Square column surmounted by urn on coved base standing on three steps. Two coloured flags (Union Flag and Regimental Colour) in metal rather than the usual stone – a one-off. The names of battles in which the regiment fought inscribed around the base – unusual in such a memorial. Unveiled on 27 January 1924 by the Prince of Wales, the regiment's honorary colonel. Relocated from the nearby central courtyard in 2002.

River Terrace, Somerset House, The Strand

LONDON – CENOTAPH ☆ ☆ ☆

A 35 ft high Portland stone pylon in the middle of a busy road. One of the best war memorials in the world. Unveiled by King George V on 11 November 1920. Built by Messrs Holland & Hannen and Cubitt Ltd.

Whitehall

LONDON – EMPIRE'S HORSES ☆

Wooden plinth for a sculpture of a heavy horse by Charles Lutyens, the architect's father. Sculpture stolen in the 1960s and replaced with a replica, which has also been stolen. The memorial is now a nearby bronze plaque by Rosemary Proctor.

Church of St Jude, Hampstead Garden Suburb

LONDON – MERCANTILE MARINE ☆ ☆ ☆

Doric temple that could equally as well be at home on the Western Front as in the heart of London. Names of the fallen on bronze panels sized to give the appearance of rusticated walling. Square stepped central attic reminiscent of the original design for the York City Memorial but surmounted by a drum rather than a War Stone. Secret gutter detailing as used on shelters in war cemeteries at Assevillers and Feuchy. Cost £20,000–25,000. Sculptor Sir William Reid Dick. Unveiled on 12 December 1928 by Queen Mary, in the absence of King George V, who was seriously ill.

Tower Hill

LONDON – ROYAL NAVAL DIVISION ☆ ☆ ☆

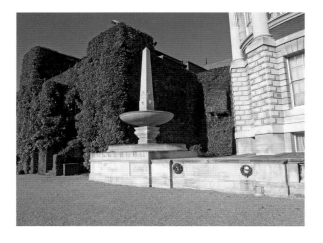

Obelisk in circular fountain bowl raised on a large square plinth linked to balustrade on adjoining building – all in Portland stone. Names of prominent regimental actions carved on base together with the badges of the regiments who made up the Division and a quotation from Rupert Brooke ('Blow out you bugles') who was a member of the Regiment's Hood Battalion. Unveiled on 25 April 1925 by Major-General Sir Archibald Paris, who commanded the Division at the defence of Antwerp. Removed in 1940 to allow construction of adjacent Citadel, re-erected in Greenwich in 1952 and restored to its original site in 2003.

Horse Guards Parade

LONDON – SOUTH AFRICA ☆ ☆

Stark 15ft-high granite cenotaph with triangular top, standing on base of two steps; the only relief being the heavy carvings of two wreaths which, unusually, also have carved supports. The empty tomb is reminiscent of Lutyens's design for the graves of Edward and Tom Thynne at Muntham Clump near Findon, Sussex. Dedicated on 30 June 1921 by the Bishop of St Albans when the memorial was accepted on behalf of South Africa by General Smuts.

Richmond Cemetery, Grove Road, Richmond

LOWER SWELL (GLOUCESTERSHIRE) ☆ ☆

Flaming urn on a pedestal standing on three steps. Nothing is known about this memorial but it is assumed that it is associated with Mark Fenwick, a regular client and for whom Lutyens did alterations and a garden layout at his nearby house, Abbotswood. The incorporation of the names of those who died in the Second World War was always a challenge and, here, the dates and names have had to be squeezed in the limited space available and the general inscription has become 'Gave their lives in the Great Wars'. The memorial appears on some lists as 'Stow-on-the-Wold' due to its proximity to the nearby town.

On green in heart of village

MAIDSTONE (KENT) – ROYAL WEST KENT REGIMENT ☆ ☆

Reduced version of the Whitehall cenotaph but without flags. Unveiled on 30 July 1921 by the Regiment's Colonel, Major General Sir Edmund Leach. Built by Messrs Wallis and Sons, a local firm.

Brenchley Gardens

MANCHESTER ☆ ☆ ☆

Cenotaph with recumbent figure, two obelisks and War Stone, all raised on a platform with a coved base. Portland stone. Contractor Nine Elms Stone Masonry Works. Cost £6,490. Unveiled by Earl of Derby with Mrs Dingle (local resident who had lost three sons in the War) 12 July 1924. Setting somewhat spoilt by catenary wires for Manchester's tram system.

St Peter's Square

MELLS (SOMERSET) ☆ ☆

Tuscan column of Portland stone with statue of St George slaying the dragon at top , similar to Wellington College. Curved flanking walls of coursed rubble in front of which are undercut ledges cum seats, standing on three steps. Walls are topped by a low yew hedge. Inscription carved by Eric Gill. Details of unveiling unknown but believed to be 1920.

High Street

MISERDEN (GLOUCESTERSHIRE) ☆

War Cross on a chunky rectangular base instead of the usual narrow one. Inscriptions in bronze applied to inset panels instead of the more usual carving stone carving. Inscription 'VH 1920' at the rear probably denotes Victor Hayward, a foreman and stonemason on the Wills Estate. It is likely that the memorial was connected with Noel Wills, who owned the nearby Misarden Park, where Lutyens designed an extension and loggia in 1919.

Opposite Church of St Andrew

MUNCASTER (CUMBRIA) ☆

War Cross of Lakeland granite. Details of unveiling unknown but believed to be 1920.

On A595 outside Ravenglass

NORTHAMPTON ☆ ☆ ☆

One of the most elaborate town memorials. Two obelisks with deep niches stand on coved bases either side of a War Stone. Each obelisk has two stone flags (the Union Flag and the flags of the three Armed Services). Low stone rail faces the memorial and contains the dedication inscription. Two sets of entrance gates and piers with urns raised on pillars. Unveiled on 11 November 1926 by General Horne

Wood Hill

NORWICH – WAR MEMORIAL ☆ ☆ ☆

Unusual low cenotaph with chest tomb similar to that on the Whitehall original set on a low wall attached to the front of which is a War Stone set on three steps. Bronze urns at either end of the wall emit flames thanks to intgral gas supply. Unveiled on 9 October 1927 by local disabled soldier Bertie Withers accompanied by Sir Ian Hamilton. Approximate cost £2,700. Resited from original location in front of Guildhall.

Market Place

NORWICH – ROLL OF HONOUR ☆ ☆

The names of the city's fallen are contained on a series of hinged wooden panels behind four wooden doors. Two wooden flags – the Union Flag and the White Ensign.

Norwich Castle

READING (BERKSHIRE) – ROYAL BERKSHIRE REGIMENT ☆

Reduced version of the Whitehall cenotaph (17ft 9in-high) but with a bowl raised on legs on the top. One painted stone flag on each side (King's Colour and Regimental Colour) with swags. Built by Messrs Wallis of Maidstone. Unveiled on 13 September 1921 by Major General E.T. Dickson. Cost *c*.£3,000.

Brock Barracks, Oxford Road (not on public view)

ROCHDALE (LANCASHIRE) ☆ ☆ ☆

Cenotaph with apsidal ends, recumbent figure and painted flags and War Stone, all raised on a dais of three steps. Cenotaph is raised by a further six steps and the War Stone by its customary three. Cornish granite. Cost £12,611. Unveiled by Earl of Derby on 26 November 1922.

The Esplanade, opposite the Town Hall

ROLVENDEN (KENT) ☆

Slender cross of Clipsham stone on octagonal base standing on three circular steps. Built by Messrs Wallis of Maidstone for £255. Unveiled on 8 November 1922 by the Archbishop of Canterbury.

In front of the Church of St Mary the Virgin

RUGBY (WARWICKSHIRE) – BRITISH THOMSON HOUSTON LTD ☆ ☆

War Cross of Portland stone on a large circular plinth that contains the names of the fallen. Built by J. Parnell and Son Ltd at a cost of £3,243. Unveiled on 28 October 1921.

Mill Road

SANDHURST (KENT) ☆ ☆ ☆

The most elaborate setting of all of Lutyens's War Crosses. Cross stands at heart of large cross formed in the grass by parallel strips of Portland stone, with stone seats at the ends of three of the arms and a circular planting bed terminating the base. Nothing is known about the commissioning of the memorial.

Junction of Bodiam Road and A268

SOUTHAMPTON ☆ ☆ ☆

Portland stone cenotaph with recumbent figure and War Stone. Short flanking walls terminated by columns with pine cones. Much carving including cross with sword in relief, the city's coat of arms, the arms of the three Services and two lions. Built by Messrs Holloway of London for £9,385. Their name, together with that of the architect, is carved on the memorial. Unveiled on 6 November 1920 by the Rt Hon J.E.B. Seely, the Lord Lieutenant of Hampshire.

Watts Park, Above Bar

SOUTHEND-ON-SEA (ESSEX) ☆ ☆

Tall obelisk of Portland stone raised on platform of eight steps, with flanking walls. Two stone flags – the Union Flag and the White Ensign. Unveiled on 27 November 1921 by Lord Lambourne. Cost £5,522. 'Lest We Forget' picked out in white chippings in the grass in front of the memorial detracts from its setting.

Clifftown Parade

SPALDING (LINCOLNSHIRE) ☆ ☆ ☆

White rendered Doric temple with pantiled roof that was a precursor to the shelter buildings on the Western Front stands behind a War Stone and a long reflecting pool. Two stone flags (Union Flag and White Ensign). Built by Hodson Ltd for £6,841. Unveiled on 8 June 1922 by Sir Ian Hamilton.

Ayscoughfee Gardens, Church Gate

STOCKBRIDGE (HAMPSHIRE) ☆

War Cross on coved base with three steps, top two of which are square and the bottom one circular. Unveiled on 3 April 1921 by Mrs Herbert Johnson, for whose husband Lutyens designed the nearby Marshcourt before their marriage.

On A3057 close to its junction with A30

TYRINGHAM (BUCKINGHAMSHIRE) ☆

Plaque of Carrera marble with verdite swags. Unveiled on 23 June 1921 by Her Highness Princess Marie Louise.

Church of St Peter

WARGRAVE (BERKSHIRE) ☆ ☆

War Cross of Portland Stone on unusual high hexagonal base to reflect the cross section of the shaft. Unveiled on 28 May 1922 by Sir William Robertson.

Mill Green

WITTERSHAM (KENT) ☆

Wooden plaque. Accreditation by local vicar in church guide from 1920s.

Church of St John the Baptist

YORK – CITY ☆ ☆

Tall Portland stone War Cross on
coved base and plinth raised on two
steps. Entrance screen and gates
also by Lutyens. Unveiled on 25
June 1925 by the Duke of York.

Station Road

YORK – NORTH EASTERN RAILWAY ☆ ☆

54ft-high obelisk of Portland stone with flanking walls and
urns, behind War Stone. Unveiled on 14 June 1924 by Field-
Marshal Lord Plumer.

Market Place

ABROAD

BERMUDA – HAMILTON ☆ ☆ ☆

Two-thirds scale version of the Whitehall original
in Bermuda limestone. Cornerstone laid by
Prince of Wales in 1920. Unveiled on 6 May 1925.

Front Street

CANADA – LONDON, ONTARIO ☆ ☆ ☆

Three-quarter scale version of the Whitehall original, 24ft
6in-high and made from Queenston limestone (a local
stone). Erected by the Imperial Order of the Daughters of
the Empire and unveiled on 11 November 1934.

Victoria Park

HONG KONG ☆ ☆

Replica of Whitehall original unveiled on 6 May 1928 by Sir Cecil Clementi, Governor General of Hong Kong.

Statue Square, Central Hong Kong

INDIA – CHENNAI (MADRAS CLUB) ☆

Simple marble tablet modelled by Eric Broadbent and made by H.J. Jenkins & Sons Ltd of Torquay. Erected in May 1924 at a total cost of £290 plus Lutyens's fee of £30. There is a sketch of a more elaborate version, similar to the Marc Noble Memorial (see page 217), in the RIBA Drawings Collection.

Madras Club, Adyar Club Road (inside – not on public display)

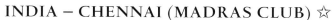

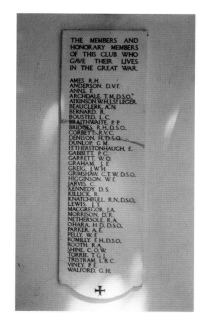

INDIA – NEW DELHI (ALL INDIA) ☆ ☆ ☆

Triumphal arch of sandstone 139ft-high with heavy attic, in the manner of the Leicester War Memorial. Lower side arches blocked by pine cones in urns. Surmounted by a shallow dome that recalls both the one on the Viceroy's House and the original plans of Thiepval. Device on top to emit smoke. Foundation stone laid by Duke of Connaught in February 1921 but moved because it was later found to be in the wrong place. Dedicated by Lord Irwin, Viceroy of India, on 12 February 1931.

Rajpath

IRELAND – DUBLIN (ALL IRELAND) ☆ ☆ ☆

Substantial landscape design incorporating War Cross, War Stone, two obelisks in fountains and two sunken rose gardens. Four Book Rooms with linking walls and stone pergolas. Constructed in the 1930s but not formally dedicated until 10 September 1988.

Con Colbert Road

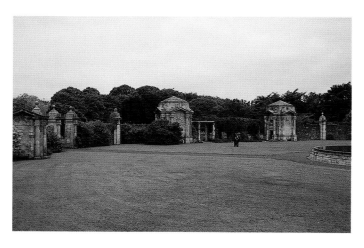

SIERRA LEONE – FREE TOWN ☆

Truncated pyramid of Portland stone with Welsh slate panels. Made in Britain by J. & H. Patterson and shipped to Freetown to be finished and assembled on site. Unveiled on 11 March 1931 by the Acting Governor. Total cost c.£700.

In front of Secretariat Building in centre of Freetown

SRI LANKA – COLOMBO ☆ ☆

Column on stepped base with brazier on top. Unveiled on 27 October 1923 by the Governor, Sir William Manning. Dismantled and moved from its original site on Galle Face Green during the Second World War.

Vihara Maha Devi Park

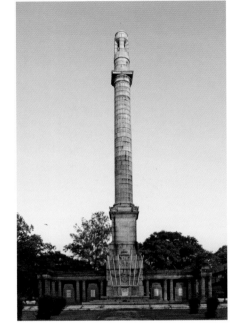

ZAMBIA – MBALA ☆

Truncated cairn completed c.1930.

On a roundabaout on the main road leading into the town from the south west.

APPENDIX 2: WESTERN FRONT CEMETERIES AND MEMORIALS TO THE MISSING

Any visitor to the Western Front is advised to do as much research as possible before setting out because, even with all of the necessary information, it can sometimes be quite difficult to find some of the more isolated cemeteries. The Michelin atlas *Cemeteries and Memorials in Belgium and Northern France*, published by, and available from, the Commonwealth War Graves Commission is an indispensable purchase and one can also download detailed route directions as well as cemetery plans from the Commission's website (www.cwgc.org). The CWGC's own local direction signs will also help once in the general location of the cemetery.

For those with limited time, the following are the key cemeteries to visit to see the best of Lutyens's work on the Western Front

Monchy: the approach
La Neuville: the entrance pavilions
Béthune: the shelter building
Dernancourt: the entrance steps and buildings
Vailly: the buildings
Croisilles: the steps
HAC: the combination of architecture and planting
Serre Road No. 2: the architecture
Bagneux: setting of the War Stone
Etaples: pure theatre
Plus, of course, Thiepval, Villers Bretonneux and Faubourg d'Amiens,

The list below is a brief description of each 'Lutyens' cemetery to help those who wish to plan their own visits. The cemeteries have been grouped into a number of different types depending upon how and when they were created:

1. Battlefield Cemetery: Close to the Front Line and distinguished by haphazard grave layouts

2. Casualty Cemetery: Behind Front Line at Dressing Stations and Field Hospitals, and hence more ordered layouts

3. Commune Cemeteries: Extensions to existing village and town cemeteries. Layouts are generally regular and follow the plots of land available.

4. Post-War Cemeteries: Created after the War by bringing in bodies from surrounding area. Completely regular layouts.

NB Epernay French National Cemetery (Architect in France N A Rew, 267 burials) was subsequently closed.

ACHIET-LE-GRAND COMMUNAL CEMETERY EXTENSION ☆ ☆
Architect in France: G.H.Goldsmith

Commune cemetery with post-War additions. Simple axial layout with an entrance pergola off the village lane leading to the Great War Stone and cross. The layout continues beyond with another pergola and a small, stone, pitched roof shelter. Stone tool house with a flat stone roof that borrows details from the pergola cross members.

1,424 casualties

ADELAIDE CEMETERY ☆
Architect in France: G.H.Goldsmith

Battlefield cemetery enlarged after War. Gentle grass ramp leads into cemetery where Cross and War Stone face each other across open area in front of graves. Pitched roof shelter with radiating tile courses around entrance doorway in the manner of, say, Greywalls. The body from one of the 'Unknown' graves was removed in 1993 and reinterred at the Australian National War Memorial in Canberra.

955 casualties

AGNY MILITARY CEMETERY ☆
Architect in France: G.H.Goldsmith

Casualty cemetery with post-War burials. Cross on middle of long side. Delightful setting in the middle of mature trees.

408 casualties

AIX-NOULETTE COMMUNAL CEMETERY EXTENSION ☆
Architect in France: A.J.S. Hutton

Commune cemetery with additional post-War burials. Central axis of Cross, War Stone and a delightful hipped roofed shelter building with a steep pitch reminiscent of Lutyens's garden buildings at Temple Dinsley and Millmead.

1,190 casualties

ALBERT COMMUNAL CEMETERY EXTENSION ☆
Architect in France: G.H.Goldsmith

Commune cemetery. Entrance pergola.

862 casualties

ANNEUX BRITISH CEMETERY ☆ ☆

Architect in France: G.H.Goldsmith

Battlefield cemetery with post-War burials. Hip roofed entrance building with three tall Doric arches forms a 'T' with Cross and War Stone.

1,006 casualties

ASSEVILLIERS NEW BRITISH CEMETERY ☆ ☆ ☆

Architect in France: W.H. Cowlishaw

Post-War cemetery. Stone entrance building with gable roof and central arch forms a 'T' with War Stone and Cross.

776 casualties

BAGNEUX BRITISH CEMETERY ☆ ☆ ☆

Architect in France: G.H.Goldsmith

Casualty cemetery. Entrance, which is down a long track, is via an entrance pergola that frames the War Stone and a matching pergola on its other side. The War Stone is raised on a terrace so that it provides a silhouette on the skyline when viewed from within the cemetery. Cross relegated to midpoint on side boundary.

1,374 casualties

BANCOURT BRITISH CEMETERY ☆ ☆ ☆

Architect in France: G.H. Goldsmith

Battlefield cemetery with substantial post-War burials. Open framed brick entrance shelters with bellied Doric columns either side of War Stone, cross at rear. Alternative site considered for New Zealand Memorial (see Grévillers below)

2,480 casualties

BARLIN COMMUNAL CEMETERY EXTENSION ☆ ☆

Architect in France: J.H. Truelove

Casualty cemetery. Entrance up steps and through limestone shelter with pyramidal roof that forms a long-armed 'T' with War Stone and Cross just inside entrance.

1,166 casualties

BEACON CEMETERY ☆ ☆

Architect in France: G.H.Goldsmith

Battlefield cemetery with post-War burials. Entrance through brick, hipped roof shelter building that acts as a hinge between views of the War Stone and the Cross.

772 casualties

BEAULENCOURT BRITISH CEMETERY ☆ ☆

Architect in France: W.H. Cowlishaw

Casualty cemetery with substantial post-War burials. Entrance, War Stone and Cross form an 'L'. War Stone is raised on substantial terrace. Excellent stone toolhouse with pyramidal roof.

715 casualties

BEAURAINS ROAD BRITISH CEMETERY ☆

Architect in France: G.H. Goldsmith

Battlefield cemetery with post-War burials. Cross in front corner alongside road.

317 casualties

BELGIAN BATTERY CORNER CEMETERY ☆

Architect in France: J.H. Truelove

Battlefield cemetery. War Stone sits unusually close to the entrance and is approached end on, facing the Cross, which is at the back of the cemetery. Unusually elaborate Tool House with limestone dressing and radial tiles to heads of blind windows.

573 casualties

BELLACOURT MILITARY CEMETERY ☆ ☆ ☆

Architect in France: W.C. von Berg

Battlefield cemetery. Gentle upward slope from entrance to back of cemetery where the War Stone and the Cross are raised on successively high terraces to overlook the cemetery. Similar in many ways to Bagneux and shows how good design can be created with only modest components.

547 casualties

BÉTHUNE TOWN CEMETERY ☆ ☆ ☆

Architect in France: G.H. Goldsmith

Commune cemetery. Cross, War Stone and shelter in close association with one another. The latter is astonishing – a tiled, hipped roof supported on twenty limestone Doric columns and a small central room with a further eight perimeter columns as decoration. A complete one-off accompanied by an elaborate toolhouse that has the Land Tablets on walls that flank a stone niche.

3,004 casualties

BIRR CROSS ROADS CEMETERY ☆

Architect in France: N.A. Rew

Battlefield cemetery enlarged by post-War burials. Cross on axis with entrance with War Stone offset to one side.

833 casualties

BLAUWEPOORT FARM CEMETERY ☆

Architect in France: W.H. Cowlishaw

Battlefield cemetery. Cross by entrance. Brick shelter with flat limestone roof, unusual for a cemetery so small, on front wall. This cemetery does not appear on the IWGC's list of Lutyens cemeteries, however, the Approval Form denotes him as the Principal Architect.

82 casualties

BONNAY COMMUNAL CEMETERY EXTENSION ☆ ☆ ☆

Architect in France: W.H. Cowlishaw

Battlefield cemetery. Brick entrance wall wraps around low terrace containing Cross. This cemetery does not appear on the IWGC's list of Lutyens cemeteries, however, the Approval Form denotes him as the Principal Architect.

106 casualties

BRONFAY FARM MILITARY CEMETERY ☆ ☆

Architect in France: G.H. Goldsmith

Casualty cemetery. Access through brick shelter with flat stone roof and shallow circular drum. Entrance, War Stone and Cross form an 'L'.

537 casualties

BROWN'S COPSE CEMETERY ☆ ☆ ☆

Architect in France: G.H. Goldsmith

Battlefield cemetery with post-War burials. Tall limestone entrance building reminiscent of Serre Road No 2 (see below). Central axis of entrance, War Stone and Cross.

2,068 casualties

BRUAY COMMUNAL CEMETERY EXTENSION ☆

Architect in France: W.C. von Berg

Commune cemetery. Open site with boundary wall on two sides, low kerb on others. Cross and War Stone on lawn, latter set against wall.

412 casualties

BRUSSELS TOWN CEMETERY ☆

Architect in France: G.H. Goldsmith

Post-War burials of people who died while prisoners of war. Graves arranged in a square 'U' around Cross. This cemetery does not appear on the IWGC's list of Lutyens cemeteries, however, the Approval Form denotes him as the Principal Architect.

54 casualties

BUCQUOY ROAD CEMETERY ☆

Architect in France: G.H. Goldsmith

Casualty cemetery. War Stone raised on terrace by entrance steps, on axis with Cross. The pair is offset from the gravestones leaving a curiously blank grassed area that has been used for World War Two burials. The size of the cemetery suggests that this area was probably reserved for some form of shelter feature that was dropped.

1,091 casualties

BULLY-GRENAY COMMUNAL CEMETERY BRITISH EXTENSION ☆

Architect in France: J.H. Truelove

Commune cemetery. Central limestone path leading to central paved area containing Cross and War Stone, the former surrounded by four inset planters containing lavender.

803 casualties

BUZANCY MILITARY CEMETERY ☆

Architect in France J.H. Truelove

Battlefield cemetery with substantial post-War burials. Entrance steps set into grassy bank look somewhat incongruous. Cross on axis with entrance, small tufa shelter with limestone dressings and pitched, tiled roof is similar to other cemeteries around Reims (see e.g. Raperie, page 209).

321 casualties

CERISY-GAILLY FRENCH NATIONAL CEMETERY ☆

Architect in France: G.H. Goldsmith

Post-War cemetery with central Cross. Sits alongside Cerisy-Gailly Military Cemetery.

393 casualties

CERISY-GAILLY MILITARY CEMETERY ☆ ☆

Architect in France: W.H. Cowlishaw

Casualty cemetery enlarged by post-War burials. Entrance, Cross and shelter form a 'T' with a central War Stone. Fine shelter with hipped roof and limestone dressings: walls cut back below eaves to give roof greater dignity.

745 casualties

CHAMBRECY BRITISH CEMETERY ☆ ☆

Architect in France: J.H. Truelove

Post-War cemetery. Cross by central entrance, square shelter with pyramidal roof offset to one side.

437 casualties

CHAUNY COMMUNAL CEMETERY BRITISH EXTENSION ☆ ☆ ☆

Architect in France: A.J.S. Hutton

Post-War cemetery. Entrance on axis with Cross and War Stone, the latter framed by two small flat roofed shelters with a linking screen wall, and all of which sit on a grass terrace with limestone feature strips. Yellow stock brick instead of the more usual red. The cemetery also contains French and German gravestones and it is interesting to compare all three types together.

902 casualties

CHESTER FARM CEMETERY ☆

Architect in France: W.H. Cowlishaw

Battlefield cemetery. Cross in central position, entrance in one corner. Brick shelter (as Blauwepoort Farm) with flat limestone roof on axis with cross.

420 casualties

CHOCQUES MILITARY CEMETERY ☆

Architect in France: W.C. von Berg

Casualty cemetery with post-War burials. Entrance on axis with Cross, War Stone in isolation at rear raised on grassy knoll above cemetery and its surrounding wall. Lutyens fretted on the Approval Form about the proximity of the Cross to the Jewish graves but they are still relatively close so it is not readily apparent whether or not his concern was acted upon.

1,800 casualties

CITADEL NEW MILITARY CEMETERY ☆

Architect in France: A.J.S. Hutton

Casualty cemetery. Sloping grass entrance path framed by generous stepped planters leading to Cross.

378 casualties

COJEUL BRITISH CEMETERY ☆

Architect in France: G.H. Goldsmith

Battlefield cemetery. Entrance leads on to a terrace that seems to form no particular function, as if it was designed for War Stone. Cross at far end of cemetery from terrace.

349 casualties

COXYDE MILITARY CEMETERY ☆ ☆

Architect in France: G.H. Goldsmith

Casualty cemetery six miles behind Front Line enlarged after War. Twin brick pavilions with low hipped roofs and limestone details frame War Stone (see Dernancourt, page 191) with Cross at rear of cemetery on axis with entrance and War Stone.

1,507 casualties

CROISILLES BRITISH CEMETERY ☆ ☆ ☆

Architect in France: G.H. Goldsmith

Battlefield cemetery with post-War burials. For some unknown reason it seems to have been decided to create a major architectural feature here. The classical limestone shelter with Doric columns and pilasters sits, with the War Stone, on a broad terrace above the cemetery. A grand dog-leg flight of steps leads down into the cemetery. Cross on axis with first treads. One of the very best and woefully ignored in works about Lutyens.

1,171 casualties

CRUCIFIX CORNER CEMETERY ☆ ☆ ☆

Architect in France: G.H. Goldsmith

Battlefield cemetery with post-War burials. Cross and War Stone at far end of cemetery on axis with entrance – Cross being raised on a terrace with a background of trees.

660 casualties

DAOURS COMMUNAL CEMETERY EXTENSION ☆ ☆

Architect in France: G.H. Goldsmith

Commune cemetery. Cross on axis with entrance, War Stone offset to one side where it is framed by two brick and stone shelter buildings with low pitched hipped roofs. The layout differs substantially from Lutyens's original drawing on page 33.

1,231 casualties

DARTMOOR CEMETERY ☆

Architect in France: G.H. Goldsmith

Casualty cemetery. Cross and War Stone are offset to one end, the latter as the focus of a curved wall. Kenyon commented on the Approval Form 'It is apparently inevitable that the Stone should be in the NW corner instead of the east'.

768 casualties

DELSAUX FARM CEMETERY ☆

Architect in France: G.H. Goldsmith

Casualty cemetery. War Stone at heart of cemetery on eastern side, Cross at corner entrance with, unusually, the cemetery name inscribed on the Cross base.

495 casualties

DERNANCOURT COMMUNAL CEMETERY EXTENSION ☆ ☆ ☆

Architect in France: G.H. Goldsmith

Casualty cemetery adjacent to existing cemetery. Notable entrance sequence in which visitor ascends broad steps to enter cemetery through one of two hipped roofed brick pavilions that frame the War Stone. Land tablet in the entrance pavilion takes form of Lutyens gravestone used for Barbara and Ernest Chaplin. Cross at far end of cemetery opposite War Stone. One of the best.

2,162 casualties

DEVONSHIRE CEMETERY ☆
Architect in France: W.H. Cowlishaw

One of the most famous battlefield cemeteries, the dead having been buried in a trench from which they advanced on the first day of the Battle of the Somme. Offset Cross close to entrance. This cemetery does not appear on the IWGC's list of Lutyens cemeteries, however, the Approval Form denotes him as the Principal Architect.

163 casualties

DICKEBUSCH NEW MILITARY CEMETERY AND EXTENSION ☆ ☆ ☆
Architect in France: W.C. von Berg

Two battlefield cemeteries sit either site of village street and are designed as one. Entrances opposite one another on axis with Cross, which is in the Extension. War Stone alongside road in New Military Cemetery raised above the level of the top of the boundary wall so that it can be seen from the Extension.

1,151 casualties

DIVE COPSE BRITISH CEMETERY ☆
Architect in France: W.C. von Berg

Casualty cemetery. War Stone and Cross placed on adjacent boundaries of cemetery. Brick shelter with pitched roof.

589 casualties

DIVISIONAL CEMETERY DICKEBUSCH ☆ ☆ ☆
Architect in France: W.H. Cowlishaw

Battlefield cemetery with entrance, 'Chester Farm' type shelter and Cross forming an 'L'.

283 casualties

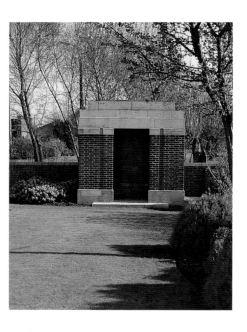

DOUCHY-LES-AYETTE BRITISH CEMETERY ☆ ☆ ☆

Architect in France: G.H. Goldsmith

Commune cemetery with post-War burials. Foursquare plan with Cross at centre. Short axis of entrance pergola (cf Achiet-le-Grand), Cross and shelter with matching pergola, long axis of tool house, Cross and War Stone. Enclosing stone wall with upper course cut back under the limestone capping. Delightful.

735 casualties

DUNKERQUE TOWN CEMETERY ☆

Architect in France: G.H. Goldsmith

Commune cemetery. Headstones in rows in front of Cross.

460 casualties

DURY MILL BRITISH CEMETERY ☆

Architect in France: W.H. Cowlishaw

Battlefield cemetery. Cross raised on low terrace overlooking graves.

335 casualties

ESQUELBECQ MILITARY CEMETERY ☆ ☆

Architect in France: A.J.S. Hutton

Casualty cemetery. Main axis of entrance, War Stone and shelter (see Adelaide, page 182) forming a 'T' with the Cross.

578 casualties

ETAPLES MILITARY CEMETERY ☆ ☆ ☆
Architect in France: G.H. Goldsmith

Casualty cemetery. The largest war cemetery in France and the largest designed by Lutyens. Near the site of the infamous training ground known as the 'Bull Ring' that featured in *The Monocled Mutineer*. The approach is through trees via the Cross on to a platform containing the War Stone and two tall quadrifon cenotaphs with stone flags – everything built in limestone. Radiating steps leading down to the graves, which are arranged in a variety of patterns showing the haphazard way in which the cemetery was developed. Designed to be seen from the adjacent railway line. Not to be missed.

10,761 casualties

ETERPIGNY BRITISH CEMETERY ☆
Architect in France: W.H. Cowlishaw

Battlefield cemetery. Steps down embankment split into two before reaching cemetery. Cross at rear. This cemetery does not appear on the IWGC's list of Lutyens cemeteries, however, the Approval Form denotes him as the Principal Architect.

66 casualties

FAUBOURG D'AMIENS CEMETERY, MEMORIAL TO THE MISSING AND FLYING SERVICES ☆ ☆ ☆

Casualty cemetery with post-War enlargement. Memorial to the Missing takes the form of a 380-ft limestone classical cloister with Doric columns that encloses the site from the busy road outside. Large brick panels on external elevation. The cloister contains the names of almost 35,000 missing and takes advantage of the irregular site shape, and is wrapped around itself to form three internal courtyards. Side axes terminated by symbolic stone gates. Four accesses from the road under tall archways give rise to a series of interpenetrating axial views focused on the Cross (which, unusually, is outside the cemetery) War Stone and the Flying Services Memorial to the Missing (which contains names of more than 1,000 airmen) incorporates a globe encircled by stars carved by Reid Dick). A much overlooked building in the Lutyens oeuvre. Essential viewing.

2,650 casualties

FAVREUIL BRITISH CEMETERY ☆ ☆
Architect in France: W.H. Cowlishaw

Battlefield cemetery with post-War burials. Entrance, Cross and flat roofed shelter are linked by limestone path with inset stone panels, the same detailing being picked up in the shelter. Unusual to find a path of this length in a cemetery. Boundary planting of poplars provides a landmark for the cemetery.

399 casualties

FEUCHY BRITISH CEMETERY ☆ ☆
Architect in France: N.A. Rew

Battlefield cemetery. Entrance through stone shelter on axis with Cross. Shelter identical to Assevillers (AIF Cowlishaw), indicating that Lutyens rather than the AIFs had strong involvement in its design. This cemetery does not appear on the IWGC's list of Lutyens cemeteries, however, the Approval Form denotes him as the Principal Architect.

209 casualties

FEUCHY CHAPEL BRITISH CEMETERY ☆
Architect in France: G.H. Goldsmith

Battlefield cemetery with post-War burials. Entrance, War Stone and Cross form an eccentric 'T'.

1,103 casualties

FIENVILLERS BRITISH CEMETERY ☆
Architect in France: A.J.S. Hutton

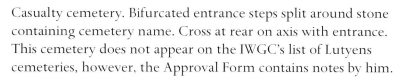

Casualty cemetery. Bifurcated entrance steps split around stone containing cemetery name. Cross at rear on axis with entrance. This cemetery does not appear on the IWGC's list of Lutyens cemeteries, however, the Approval Form contains notes by him.

124 casualties

FOSSE NO. 10 COMMUNAL CEMETERY EXTENSION ☆

Architect in France: G.H. Goldsmith

Casualty cemetery. Long and thin with Cross towards rear. The memorial to the French dead in the adjacent Communal Cemetery, with a recumbent soldier resting on a pile of stone rubble is a stark constrast to the memorials in UK towns and villages. It was the fear of such memorials that had helped to prompt the 1919 exhibition at the Victoria & Albert Museum (see page 49).

471 casualties

FOUQUIÈRES CHURCHYARD EXTENSION ☆

Architect in France: A.J.S. Hutton

Casualty cemetery. Awkward shape, with entrance at an angle via paired staircases. Cross and War Stone on adjacent boundaries, latter on the west rather than the east.

387 casualties

GÉZAINCOURT COMMUNAL CEMETERY EXTENSION ☆

Architect in France: G.H. Goldsmith

Casualty cemetery. War Stone raised on a terrace at entrance of site with Cross in opposite corner of cemetery. Gargoyle detail on tool house comes from Lindisfarne Castle.

596 casualties

GONNEHEM BRITISH CEMETERY ☆

Architect in France: W.H. Cowlishaw

Casualty cemetery with some post-War burials. Entrance in one corner, graves face Cross which has curved planting area behind.

200 casualties

GRÉVILLERS BRITISH CEMETERY AND NEW ZEALAND MEMORIAL TO THE MISSING ☆ ☆ ☆

Architect in France: G.H. Goldsmith

Casualty cemetery with post-War burials. Tall brick, hip roofed entrance shelter on central axis with War Stone and Cross. Rear wall of cemetery formed by New Zealand Memorial to the Missing, which is a stone wall with niches terminated by shelter building and matching toolhouse with pyramidal roofs.

2,086 casualties

GROVE TOWN CEMETERY ☆ ☆

Architect in France: A.J.S. Hutton

Casualty cemetery. Entrance, War Stone and Cross on axis, shelter with severe stone pitched roof offset at right angles on alignment with War Stone. Cross raised on terrace at rear of cemetery.

1,392 casualties

H.A.C. CEMETERY ☆ ☆ ☆

Architect in France: G.H. Goldsmith

Battlefield cemetery with post-War burials. A gentle flight of steps, with each tread treated as a brick platform with stone edging, leads into the cemetery. The War Stone and Cross are at the entrance and form an elongated 'L' with the shelter, which is at the rear on axis with the entrance. Despite appearances from the front, the brick and hipped roofed shelter, with its bellied Doric columns, is U shaped. The poplars that surround the cemetery form an arresting silhouette and the planting provides a good example of the Commission's policy of using larger shrubs at the end of rows of headstones to mark the mark pathways, in this case leading from the entrance to the shelter.

1,832 casualties

HAMEL MILITARY CEMETERY ☆ ☆

Architect in France: A.J.S. Hutton

Casualty cemetery. Stone shelter with very shallow pitched stone roof on small terrace facing Cross on similar terrace.

487 casualties

HANGARD COMMUNAL CEMETERY EXTENESION ☆ ☆

Architect in France: G.H. Goldsmith

Battlefield cemetery with post-War burials. Rubble stone entrance bastion wrapped around steps that make two right-angled turns before the cemetery is entered, wrapping around the Cross in the process.

563 casualties

HAPPY VALLEY BRITISH CEMETERY ☆

Architect in France: W.H. Cowlishaw

Battlefield cemetery. Cross offset in one corner.

76 casualties

HEILLY STATION CEMETERY ☆ ☆

Architect in France: G.H. Goldsmith

Casualty cemetery. Flat-roofed brick entrance cloister with combination of arches and square openings, the latter with heavy stone quoins. The dense nature of the burials (sometimes three to a grave) means that there was insufficient space on the gravestones for the regimental badges, which are inset into the cloister wall. War Stone and Cross on adjacent external boundaries of cemetery.

2,890 casualties

HEM FARM MILITARY CEMETERY ☆

Architect in France: G.H. Goldsmith

Battlefield cemetery with post-War burials. War Stone on grass terrace between twin entrance gates with, unusually, the inscription facing the road rather than the cemetery. Cross on axis at rear of cemetery.

596 casualties

HÉNINEL-CROISILLES ROAD CEMETERY ☆

Architect in France: N.A. Rew

Battlefield cemetery with post-War burials. Classic small cemetery with low stone walls and Cross at rear.

307 casualties

HERSIN COMMUNAL CEMETERY EXTENSION ☆

Architect in France: W.H. Cowlishaw

Commune cemetery. Cross at rear on low platform. Entrance from Communal Cemetery framed by beech hedges and yew trees.

224 casualties

HOOGE CRATER CEMETERY ☆ ☆ ☆

Architect in France: N.A. Rew

Battlefield cemetery greatly enlarged after the War. Dramatic entrance with War Stone at the centre of a circular symbolic crater with two open pitched roofed pavilions framing Cross and entrance to graves on downward slope. The image from the road at the rear of the site, with the regular rows of graves set against the hillside is particularly memorable.

5,922 casualties

HOUCHIN BRITISH CEMETERY ☆

Architect in France: J.R. Truelove

Casualty cemetery. Limestone steps up grass bank into cemetery, steps, War Stone and Cross forming an 'L'. Boundary trees provide an identifying landmark.

700 casualties

HUTS MILITARY CEMETERY, DICKEBUSCH ☆

Architect in France: G.H. Goldsmith

Battlefield cemetery. Entrance, Cross and War Stone form an 'L' with a brick, pitched roof shelter with stone classical detailing in the corner of the cemetery.

1,094 casualties

JONCHERY-SUR-VESLE BRITISH CEMETERY ☆ ☆

Architect in France: J.R. Truelove

Post-War cemetery. Entrance, Cross and shelter with pyramidal roof on axis linked by narrow limestone path.

361 casualties

KEMMEL CHATEAU MILITARY CEMETERY ☆ ☆

Architect in France: G.H. Goldsmith

Battlefield cemetery. Axial alignment of entrance, War Stone (facing the entrance rather than the graves) and Cross. Entrance feature formed by twin brick arches, one of which is open and one containing a niche with a seat.

1,135 casualties

KEMMEL NO. 1 FRENCH CEMETERY ☆ ☆

Architect in France: W.H. Cowlishaw

Battlefield cemetery with later burials. Sits on top of planted embankment, approached by straight flight of stairs leading to Cross. Combined shelter cum toolshed similar in design to Chester Farm.

296 casualties

KLEIN VIERSTRAAT BRITISH CEMETERY ☆ ☆ ☆

Architect in France: J.R. Truelove

Battlefield cemetery with later burials, adjacent to Kemmel No 1. Distinctive flat roofed shelter with alternating bands of limestone and grey/brown stone and twin Doric columns. Feature windows inside shelter with decorative grilles. Shelter, War Stone and Cross form a loose 'L'. Shelter is a 'one-off' and one of the best.

804 casualties

LA CLYTTE MILITARY CEMETERY ☆ ☆

Architect in France: N.A. Rew

Casualty cemetery with post-War burials. Twin flat-roofed brick pavilions at entrance frame War Stone with Cross at far end of cemetery. Height of pavilions has been lowered since originally constructed.

1,082 casualties

LA LAITERIE MILITARY CEMETERY ☆ ☆

Architect in France: G.H. Goldsmith

Battlefield cemetery with later burials. Entrance, War Stone and 'Dive Copse' type shelter form an 'L' with the Cross in the middle of cemetery.

751 casualties

LA NEUVILLE BRITISH CEMETERY ☆ ☆ ☆

Architect in France: G.H. Goldsmith

Casualty cemetery with twin entrance pavilions that are a complete 'one-off' – limestone, flat roofed and angular. They are the most extreme form of Lutyens's 'Elemental Mode' on the Western Front and could almost be the work of Holden. The pavilions are at the two front corners of the site – one framing the view of the War Stone and the other, the Cross. The style of the pavilion was used by Goldsmith in his design for the shelter at the Glageon Communal Cemetery Extension.

866 casualties

LAPUGNOY MILITARY CEMETERY ☆

Architect in France: G.H. Goldsmith

Casualty cemetery. Slopes gently downhill from entrance with War Stone halfway. Cross in corner near entrance

1,323 casualties

LARCH WOOD (RAILWAY CUTTING) CEMETERY ☆ ☆

Architect in France: W.H. Cowlishaw

Battlefield cemetery with post-War burials. Feature with steps and planters leads down to a grass path to cemetery proper. Entrance, Cross and War Stone form an 'L'. War Stone framed by open and blind brick arches, all three sitting on a raised terrace.

856 casualties

LA VILLE-AUX-BOIX BRITISH CEMETERY ☆ ☆

Architect in France: J.R. Truelove

Post-War cemetery. War Stone by entrance flanked by pitched roof shelters, Cross at rear on axis with entrance. Unusually low boundary wall.

564 casualties

LE TOUQUET-PARIS-PLAGE COMMUNAL CEMETERY ☆

Architect in France: W.H. Cowlishaw

Commune cemetery. Limestone entrance paving around steps at entrance reminiscent of that at Marshcourt.

142 casualties

LILLERS COMMUNAL CEMETERY AND EXTENSION ☆ ☆ ☆

Architect in France: A.J.S. Hutton

Commune cemetery. Cross and War Stone, both raised on podia, face each other across the cemetery. Lutyens had originally wanted the latter to be sited in the stream that forms the eastern boundary of the cemetery.

894 casualties

LONDON CEMETERY, NEUVILLE-VITASSE ☆ ☆

Architect in France: G.H. Goldsmith

Battlefield cemetery with post-War burials. Cross just inside entrance with stone flat roofed shelter (see Pernes page 207) offset to one side.

747 casualties

MAPLE COPSE CEMETERY ☆ ☆

Architect in France: N.A. Rew

Battlefield cemetery that is unusually large given the relatively few burials, the explanation being that 230 bodies that it originally contained were destroyed in later fighting. Solid flat roofed entrance building cum shelter aligned with Cross. Enclosed by ha-ha.

308 casualties

MARFAUX BRITISH CEMETERY ☆ ☆

Architect in France: A.J.S. Hutton

Post-War cemetery. Entrance (overshadowed by large lime trees), War Stone and stone shelter on successively higher terraces, Cross in opposite corner from entrance. Shelter contains memorial tablet (not by Lutyens) to ten Missing from the New Zealand Cyclist Battalion.

1,109 casualties

MAZINGARBE COMMUNAL CEMETERY EXTENSION ☆ ☆

Architect in France: W.H. Cowlishaw

Commune cemetery. Extensive use of brick for the surrounding walls and the paving that divides the cemetery into four. Cross, surprisingly is not in central position has one of the 'quarters' by itself. Brick shelter with flat stone roof. Nicely detailed wall containing integral planters at corners and midpoints. This cemetery does not appear on the IWGC's list of Lutyens cemeteries, however, the Approval Form denotes him as the Principal Architect.

248 casualties

MÉAULTE MILITARY CEMETERY ☆

Architect in France: A.J.S. Hutton

Battlefield cemetery. Cross is at one end, offset from the entrance. Surrounded by low brick wall inside which is a taller hedge. Unusual red sandstone headstones.

312 casualties

MÉRICOURT L'ABBÉ COMMUNAL CEMETERY EXTENSION ☆

Architect in France: A.J.S. Hutton

Commune cemetery. Cross in central position on axis with entrance.

441 casualties

MOEUVRES COMMUNAL CEMETERY EXTENSION ☆ ☆

Architect in France: G.H. Goldsmith

Commune cemetery with post-War burials. Entrance through stone shelter with pitched roof on axis with Cross, War Stone offset to the east. Low-angled stone edging (reminiscent of Lutyens's grave for Julius Drewe at Holy Trinity Church, Drewsteignton, Devon) defines a plot of German graves.

565 casualties

MONCHY BRITISH CEMETERY ☆ ☆ ☆

Architect in France: G.H. Goldsmith

Battlefield cemetery. Splendid axial view of entrance piers, arch, War Stone and blind arch, all in limestone, the more unexpected by being approached from an oblique angle. Cross in central position towards rear of cemetery. The brick shelter building (identical to Huts) seems curiously out of place.

581 casualties

MONS COMMUNAL CEMETERY ☆

Architect in France: W.H. Cowlishaw

Commune cemetery of post-War burials. Cross
and War Stone either side of access road.

393 casualties

MORY ABBEY MILITARY CEMETERY ☆

Architect in France: G.H. Goldsmith

Battlefield cemetery with post-War burials. Stone staircase
turns through right angles to focus on stone seat at rear
of cemetery. Cross by entrance, War Stone on eastern side
with no apparent relationship between the two.

619 casualties

NEUVILLE-SOUS-MONTREUIL
INDIAN CEMETERY ☆

Architect in France: W.H. Cowlishaw

Casualty cemetery. Small feature stone wall cum
seat. No Cross. This cemetery does not appear on the
IWGC's list of Lutyens cemeteries, however, the
Approval Form denotes him as the Principal Architect.

25 casualties

NOEUX-LES-MINES COMMUNAL
CEMETERY AND EXTENSION ☆ ☆

Architect in France: J.R. Truelove

Commune cemetery. Two strips of plots arranged as an 'L'
around the existing civil graves. Twin pavilions linked by a
curved brick wall frame the War Stone and broad steps down
to the main graves. Cross at the end of the other leg of the
'L'. As ever, the repose of the British graves forms a stark
contrast to the haphazard arrangement of the civil graves.

1,284 casualties

NOYELLES-SUR-MER CHINESE CEMETERY ☆ ☆

Architect in France: J.R. Truelove

Casualty cemetery. Chinese style entrance gateway surmounted by pine cone.

842 casualties

ONTARIO CEMETERY ☆ ☆

Architect in France: G.H. Goldsmith

Battlefield cemetery with post-War burials. Circular limestone paving entrance feature with inset stone panels. Entrance, Cross and twin stone shelters with flat roofs form a 'T'.

336 casualties

OOSTTAVERNE WOOD CEMETERY ☆ ☆ ☆

Architect in France: N.A. Rew

Battlefield cemetery enlarged after the War. Handsome hipped roofed entrance building cum shelter, bottom half in limestone, top half in local stone, on axial alignment with War Stone and Cross.

1,119 casualties

ORANGE TRENCH CEMETERY ☆

Architect in France: W.H. Cowlishaw

Battlefield cemetery. Cross in corner opposite offset entrance. This cemetery does not appear on the IWGC's list of Lutyens cemeteries. However, the Approval Form denotes him as the Principal Architect.

118 casualties

PERNES BRITISH CEMETERY ☆ ☆
Architect in France: W.C. von Berg

Casualty cemetery. Gently curved approach up steps into the cemetery through the flat roofed stone shelter, similar to London Cemetery, Neuville-Vitasse. Cross on axis with shelter, War Stone at centre of eastern boundary raised on level grass terrace on this sloping site.

1,075 casualties

PERTH CEMETERY (CHINA WALL) ☆
Architect in France: J.R. Truelove

Battlefield cemetery substantially enlarged by post-War burials. Axial alignment of entrance, War Stone and Cross. Shelter (similar to Ontario but in brick) offset to one side.

2,791 casualties

PUCHEVILLERS BRITISH CEMETERY ☆
Architect in France: W.H. Cowlishaw

Casualty cemetery. Cross and War Stone uncomfortably close together in front corner of cemetery. Brick shelter with stone quoins gives access to separate enclosure at rear containing later burials – an unusual arrangement

1,763 casualties

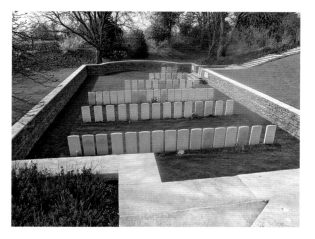

QUARRY CEMETERY, MARQUION ☆ ☆
Architect in France: G.H. Goldsmith

Battlefield cemetery. Steps lead down to reveal enclosing walls designed as a church with an apsidal end. Cross is raised on a substantial stone platform where the altar would be. Charming.

68 casualties

QUÉANT COMMUNAL CEMETERY BRITISH EXTENSION ☆

Architect in France: G.H. Goldsmith

Battlefield cemetery. Open entrance on to limestone platform with Cross.

276 casualties

QUÉANT ROAD CEMETERY ☆ ☆

Architect in France: G.H. Goldsmith

Casualty cemetery with substantial post-War burials. Cross and War Stone either side of entrance, brick, hip roofed shelter at rear on axis with entrance.

2,377 casualties

RAILWAY DUGOUTS BURIAL GROUND ☆ ☆ ☆

Architect in France: J.R. Truelove

Battlefield cemetery with unusually haphazard layout of graves. Order is given to the apparent chaos with two entrance arches leading to a *rond point* at the centre of which is a War Stone. Cross in middle of cemetery.

2,459 casualties

RAMSCAPPELLE ROAD MILITARY CEMETERY ☆

Architect in France: G.H. Goldsmith

Battlefield cemetery considerably enlarged after the War. Entrance, Cross and War Stone form a 'T' with octagonal stone shelter tucked in the corner. Steps from entrance lead down to a mini terrace from which access to the cemetery proper incorporates the familiar Lutyens device of a concave cutaway leading down to a full circle, for example, Folly Farm.

841 casualties

RAPERIE BRITISH CEMETERY ☆

Architect in France: J.R. Truelove

Post-War cemetery. Entrance, Cross and War Stone on axis with twin pitch roofed stone 'Buzancy' shelters either side of Cross inside entrance.

600 casualties

RIBEMONT COMMUNAL CEMETERY EXTENSION ☆

Architect in France: G.H. Goldsmith

Casualty cemetery with post-War burials. Entrance leads to War Stone, raised on a terrace, which faces Cross, similarly treated, across the cemetery.

498 casualties

RIDGE WOOD MILITARY CEMETERY ☆

Architect in France: G.H. Goldsmith

Battlefield cemetery. Entrance, War Stone and Cross form an 'L' with the latter two being at opposite ends of the cemetery. Twin pavilions, similar to La Clytte, that framed the War Stone have been demolished.

619 casualties

ROSIÈRES COMMUNAL CEMETERY EXTENSION ☆

Architect in France: G.H. Goldsmith

Casualty cemetery with substantial post-War burials. Cross on axis with entrance.

426 casualties

STE EMILIE VALLEY CEMETERY ☆

Architect in France: A.J.S. Hutton

Battlefield cemetery with post-War burials. Central cross aligned with entrance from quadrant of seven steps set into grass bank, with further steps inside between low planters.

513 casualties

ST MARTIN CALVAIRE BRITISH CEMETERY ☆

Architect in France: G.H. Goldsmith

Battlefield cemetery. Notable entrance steps, the lower ones projecting beyond the boundary wall, the upper ones deeply recessed into the embankment upon which the cemetery is built.

228 casualties

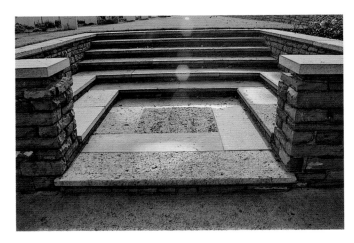

ST PIERRE CEMETERY, AMIENS ☆

Architect in France: W.C. von Berg

Commune cemetery with central War Stone and Cross.

676 casualties

SANCTUARY WOOD CEMETERY ☆ ☆ ☆

Architect in France: N.A. Rew

Battlefield cemetery considerably enlarged after the War. Dramatic shape of a quarter circle with the entrance through a large, hipped roofed shelter building with Doric columns that are paired on the cemetery side. Axial composition of entrance, War Stone and Cross.

1,989 casualties

SANDPITS BRITISH CEMETERY ☆

Architect in France: G.H. Goldsmith

Battlefield cemetery. Inset 'L'-shaped stairs gives access to this triangular cemetery with Cross at apex. Unusually the Land Tablet is combined on a plaque with the cemetery name.

394 casualties

SERRE ROAD CEMETERY NO. 2 ☆ ☆ ☆

Architect in France: G.H. Goldsmith

Battlefield cemetery surrounded by substantial post-War burials. Classical limestone entrance pavilion framing axis to War Stone, which sits at the front of the original burials, at the Cross, on a terrace at the rear of the cemetery. The Cross is itself framed by two open classical pavilions with slightly upswept roofs in a subtle Japanese style. One of the best: see this if nothing else.

7,126 casualties

SPOILBANK CEMETERY AND EXTENSION ☆

Architect in France: W.H. Cowlishaw

Battlefield cemetery enlarged after the War. Cross on axis with entrance. Lutyens's nephew, Charles John Lutyens is buried in the cemetery.

520 casualties

SUNKEN ROAD CEMETERY, BOISLEUX ST MARC ☆

Architect in France: G.H. Goldsmith

Casualty cemetery. Broad entrance steps twist through 90° around the Cross into the cemetery.

416 casualties

THIEPVAL ANGLO-FRENCH CEMETERY AND MEMORIAL TO THE MISSING OF THE SOMME ☆ ☆ ☆

Architect in France: G.H. Goldsmith

Tall brick multi-arched structure with limestone dressings and panels on to which are carved the names of the 72,099 men, the majority of whom died in the battles for the surrounding area and whose bodies were not found and identified. War Stone at the heart of the memorial. The Cross is at the far end of a small cemetery that was designed as a symbolic gesture on conjunction with the Memorial and contains 600 graves (300 Commonwealth, 300 French).

600 casualties

TILLOY BRITISH CEMETERY ☆ ☆

Architect in France: G.H. Goldsmith

Casualty cemetery with post-War burials. Entrance, brick hipped roofed shelter (similar to Queant Road but with three arches) and Cross form an 'L' with the War Stone being offset.

1,642 casualties

VAILLY BRITISH CEMETERY ☆ ☆ ☆

Architect in France: N.A. Rew

Post-War cemetery. Entrance shelter and matching toolshed with niche stand either side of War Stone, which faces Cross across the cemetery. The buildings, which have battered limestone walls and pitched limestone roofs, are particularly fine.

675 casualties

VAULX HILL CEMETERY ☆ ☆

Architect in France: G.H. Goldsmith

Battlefield cemetery with post-War burials. Shallow entrance steps focussed on War Stone, which is at the midpoint of the eastern boundary, facing the Cross on the western one. The two rear corners have 'sentry box' shelters with shallow pitched, hipped roofs with false timber rafter feet made from concrete. The sentinel theme is continued by the clipped yews around the boundary.

856 casualties

VENDRESSE BRITISH CEMETERY ☆ ☆

Architect in France: J.R. Truelove

Post-War cemetery. Shallow flight of bifurcated entrance steps around Cross. 'Buzancy' style shelter at rear on axis with Cross.

667 casualties

VILLERS-BOCAGE COMMUNAL CEMETERY EXTENSION ☆

Architect in France: G.H. Goldsmith

Casualty cemetery. Twin square stepped entrance platforms provide access to cemetery through low wall. Cross at entrance.

60 casualties

VILLERS-BRETONNEUX MILITARY CEMETERY AND AUSTRALIAN MEMORIAL TO THE MISSING ☆ ☆ ☆

Architect in France: G.H. Goldsmith

Post-War cemetery. Large twin classical pavilions in limestone (the largest designed by Lutyens) flank the War Stone and frame the approach up the gently curving convex slope, between rows of graves made after the Armistice to the Cross and Australian Memorial. Over 10,700 names are carved on the walls flanking the tower that forms the centrepiece of the Memorial. The wall is terminated by loggias with aedicules and stone flags, as on the tower. The tower, loggias, pavilions and toolsheds all have pyramidal roofs. Visitors should find time to walk around the back of the memorial to see the battered brick back of the memorial wall. Not to be missed.

2,141 casualties

VOORMEZEELE ENCLOSURES NO. 1 AND NO. 2 ☆ ☆ ☆

Architect in France: W.C. von Berg

Battlefield cemetery within village envelope. Unusual twin double pitch hipped roofed limestone pavilions frame War Stone and form a 'T' with the Cross.

593 casualties

VOORMEZEELE ENCLOSURE NO. 3 ☆

Architect in France: W.C. von Berg

Battlefield cemetery with post-War burials. Entrance, Cross and War Stone form a 'T'. Surprisingly, given its size, there is no shelter.

1,611 casualties

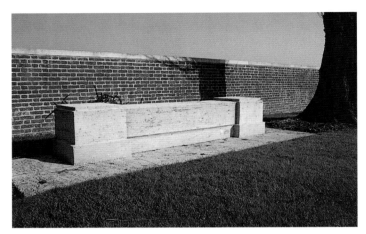

WANCOURT BRITISH CEMETERY ☆ ☆

Architect in France: G.H. Goldsmith

Battlefield cemetery with post-War burials. Flat roofed brick entrance building set back from entrance piers to form small courtyard frames view to War Stone, which forms an 'L' with the Cross.

1,934 casualties

WARLENCOURT BRITISH CEMETERY ☆ ☆ ☆

Architect in France: G.H. Goldsmith

Post-War cemetery. Substantial entrance building, almost a mini version of the Menin Gate, containing brick herringbone paving. Cross at far end on axis with entrance, War Stone in middle of long side.

3,505 casualties

WINDMILL BRITISH CEMETERY ☆

Architect in France: W.H. Cowlishaw

Battlefield cemetery. Cross raised on terrace overlooking graves. Pleached trees to screen adjacent building.

402 casualties

WOODS CEMETERY, ZILLEBEKE ☆ ☆

Architect in France: W.H. Cowlishaw

Battlefield cemetery. Shelter cum tool store as Chester Farm. The entrance and shelter form an obtuse angle with the Cross as a hinge.

326 casualties

WYSCHAETE MILITARY CEMETERY ☆

Architect in France: W.H. Cowlishaw

Post-War cemetery. Entrance steps, Cross and War Stone form a loose 'L'.

1,002 casualties

ZUYDCOOTE MILITARY CEMETERY ☆

Architect in France: G.H. Goldsmith

Casualty cemetery. Entrance and Cross raised on terrace overlooking graves.

326 casualties

APPENDIX 3:
PRIVATE MEMORIALS

RAYMOND ASQUITH ☆

Bronze wreath above Latin inscription carved directly into the wall of the church by Eric Gill. The son of the Prime Minister, Asquith died in an attack on the Somme on 15 September 1916 and is buried in Guillemont Road, Cemetery

Church of St Andrew, Mells, Somerset

WILLIAM CONGREVE ☆

Congreve has the unusual distinction of two Lutyens designed marble wall tablets – one, with a broken pediment, at his home in Staffordshire and another, simpler affair, in Corbie, near to where he is buried. Congreve was a Major in the Rifle Brigade and won the VC, DSO and MC. He is one of only a handful of sons with fathers who had been similarly honoured. He died on 20 July 1917 and is buried in the Corbie Communal Cemetery Extension.

a) Church of St John the Baptist, Stowe-By-Chartley, Staffordshire
b) Church of St Etiennes, Corbie, Somme, France

EDWARD HORNER ☆

Bronze equestrian statue by the painter Sir Alfred Munnings, on a tall plinth by Lutyens. The plinth contains his original wooden grave marker. Relocated from the family chapel in 2007. Horner was a Lieutenant in the 18th (Queen Mary's Own) Hussars. Horner died on 21 November 1917 and is buried in Rocquigny-Equancourt Road British Cemetery

Church of St Andrew, Mells, Somerset

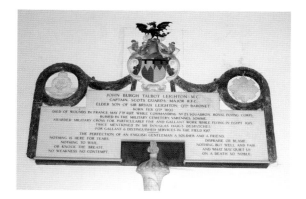

JOHN LEIGHTON ☆

Marble wall tablet below the propeller from his plane. Leighton was a Captain in the Scots Guards who had transferred to the Royal Flying Corps, winning the Military Cross in Egypt in 1915. He died of wounds on 7 May 1917 on the Somme and is buried in Varennes Military Cemetery on the Somme.

Church of St Michael and All Angels, Alberbury, Shropshire

DEREK LUTYENS ☆

Stone cross with flared shaft on square stone base. The cross contained bronze wings that, at the time of writing, had been stolen. Derek was one of five of Lutyens's nephews to die in the War. A member of the Royal Air Force he died when his plane crashed at Mytchett Heath, Surrey on 8 May 1918.

Church of St Michael, Busbridge, Surrey

FRANCIS MCLAREN ☆

An unusual wooden headboard surmounted by a carved badge of the Royal Flying Corps, in which McLaren was a Second Lieutenant. He died on 30 August 1917 after his plane crashed into the sea near Montrose. McLaren was the sitting MP for Spalding, which connection gave rise to Lutyens's commission to design the town's war memorial.

Church of St John the Baptist, Busbridge, Surrey

MARC NOBLE ☆

Elegant marble wall tablet. Noble was a Second Lieutenant in the Royal Field Artillery and died near Ypres on 1 July 1917. He is buried in Ferme-Olivier Cemetery.

Church of St Ethelbert, East Wretham, Norfolk

HENRY TENNANT ☆

An unusual memorial mounted at the head of the arch to the North Chapel and designed to be seen from both sides. It incorporates his wooden grave marker and used to contain his sword too, until it was stolen. Tennant was a Second Lieutenant in the Royal Flying Corps who died on 27 May 1917 and is buried in La Chapelette British and Indian Cemetery.

Church of St Mary the Virgin, Rolvenden, Kent

NOTES

One: Tyringham

1 Letter from Private Raymond H. Dorrough reported in the *Bucks Standard*, 30 September 1916.

2 Reported in the *Bucks Standard*, 21 April 1917.

3 His body was later transferred to the Dar Es Salaam War Cemetery when graves from transferred from a number of isolated sites throughout Tanzania to safeguard maintenance. Curiously, the plaque on Tyringham Church records the date of Gubbins's death as 18 May but the CWGC records confirm the date as 13 May so it is presumed that that somewhere along the line an 8 got mistaken for a 3.

Two: The Architect Established

1 Jane Ridley, *The Architect And His Wife: A Life of Sir Edwin Lutyens* (Chatto and Windus, 2002), p.56.

2 The memorial has a curious history in that its foundation stone was laid as an expedient during the Duke of Connaught's visit in 1910, before the memorial itself had been designed. It cost £18,000 and Lutyens received a fee of £300. It stands in Herman Eckstein Park, Johannesburg.

3 Clayre Percy and Jane Ridley (editors), *The Letters of Edwin Lutyens to his wife Lady Emily* (Collins, 1985), p.300.

4 Milner lies in a Lutyens designed grave in the churchyard of St Mary the Virgin, Salehurst, Sussex.

Three: The War Stone

1 Milner is buried in a tomb designed by Lutyens in the churchyard of St Mary the Virgin, Salehurst, Sussex.

2 The Belgian Government passed similar legislation in October 1917.

3 Quoted in Philip Longworth, *The Unending Vigil* (Leo Cooper, 2003), p.20.

4 *Ibid.*, p.21.

5 Lord Derby's daughter-in-law, Maureen Stanley, is buried with his son, Oliver, in a grave with a Lutyens designed headstone in the churchyard of St Lawrence in Waltham St Lawrence.

6 Edwin Lutyens to Fabian Ware, letter of 27 May 1917, CWGC archives.

7 Letter of 27 May 1917, *ibid.*

8 Percy and Ridley, *op. cit.*, p.349.

9 Minutes of Meeting held at DGR&E, GHQ 14 July 1917, CWGC archives.

10 *Ibid.*

11 *Ibid.*

12 *Ibid.* (additional notes).

13 Percy and Ridley, *op. cit.*, p.352 (letter of 24 August 1917).

14 Herbert Baker to Fabian Ware, letter of 27 July 1917, CWGC archives.

15 *Ibid.*

16 Charles Aitken, undated comments on Minutes of Meeting on 14 July 1917, CWGC archives.

17 Edwin Lutyens to Fabian Ware, letter of 3 August 1917, CWGC archives.

18 James Barrie to Fabian Ware, letter of 25 July 1917, CWGC archives.

19 Percy and Ridley, *op. cit.*, p.351 (letter of 23 August 1917).

20 Barrie's proposal for the bells had been circulating for some time because Lutyens referred to it in his letter of 27 May 1917 to Ware. Somewhat uncharitably perhaps, in view of the support that Barrie was to give him, although Lutyens supported the principle of the bells to Ware he suggested that the idea should be ruled out because of the wear and tear that a swaying bell would cause to its bearings.

21 Lord Lytton to Fabian Ware, letter of 6 August 1917, CWGC archives.

22 Edwin Lutyens to Fabian Ware, letter of 3 August 1917, CWGC archives.

23 Ibid.

24 Edwin Lutyens to Fabian Ware, letter of 7 August 1917, CWGC archives.

25 Edwin Lutyens to Fabian Ware, letter of 20 August 1917, CWGC archives.

26 *Ibid.*

27 Percy and Ridley, *op cit.*, p.355 (letter of 29 August 1917).

28 *Ibid.* p.355 (letter of 5 September 1917).

29 Edwin Lutyens, 'Graveyards of the Battlefields', 28 August 1917, CWGC archives

30 *Ibid.*

31 Percy and Ridley, *op. cit.*, p.355 (letter of 14 October 1917).

32 *Ibid.*, p.356 (letter of 14 October 1917).

33 Fabian Ware, File Note of Meeting of 17 October 1917, CWGC archives.

34 Minutes of Meeting of 21 September 1917, CWGC archives.

35 Fabian Ware to Charles Aitken, letter of 11 November 1917, CWGC archives.

36 Sir Frederic Kenyon, 'War Graves: How the Cemeteries Abroad Will Be Designed', Report to the Imperial War Graves Commission, 1918.

37 Percy and Ridley, *op. cit.*, p.363.

38 *Ibid.*, p.367 (letter of 3 September 1918).

39 *Ibid.*, p.402 (letter of 11 September 1924).

40 Quoted in Gavin Stamp, *The Memorial to the Missing of the Somme* (Profile Books, 2006), p.82.

41 Hussey, *The Life of Sir Edwin Lutyens* (Country Life, 1950), p.375.

42 Sir Edwin Lutyens to Fabian Ware, letter of 13 February 1920, CWGC archives.

Four: Southampton and London: A Tale of Two Cenotaphs

1 Sir Frederic Kenyon to Colonel Durham, letter of 24 April 1920, CWGC archives.

2 Sir Sidney Kimber, *Thirty-Eight Years Of Public Life In Southampton 1910–1948*, (Privately Published, 1949).

3 *Ibid.*

4 Earl of Derby to Lionel Earle, Letter of 17 May 1919, National Archives WORK 21/74.

5 War Cabinet Peace Celebrations Committee, Minutes of Meeting of 1 July 1919, National Archives CAB 52/27.

6 Allan Greenberg, 'Lutyens's Cenotaph', *The Journal of the Society of Architectural Historians*, Vol. 48 No. 1 March 1989, pp.5–23.

7 Sir Edwin Lutyens, Journal of Remembrance, 1931, National Archives (WORK 20/226).

8 *The Times*, 18 July 1919.

9 *The Times*, 19 July 1919.

10 *The Builder*, 25 July 1919.

11 Sir Edwin Lutyens, *op. cit.*

12 Admiral of the Fleet and geologist.

13 Edwin Lutyens to Alfred Mond, Letter of 1 November 1919, National Archives (WORK 20/139).

14 Her pet name for Lutyens, referring back to the name by which he was universally known. In return, she was known as 'MacSack'.

15 Greenberg, *op. cit.*

16 'The Cenotaph', Viscount Lee of Fareham, 19 January 1920, National Archives (WORK 20/139).

17 Sir Edwin Lutyens, *op. cit.*

Five: Spalding

1 Exhibition Catalogue, War Memorials Exhibition 1919, Royal Academy.

2 Edwin Lutyens to Lady Emily Lutyens, letter of 21 September 1929, RIBA.

3 For example, the Brookfield Estate, St Pancras 1922–30.

4 Edwin Lutyens to Lady Emily Lutyens, letter of 27 August 1919, RIBA.

5 The house was one of a pair together with 8 Little College Street, which was designed for McLaren's sister, Lady Norman.

6 This quotation, together with those that immediately follow, are all taken from the *Lincolnshire, Boston and Spalding Free Press*, 5 August 1919.

7 *Lincolnshire, Boston and Spalding Free Press*, 13 June 1922.

8 *Ibid.*

Six: Civic Pride

1 Hugh Murray, *Dr Evelyn's York* (William Sessions, 1983), p.42.

2 *Ibid.*, p.42.

3 *Ibid.*, p.40. The question of the drawings is confusing. It is recorded that the War Memorial Committee asked Lutyens for a set of black and white drawings, and that he sent a perspective by the end of October 1922. It is presumed that the drawings on display at the *Yorkshire Herald* were elevations and plans and that, what Dr Evelyn and others wanted, was an artist's impression, which is the drawing shown on page 61. The matter is further complicated by a drawing in the RIBA Drawings Collection that purports to be a preliminary design for the memorial (see Margaret Richardson, *Sketches by Edwin Lutyens*, Academy Editions, 1994, p.89). It shows a pair of cenotaphs supporting a recumbent figure but bears no relation to the York City Memorial as proposed. The attribution appears to have been made after Lutyens's death and would seem to be incorrect. Unfortunately it is not readily apparent what other memorial it might be: Rochdale is probably the most likely, but Leicester is another possibility, as there is a small sketch on the drawing indicative of a church.

4 *Yorkshire Herald*, 26 November 1921.

5 *Ibid.*

6 Lord Grey was the Foreign Secretary at the time of the outbreak of the War and famously stated that 'The lamps are going out all over Europe; we shall not see them lit again in our lifetime' is attributed. Lutyens designed a memorial plaque to him, incorporating a relief carving of Lord Grey by Sir William Reid Dick on the wall outside the Ambassadors' Entrance at the Foreign Office.

7 *North Eastern and Scottish Magazine*, July 1924

8 Murray, *op. cit.*, p44

9 *Ibid.*, p.40.

10 Advice from Lutyens's office dated 11 June 1925.

11 Leicester War Memorial Committee (Site and Design Sub-Committee), meeting of 20 January 1920.

12 Description by Lutyens for public meeting on 25 October 1920.

13 Leicester War Memorial Committee, meeting of 10 June 1921.

14 Leicester War Memorial Committee (Finance Sub-Committee), meeting of 21 March 1922.

15 Leicester War Memorial Committee, meeting of 29 March 1922.

16 *Ibid.*, 23 April 1923.

17 *Ibid.*

18 *Ibid.*

19 *Leicester Advertiser*, 4 July 1925.

20 Now part of the Royal Bank of Scotland.

21 Leicester War Memorial Committee, meeting of 31 May 1923.

22 *Illustrated Leicester Chronicle*, 11 July 1925.

23 Leicester War Memorial Committee, meeting of 30 June 1926.

24 'Norwich War Memorial: Erection of War Memorial', Lord Mayor's files (N/LM/1/72), Norfolk Records Office.

25 Sir Edwin Lutyens, letter to Lady Emily Lutyens, 13 June 1927, RIBA.

26 *Ibid.*

27 Percy and Ridley, *op. cit.*, p.409 (letter of 16 July 1927).

28 *Norfolk News*, 16 July 1927.

29 'Norwich War Memorial: Erection of War Memorial', Lord Mayor's files (N/LM/1/72), Norfolk Records Office.

30 Faculty Petition of 11 July 1922.

31 The inscription is a mis-quotation as the original is 'Hand of God'

32 Lieutenant-Colonel A.S. Blair to Sir Fabian Ware, Letter of 13 April 1926, CWGC archives.

33 H.F. Robinson to Sir Fabian Ware, Memorandum of 20 April 1926, CWGC archives.

34 Lieutenant-Colonel A.S. Blair to Sir Fabian Ware, letter of 24 April 1926, CWGC archives.

35 *Ibid.*

36 Sir Robert Lorimer to Sir Fabian Ware, letter of 17 May 1927, CWGC archives.

37 *Ibid.*

38 This and the quotes immediately following are from Lieutenant-Colonel A.S. Blair to Sir Edwin Lutyens, letter of 1 June 1927 CWGC archives.

39 Albert Thomas to Lieutenant-Colonel A.S. Blair, letter of 14 June 1927, CWGC archives.

40 This and the quotes immediately following are from Lieutenant-Colonel A.S. Blair to Sir Edwin Lutyens, letter of 17 June 1917, CWGC archives.

41 Sir Edwin Lutyens to Lieutenant-Colonel A.S. Blair, letter of 20 June 1927, CWGC archives.

42 Lieutenant-Colonel A.S. Blair to Sir Edwin Lutyens, letter of 21 June 1917, CWGC archives.

43 *Ibid.*

44 Sir Edwin Lutyens to Lieutenant-Colonel A.S. Blair, letter of 22 June 1927, CWGC archives.

45 Lieutenant-Colonel A.S. Blair to Sir Edwin Lutyens, letter of 23 June 1927, CWGC archives.

46 F.C. Gilter to E.J. Macrae, letter of 30 July 1927, CWGC archives.

47 *Ibid.*

48 Lieutenant-Colonel A.S. Blair to F.C. Gilter, letter of 1 August 1927, CWGC archives.

Chapter Seven: Village Voices

1 Lutyens returned to Tyringham in the mid-1920s to design one of his most famous garden layouts – a long canal flanked by a Temple of Music and a Bathing Pavilion.

2 Hussey, *op. cit.*, p.100.

3 *Hampshire Chronicle*, 22 February 1919.

4 *Hampshire Chronicle*, 2 April 1919.

5 Percy and Ridley, *op. cit.*, p.371.

6 The grave and memorial to Lord Muncaster's father, Sir Josslyn Pennington, the fifth Baron Muncaster, are in the Church of St Michael, Muncaster.

7 Lutyens also designed the gravestone for Mary Gribble (d 1924), which stands alongside Wolverley Fordham's grave.

8 The memorial is sometimes incorrectly listed as being in nearby Stow on the Wold.

9 Barham's son, Wilfrid, had died in the War and Barham ensured that he was remembered in a number of ways – memorial gates at the family home, Hole Park, a memorial screen to the family pew in Rolvenden Church, a bursary at Malvern College and the family coat of arms in a corner of the Memorial Court at Clare College, Cambridge.

10 The reason for the fall is unexplained in the Minutes but it is presumed that it must have been connected with the purchase of the site.

11 *Kentish Express*, date unknown.

12 Letter contained in file of the Rolvenden War Memorial Committee.

Chapter Eight: Soldiers, Sailors, Scholars and Company Men

1 Sir Edwin Lutyens to Lady Emily Lutyens, letter of 2 September 1920, RIBA.

2 *Ibid.*

3 The James Hackett grave is in Woodlawn Cemetery in New York; the Sidney Myer grave is in Box Hill Cemetery, Melbourne

and the graves of Claude and Niall Beddington are in the United Synagogue Cemetery, Willesden, London.

4 Edward Horner is buried in Rocquigny-Equancourt Road British Cemetery, Manancourt and Raymond Asquith in Guillemont Road Cemetery, Guillemont. Both additionally are commemorated on plaques by Eric Gill in Cambria and Amien Cathedrals respectively, to which Lutyens took Lady Horner and her daughter Katherine Asquith on one of his visits to the Western Front in July 1933.

5 Church of St John the Baptist.

6 His grave is in the Ferme-Olivier Cemetery.

7 Percy and Ridley, *op. cit.*, p.358.

8 Walter Congreve served with distinction in the First World War and subsequently became Governor of Malta, where he died in 1927. He was buried at sea at his request.

9 Sir Edwin Lutyens to Fabian Ware, letter of 9 June 1926, CWGC archives.

10 Sir Edwin Lutyens to Fabian Ware, letter of 28 June 1926, CWGC archives.

11 Baker designed the South Africa War Memorial at Delville Wood on the Somme.

12 British Thomson Houston was ultimately absorbed into the General Electric Company (GEC) which, in turn, became Marconi.

Chapter Nine: Meanwhile Abroad

1 A similar situation occurred with the Rand Regiments Memorial

2 Edwin Lutyens to Ernest Owens, Crown Agents for the Colonies, letter of 21 June 1922, National Archives (Ref. CAOG 10/87).

3 Edwin Lutyens to Ernest Owens, Crown Agents for the Colonies, letter of 26 July 1922, National Archives (Ref. CAOG 10/87).

4 Edwin Lutyens to Ernest Owens, Crown Agents for the Colonies, letter 1922, National Archives (Ref. CAOG 10/87).

5 Percy and Ridley, *op. cit.*, p.343 (letter of 27 March 1917).

6 Robert Grant Irving, *Indian Summer: Lutyens Baker and Imperial India* (Yale University Press, 1981), p.347.

7 Percy and Ridley, *op. cit.*, p.387.

8 Ridley, *op. cit.*, p.339.

9 Lutyens did not have much luck with bridges in Dublin. He had designed an art gallery for Hugh Percy Lane in 1913 that took the form of a Palladian Bridge over the Liffey in the heart of Dublin but, amid controversy, the scheme did not receive official backing and did not proceed.

10 Burnet was appointed as the IWGC's Principal Architect with responsibility for Palestine and Gallipoli on 13 August 1919.

11 Officer Commanding, West African Regiment to Secretary Imperial War Graves Commission, letter of 24 May 1927, CWGC archives.

12 *Ibid.*

13 The former name of Zambia.

14 Hector Croad, the local District Commissioner.

15 G.A.M. Alexander, 'The Evacuation of Kasama in 1918', *Northern Rhodesia Journal*, Vol. IV, No. 5 (1961).

Chapter Ten: Permanent Sepulture

1 Longworth, *op. cit.*, p.32.

2 Frederick Kenyon, Memorandum on the Services of Architects, CWGC archives.

3 Mary Lutyens, *Edwin Lutyens: By His Daughter* (Black Swan, 1991), p.178.

4 Percy and Ridley, *op. cit.*, p.356 (letter of 14 October 1917).

5 Longworth, *op. cit.*, p.37.

6 Frederic Kenyon to Fabian Ware, letter of 26 February 1918, CWGC archives. 'Berrington' was possibly Adrian Berrington, who died in 1921, 'Pearson' was Lionel Pearson, the partner of Charles Holden.

7 Letter to Gavin Stamp, 13 August 1977.

8 *The Times*, 2 September 1920, quoted in Longworth, *op. cit.*, p.67.

9 *The Daily News*, 5 May 1920, quoted in Longworth, *op. cit.*, p.52.

10 *Ibid.*, p.54.

11 Kenyon wrote to Colonel Durham (the Commission's Director of Works) on 24 April 1920 regarding the naming of these two key items: 'I think I should use the terms 'The War Stone' and 'The Great Cross', not 'War Cross'. The terms 'Stone of Remembrance' and 'Cross of Sacrifice' should not be used as titles but only as descriptions' (CWGC archives). Despite Kenyon's desire, however, they became known as the 'Stone of Remembrance' and the 'Cross of Sacrifice'.

12 Sir Frederic Kenyon, Memorandum on the Cross as Central Monument, 28 January 1919, CWGC archives.

13 *Ibid.*

14 Hussey, *op. cit.*

15 *Ibid.*, p.375.

16 This reached its extreme with the cross for David Thomas, Lord Rhondda, in the Churchyard of St Mary, Llanwern, where the arms of the cross barely protrude beyond the width of the shaft. Lord Rhondda was sent to the United States by Lloyd George to help to arrange for the supply of munitions for the British forces. He survived the sinking of the *Lusitania* and was Minister of Food from 1917 until his death in 1918.

17 Wilfred von Berg to Gavin Stamp, letter of 13 September 1977.

18 It is often forgotten that the main source of Jekyll's income was not from the landscape plans that she designed but from the sale of plants from her nursery at her home in Munstead Wood. On one occasion, at least, she sent plants (1,800 white thrift – *Armeria maritime* 'Alba') to the Western Front.

19 Sir Fabian Ware, *The Immortal Heritage* (Cambridge University Press, 1937) p.56–8.

20 The term 'Silent Cities' was coined by Rudyard Kipling to describe the war cemeteries.

21 Wilfred von Berg to Gavin Stamp, letter of 13 August 1977.

22 *Ibid.*

23 *Ibid.*

24 *Ibid.*

25 Parker died in 1938 and his colleagues at

the IWGC paid for a memorial to him, designed by Lutyens, in the Church of St Mary, Bitton, Gloucestershire.

26 As an interesting adjunct, the form of the La Neuville entrance pavilion was used by Goldsmith on his own account for his design of the shelter at Glageon Communal Cemetery Extension. This was echoed elsewhere – the shelter in Cowlishaw's Condé-sur-l'Escaut Communal Cemetery is a copy of the one at Favreuil.

27 In the Churchyard of St Andrews, Whissendine, Leicestershire. Margaret (Barbara's mother) was the daughter of Mark Fenwick (cf Lower Swell War Memorial). Perhaps this was also what Lutyens had in mind in making his suggestion in connection with the Edinburgh War Memorial.

28 H.F. Robinson to Fabian Ware, Memorandum of 10 May 1933, CWGC archives.

29 The cemeteries are Blauwepoort Farm Cemetery, Bonnay Communal Cemetery Extension, Brussels Town Cemetery, Devonshire Cemetery, Eterpigny British Cemetery, Feuchy British Cemetery, Fienvillers British Cemetery, Gonnehem British Cemetery, Mazingarbe Communal Cemetery Extension, Neuville-sous-Montreuil Indian Cemetery, Orange Trench Cemetery.

30 Sir Edwin Lutyens to Colonel H.F. Robinson, letter of 8 September 1938, CWGC archives.

31 Colonel H.F. Robinson to Sir Edwin Lutyens, letter of 9 September 1938, CWGC archives.

32 In recent times small stainless steel panels have been included within the cemeteries to explain how they came to be created and to put them into the overall context of the War. Often they will credit the name of the Principal Architect but they make no mention of the Architect in France, a situation that would have disappointed Sir Frederic Kenyon who, at the Commission's meeting on 14 September 1938, argued that the naming proposals 'should be applied to all the Cemeteries and Memorials, in order that the junior architects might have credit for the part they had played in the design'.

Chapter Eleven: Known Unto God

1 The New Zealand Government was given a choice of two potential locations – Grévillers and Bancourt British Cemetery. The former was chosen after a site visit as it had better road access and because the background to the cemetery, consisting of existing trees and shrubs, was preferable to the open aspect of Bancourt. There is also a plaque (not designed by Lutyens), to commemorate ten missing members of the New Zealand Cyclist Battalion in the shelter building at Lutyens's Marfaux British Cemetery.

2 Fabian Ware to Frederic Kenyon, letter of 8 August 1919, CWGC archive.

3 Frederic Kenyon to Fabian Ware, letter of 12 August 1919, CWGC archive.

4 The main standalone Memorials to the Missing are Nieuport (Architect William Binnie – the Commission's Deputy Director of Works/Sculptor Charles Sargeant Jagger), Ypres – Menin Gate (Blomfield/Reid Dick), Ploegstreet (W. Chalton Bradshaw/Gilbert Ledward), La Ferté-sous-Jouarre (Goldsmith), Soissons (V.O. Rees and G.H. Holt). There are major memorials in the cemeteries at Tyne Cot (Baker), Louverval (Bradshaw/Jagger), Le Touret (Truelove), Vis en Artois (Truelove/Ernest Gillick), Poziéres (Cowlishaw/Laurence Turner), Dud Corner (Baker).

5 Lafontaine was responsible for designing the 'Cathedral Tablets' that were placed in over thirty cathedrals in France and Belgium to record the contribution of the British Empire to the War.

6 Cart de Lafontaine, Undated File Note, CWGC archives.

7 The fee was payable in four instalment: 1/3 on acceptance of the builder's tender price, 1/3 once half of the contract sum had been paid to the builder, 1/6 on issuing the final certificate of completion and 1/6 within three months of the final payment to the builder.

8 Note of meeting of Anglo-French Mixed Committee 25 June 1926, CWGC Archives

9 The location was subsequently changed from the brow of the hill to avoid the cost of building a podium upon which the memorial could sit.

10 Stamp, *The Memorial to the Missing of the Somme*, Profile Books, 2006, p.3.

11 *Ibid.*, p13.

12 Malcolm Shepherd, undated note (possibly 1921), CWGC archives.

13 Fabian Ware to Malcolm Shepherd, letter of 27 July 1923, CWGC archives.

14 Villers-Bretonneux Design Competition Rules, CWGC archives.

15 Malcolm Shepherd to William Lucas, letter of 18 February 1930, CWGC archives.

16 Fabian Ware to Sir Granville de Laurie Ryrie, letter of 14 January 1931, CWGC archives.

17 Lutyens's formal appointment had ceased on 31 December 1930 and he had been retained in an advisory capacity.

18 Early in his career, Lutyens had replaced Halsey Ricardo as the architect for Orchards, a large house near Munstead Wood, thanks to an introduction to the clients William and Julia Chance by Gertrude Jekyll.

19 Herbert Creedy to Fabian Ware, letter of May 1932, CWGC archives.

20 Undated file note, recollection of letter from Sir Edwin Lutyens to William Lucas, 26 June 1925, CWGC archives.

21 Sir Edwin Lutyens to Sir Fabian Ware, letter of 10 October 1935, CWGC archives.

22 H.F. Robinson to Sir Edwin Lutyens, letter of 13 September 1933, CWGC archives.

23 William Lucas to Rt Hon Joseph Lyons, letter of 25 Mach 1938, CWGC archives.

24 In a sad postscript Major General Sir Talbot Hobbs, who had been the Chairman of the assessors for the original architectural competition, died at sea *en route* to the unveiling.

Chapter Twelve: The Unbuilts

1 Sir Edwin Lutyens to Lord Provost, Glasgow Corporation, Letter of 28 April 1921, Glasgow City Council Archives Ref. G1/3/1.

2 *Ibid.*

3 Meeting of the Executive Committee on the Glasgow War Memorial, 9 May 1921, Glasgow City Council Archives Ref. G4/1.

4 Meeting of the Executive Committee on the Glasgow War Memorial, 6 June 1921, Glasgow City Council Archives Ref. G4/1.

5 Lutyens designed the key civic buildings (two churches and an institute) as well as some houses as a focus for the suburb (1908–11).

6 George Barnes was a Labour MP and H.M. Hyndman an influential socialist.

7 George Lansbury was a prominent member of the Labour Party and editor of the *Daily Herald*.

8 Percy and Ridley, *op. cit.*, p.360.

9 John H. Hills, letter to *The Times*, 27 October 1925.

10 Reference needed

11 Minutes of the RAWCF, meeting of 28 October 1920.

12 Minutes of the RAWCF, meeting of 9 December 1920.

13 Minutes of the RAWCF, meeting of 28 February 1921,

Chapter Thirteen: Their Name Liveth for Evermore

1 *The Times*, 1 February 1922.

2 At York a plaque has been put up alongside the memorial to inform visitors that a list of the Fallen is contained within an adjacent building.

3 The unusual name arises from the backwards spelling of 'Iron' to reflect the brick's hardness.

4 Reported in the *Bristol Evening Post*, 24 September 2002.

5 http://www.eveningnews24.co.uk, 20 September 2007.

Chapter Fourteen: Endgame

1 Simon Bradley and Nikolaus Pevsner, *The Buildings of England: London 6: Westminster* (Yale University Press, 2003), p.558.

2 Nikolaus Pevsner, 'Building With Wit: The Architecture of Sir Edwin Lutyens', *Architectural Review* 109, April 1951, p.217–25.

L'Envoi

1 Lutyens had been knighted in the New Year Honours list in 1918.

2 Minutes of IWGC meeting, 19 January 1944, CWGC archives.

3 *Ibid.*

BIBLIOGRAPHY

Amery, Colin and Richardson, Margaret, *Lutyens: The Work Of The English Architect Sir Edwin Lutyens (1869–1944)*, Arts Council Of Great Britain, 1981

anon., *The History Of Miserden*, Privately Published, 2000

Ashley, Peter, *Lest We Forget*, English Heritage, 2004

Aslet, Clive, *Landmarks of Britain: The Five Hundred Places That Made Our History*, Hodder & Stoughton, 2005

Atkinson, C.T., *The Queen's Own Royal West Kent Regiment*, Simpkin Marshall, 1924

Barker, Michael, *Sir Edwin Lutyens*, Shire Publications, 2005

Bell, J. & Ivatt, A.W., *A Brief Sketch of the History of the Parish of Fordham*, Soham, 1923

Boorman, Derek, *At the Going Down of the Sun: British First World War Memorials*, Derek Boorman, 1988

Borg, Alan, *War Memorials: From Antiquity To The Present*, Leo Cooper, 1991

Bott, Alan, *A Guide to the Parish Churches of Witley and Thursley, Surrey*, Privately Published, 2003

Brown, Jane, *Gardens of a Golden Afternoon*, Penguin Books, 1985

_____, *Lutyens and the Edwardians: An English Architect And His Clients*, Viking, 1997

Burke's & Savills Guide to Country Houses Volume III: East Anglia, Burke's Peerage, 1981

Butler, A.S.G, with George Stewart and Christopher Hussey, *The Architecture of Sir Edwin Lutyens*, Country Life, 1950

Cecil, Hugh and Mirabel, *Imperial Marriage: An Edwardian War and Peace*, John Murray, 2002

Compton, Ann, *The Sculpture of Charles Sargeant Jagger*, The Henry Moore Foundation in Association with Lund Humphries, 2004

Drew, Bernard, *The London Assurance: A Second Chronicle*, London Assurance, 1949

Gliddon, Gerald, *Aristocracy and the Great War*, Gliddon Books, 2002

Gradidge, Roderick, *Edwin Lutyens: Architect Laureate*, Allen & Unwin, 1981

Gray, Rosemary and Griffiths, Sue, *The Book Of Wargrave*, Wargrave Local History Group, 1987

Greenberg, Alan, *Lutyens and the Modern Movement*, Papadakis Publisher, 2007

Hopkins, Andrew and Stamp, Gavin (eds), *Lutyens Abroad*, The British School at Rome, London, 2002

Hunt, J. and Thorpe, D., *Gerrards Cross*, Phillimore, 2006

Hurst, Sidney C, *Silent Cities*, Naval & Military Press, 1993

Hussey, Christopher, *The Life of Sir Edwin Lutyens*, Country Life, 1950

Irving, Robert Grant, *Indian Summer: Lutyens, Baker, and Imperial Delhi*, Yale University Press, 1981

Jeffery, Keith, *Ireland and the Great War*, Cambridge University Press, 2000

Kimber, S.G., *Thirty-Eight Years of Public Life in Southampton*, Privately Published, 1949

King, Alex, *Memorials of the Great War in Britain: The Symbolism and Politics of Remembrance*, Berg, 1998

King, Tom and Furbank, Kevan, *The Southend Story: A Town and its People 1892-1992 Borough Centenary*, Southend Standard Recorder, 1992

Knight, Jill, *The Civil Service Rifles in the Great War: 'All Bloody Gentlemen'*, Pen & Sword, 2004

Longworth, Philip, *The Unending Vigil: The History of the Commonwealth War Graves Commission*, Leo Cooper, 2003

Lutyens, Lady Emily, *Candles in the Sun*, Hart-Davis, 1957

Lutyens, Mary, *Edwin Lutyens by his Daughter*, Black Swan, 1991

Mee, Arthur, *The King's England*, Hodder and Stoughton

Murray, Hugh, *Dr Evelyn's York*, William Sessions Of York, 1983

Newsome, David, *A History of Wellington College 1859–1959*, John Murray, 1959

Percy, Clayre and Ridley, Jane (eds), *The Letters of Edwin Lutyens to his Wife Lady Emily*, Collins, 1985

Pevsner, Nikolaus et al., *The Buildings of England*, Penguin Books/Yale University Press

Richardson, Margaret, *Sketches by Edwin Lutyens*, Academy Editions, 1994

Ridley, Jane, *The Architect and his Wife*, Chatto & Windus, 2002

Sheldrick, Albert W., *'Fourpenny Phyllis' Phyllis Fordham of Ashwell Bury 1882–1958*, The Friends of Ashwell Village Museum, 1987

Sherburne, K. Chester, *Gerrards Cross and District*, Suburban and Provincial Association, undated

Stamp, Gavin, *Silent Cities: An Exhibition Of The Memorial And Cemetery Architecture Of The Great War*, Royal Institute of British Architects, 1977

_____, *Edwin Lutyens: Country Houses*, Aurum Press, 2001

_____, *The Memorial to the Missing of the Somme*, Profile Books, 2006

Summers, Julie, *Remembered: The History of the Commonwealth War Graves Commission*, Merrell, 2007

Von Donop, Maj. Gen. Sir Stanley, *Royal Artillery War Memorial Unveiling and Dedication Ceremony*, HMSO, 1925

Weaver, Lawrence, *Houses and Gardens by E.L. Lutyens*, Antique Collectors' Club, 1981

Wilhide, Elizabeth, *Sir Edwin Lutyens: Designing in the English Tradition*, Pavilion Books, 2003

Websites

Commonwealth War Graves Commissions (www.cwgc.org.uk)

North East War Memorials Project (www.newmp.org.uk)

Public Monuments and Sculpture Organisation (www.pmsa.org.uk)

The Lutyens Trust (www.lutyenstrust.org.uk)

United Kingdom National Inventory Of War Memorials (www.ukniwm.org.uk)

INDEX

References in *italics* refer to illustrations

ACKNOWLEDGMENTS

Books such as ours can only be written with the support of a group of people who have given freely of their time and energies to unearth obscure information for us or to offer guidance and support as our research progressed.

The primary burden, of course, falls upon the authors' families, who soon learn to develop the skill to mop a fevered brow as and when necessary and to grow broad shoulders as their loved one disappears to look at and photograph yet another obscure memorial ('Mum, how many photographs can Dad take of one war memorial?' – Mark Skelton, aged nine, Holy Island, 9 August 1998). So, grateful thanks are due to Alison, Jo and Mark Skelton for having lived with Lutyens for so long (in the case of Jo and Mark, for all of their lives) and to Wynne Gliddon for her advice and support.

A Mention in Despatches is given to Nigel Skelton, for not only suggesting the trip to the Somme in 1999 that directly led to this book, but also for acting as a loyal and faithful driver on the six subsequent trips. Nigel remained completely unruffled on those occasions when his map-reader was at fault: his skill in turning round the car on the narrow muddy track barely wider than a car that leads to Dury Mill Cemetery will remain long in Tim's memory. He was also sufficiently appreciative of the wishes of the photographer to ensure that he was out of shot as soon as the camera was raised to his brother's eye. Needless to say, having seen so many of the cemeteries, he was also able to offer valuable comments upon the text as it emerged from Tim's computer.

Special campaign medals are awarded to the staff of the Commonwealth War Graves Commission and, in particular, Maria Choules (for dealing so patiently with our enquiries and locating the appropriate files for our research); Cheryl Arnold of the Spalding Western Front Association (for unearthing the wonderful story of the Spalding War Memorial); David Barham of the Rolvenden War Memorial Trust (for providing us with the records for Rolvenden); Andrew Barnett (for providing photos to fill the gaps in Tim's collection); Gavin Chappell (for his help and advice throughout); the staff of the National Archives at Kew; the staff of the Imperial War Museum Department of Printed Books; Debbie Francis at The Institute of Civil Engineers and Fiona Orsini and the staff at the Royal Institute of British Architects Drawings Collection at the Victoria and Albert Museum.

The following assisted Gerald with particular aspects of his research: Peter E. Batchelor; Dr Graham Keech; Chris Preston; Sarah Talbutt and Ray Westlake.

The following individuals helped with specific memorials: Peter Greener and Dr Mervyn Miller (Ashwell); Gareth Wood (Fordham); Jenny Brown of the North East War Memorials Project (Hartburn and Holy Island); Gordon Pearson and Mary Pollock (King's Somborne); Rosalynd Goulbourne and Major M.T.N.H. Wills (Miserden); Sarah Bridges (Northampton); the Dean and Chapter of Canterbury Cathedral (Rolvenden); Mrs Rich (Shere); Dr Andy Russel, Joanne Smith and Sue Woolgar (Southampton); James Brazier and Tony Stubbs (Spalding); Philip Mallet (Wittersham); Sarah Palmer (York); Kathie Dickie of the Corporation of the City of London (London, Ontario); Ravi Katari and Smuthiah (Madras Club); Jenny Brown (Billy Congreve); Marion Roberts (John Leighton); David Cowdery (Cavalry Club); Lt Col.

G. Bennett (Lancashire Fusiliers); Daniel Sudron (Leeds Rifles); Dino Lemonofides (Oxfordshire and Buckinghamshire Light Infantry); Lee Sands (British Medical Association); G.M.D. Booth, Douglas Byrne and John Williams (British Thomson Houston Company); Greg Beechcroft (North Eastern Railways); Lesley Whitelaw (Middle Temple); K.J. Durham (Wellington College) and Dick Rayner (Norwich and Great Yarmouth).

Grateful thanks are given to the Commonwealth War Graves Commission and the RIBA Drawings & Archives Collection for being able to quote so freely from the various Lutyens correspondence in their archives; and to N.G. Bailey Group, Sir Robert and Lady Clark and Dominic and Stephanie Parker, for their help with particular photos.

Last, but by no means least, thanks are due to John Nicoll at Frances Lincoln who, having thought about publishing a book on the architecture of the Western Front, readily acceded to our proposal that he should really be publishing a book about Lutyens instead.

We are aware that, despite our research, there will still be stories relating to the memorials in this book that we were unable to uncover (like who, for example, was the sculptor for the recumbent figures at Southampton *et al.*). We would therefore encourage anybody with any information that we may have overlooked to contact us via the publishers, so that we can take account of it in any future updating of this book.

ILLUSTRATIONS
All photographs were taken by Tim Skelton, with the following exceptions: Andrew Barnett (p.16, p.18 right and bottom, pp.20–1, p.111, p.121 middle, p.136, p.138 top, p.139, p180 middle; Gavin Chapell (p.92 right, p.217 left middle); Commonwealth War Graves Commission (p.103, p.104, p.105, p.108, p.132, 180 top and bottom, p.187 second from top, p.192 top, p.205 top); Peter Howard (p.98 and p.179); Ravi Katari (p.178 second from top); Einar Einarsson Kvaran (p.178 bottom); Carl Purcell/Painet Inc. (p.178 third from top); Red Images/Waldemar Wellmann (p.20); Jo Skelton (p.46); Nigel Skelton (p.205 third from top); Xiaowei (p.179 top).

Grateful thanks are given to the following for allowing the reproduction of particular images:

Auckland War Memorial Museum (p.100); Record Office, Bristol City Council (p.158); *Building* magazine (in succession to *The Builder*) (p.94, p.133, p.141, p.149); City of York Council (p.61); Commonwealth War Graves Commission (p.25, p.33 left, p.113, p.142); Corporation of Lloyd's (p.153); *Country Life* (p.146); Department of the Environment, Heritage, and Local Government, Irish Republic (p.102); Gertrude Jekyll Collection (1955-1) Environmental Design Archives, University of California, Berkeley (p.33 right); *Lincolnshire Free Press* (p.50, p.57); Norfolk County Council (p.151); RIBA Library and Drawings & Archives Collection (p.38, p.64 bottom, p.80 left); Jane Ridley (p.42 right); University College School (p.156); *The Times* (p.150).

Every attempt has been made by the authors to trace the copyright holders of images contained in this book and any necessary corrections will be made in future editions.